Chatelaine

MODERN CLASSICS

Chatelaine

MODERN CLASSICS

250 FAST, FRESH RECIPES FROM
THE CHATELAINE KITCHEN

RECIPES COMPILED AND EDITED BY VICTORIA WALSH

John Wiley & Sons Canada, Ltd.

Library and Archives Canada Cataloguing in Publication Data

Chatelaine's modern classics : 250 fast, fresh recipes from the Chatelaine kitchen

Includes index.

ISBN 978-0-470-73982-2

   1. Cookery.

TX714.C465 2010   641.5   C2010-901592-4

Production Credits
Editor: Leah Marie Fairbank
Creative direction and interior design: Ian Koo
Composition: Interrobang Graphic Design
Photography: Yvonne Duivenvoorden
Cover design: Sandy Kim
Managing Editor: Alison Maclean
Production Editor: Lindsay Humphreys
Production Assistant: Sarah Lichter
Food styling: Ashley Denton/Judy Inc.
Prop styling: Carolyn Souch/Judy Inc.
Printer: Printplus Ltd.

John Wiley & Sons Canada, Ltd.
6045 Freemont Blvd.
Mississauga, Ontario
L5R 4J3

Printed in China
1 2 3 4 5 PP 14 13 12 11 10

table of contents

acknowledgements

THE CHATELAINE TEAM

This book was made possible through the efforts of the talented team at *Chatelaine*: Rebecca Caldwell, Philina Chan, Anna Cipollone, Katie Dupuis, Jane Francisco, Rachel Giese, Megan Griffith-Greene, Maureen Halushak, Sandy Kim, Alicia Kowalewski, Alex Laws, Sue Marteleira, Myles McCutcheon, Vanessa Milne, Melanie Morassutti, Jen O'Brien, Erika Oliviera, Marnie Peters, Erinn Steringa, Doug Wallace, Cameron Williamson, Heather Trim and Meaghan Baron.

THE CHATELAINE KITCHEN

Thank you to the many talented cooks who develop and test recipes in the Chatelaine Kitchen every day. Special thanks to former food editor Monda Rosenberg for 30 years of contributions to kitchens across the country.

BEHIND THE SCENES

We are grateful for the hard work and support of our friends at John Wiley & Sons Canada: Meghan Brousseau, Leah Fairbank, Ian Koo, Alison Maclean, Lindsay Humphreys, Judy Phillips and Jennifer Smith.

SPECIAL THANKS

Thanks to friends and family for their support: Eleanor Anckaert, Brunch Club, Michael Erickson, Jennifer Goldberg, Betty Jarvie, the Jarvie family, George Kiddell, Isla Macpherson, Susan Macpherson, Scott McCallum, the Millet family, Leanne Stanton, Tara Sullivan, Brianne Walsh, Katrina Walsh, David Williams, Lou Williams and Margaret Williams.

introduction

FROM THE CHATELAINE KITCHEN

We know this sounds familiar: It's 2 p.m. and you suddenly wonder, what's for dinner? It has to be delicious, easy, fast, nutritious and affordable . . . easier said than done! So what's on the menu?

At *Chatelaine*, we hear you. Every night we go home to our own kitchens to face the same dilemma. But we believe that everyday cooking can be satisfying and fun, a pleasure instead of a chore. So, even after more than 80 years of fabulous recipes, the Chatelaine Kitchen continues to develop simple, mouth-watering solutions for every meal of the day.

Of course, like you, we have high expectations of our recipes, so we test and retest each one to make sure it's as reliable as it is tasty. For this collection, we've chosen 250 of our best triple-tested recipes that have earned our seal of approval. We hope they'll soon become family favourites for you.

Cheers!

breakfast and brunch

Never skip breakfast again! Weekdays start better with homemade spiced granola and quinoa porridge. And weekend brunches are fun and effortless with stuffed French toast and easy eggs Benedict.

Perfect Omelette

PREPARATION TIME 5 MINUTES
COOKING TIME 3 MINUTES
MAKES 1 SERVING

FILLINGS
Keep it fresh with

- Prosciutto, sliced roasted red pepper and snipped chives

- Chopped tomatoes, chopped fresh dill and sliced bocconcini (shown at right).

- Sliced strawberries, crème fraîche or sour cream, shredded basil and freshly ground black pepper

- Chopped fresh mint and ricotta cheese

3 eggs
Salt
2 tsp (10 mL) butter
Filling (see sidebar for suggestions)

1. In a bowl, gently whisk eggs with salt and 1 tbsp (15 mL) water. Melt butter in a medium non-stick frying pan with sloping sides over medium heat. Swirl as it melts to coat both the bottom and sides of pan.

2. Add egg mixture, but don't stir. When edge is set, after 1 minute, use a spatula to lift edge of omelette, pulling toward the centre, and tilting pan so uncooked, liquid egg mixture runs underneath. Slowly repeat until mixture is set, 2 to 3 more minutes.

3. Sprinkle filling, if using one, across centre of omelette.

4. Tilt pan beside a plate. For a three-fold rolled omelette, lift top third of omelette over filling, then tilt pan so omelette rolls onto itself and onto plate, smooth-side up. For a folded omelette, slip spatula under unfilled side and fold over filling.

NUTRIENTS PER SERVING 19 G PROTEIN 23 G FAT
1 G CARBOHYDRATES 0 G FIBRE 2 MG IRON
78 MG CALCIUM 237 MG SODIUM 285 CALORIES

Baked Croque Monsieur

PREPARATION TIME 15 MINUTES
TOASTING TIME 20 MINUTES
REFRIGERATION TIME 8 HOURS
BAKING TIME 45 MINUTES
MAKES 6 SERVINGS

12 slices regular white bread

8 eggs

2 tbsp (30 mL) Dijon mustard

2 cups (500 mL) 2% milk or half-and-half cream

1 tsp (5 mL) salt

8 thin slices ham or prosciutto

3 cups (750 mL) grated swiss or cheddar cheese

WHAT IS IT?

The traditional French croque monsieur is a ham-and-cheese sandwich that's dipped in egg, then cooked in butter just like French toast. A croque madame has the addition of a fried egg, but in North America this sandwich often lends itself to creative twists, with the substitution of various cheeses, or chicken.

1. Preheat oven to 350°F (180°C). Remove crusts from bread if you wish. Place slices on a large baking sheet. It's okay if they overlap a little. Toast in centre of preheated oven for 20 minutes. Turn slices over halfway through toasting time. Meanwhile, lightly coat or spray a 9- × 13-inch (3 L) glass baking dish with oil. In a large bowl, whisk eggs with Dijon. Whisk in milk and salt. Cut ham into thick strips.

2. Place 6 slices toasted bread in a single layer on bottom of baking dish. It's okay to squish them in. Pour one-third of egg mixture evenly overtop. Sprinkle with 1 cup (250 mL) cheese. Scatter ham over cheese, then sprinkle with another 1 cup (250 mL) cheese. Cover with remaining 6 bread slices. Firmly press bread down with your hands. If it's not lying flat, trim edges. Pour remaining egg mixture evenly overtop. Sprinkle with remaining 1 cup (250 mL) cheese. Cover and refrigerate at least 8 hours or overnight.

3. When ready to bake, place oven rack in bottom third of oven. Preheat oven to 350°F (180°C). Bake cold casserole, uncovered, until top is golden, about 45 minutes. Slice and serve immediately. Great served with our Easy Arugula and Hazelnut Salad (page 86).

NUTRIENTS PER SERVING 39 G PROTEIN 28 G FAT
33 G CARBOHYDRATES 1 G FIBRE 3 MG IRON
742 MG CALCIUM 1543 MG SODIUM 545 CALORIES

Chocolate-Stuffed French Toast

PREPARATION TIME 25 MINUTES
REFRIGERATION TIME 1 HOUR
BAKING TIME 16 MINUTES
MAKES 14 PIECES

1 large baguette
2 52-g caramel-filled chocolate bars, broken into squares
3 eggs
1 cup (250 mL) milk
2 tbsp (30 mL) granulated sugar
1 tsp (5 mL) vanilla extract
¾ tsp (4 mL) cinnamon or ground cardamom
½ tsp (2 mL) salt
3 tbsp (45 mL) unsalted butter, melted

COOKING TIP

Use up your day-old bread for this recipe — the results are even better than using fresh.

1. Slice baguette into 1 ½-inch- (4 cm) thick rounds. Using a serrated knife, cut through the middle of bottom crusty side of each round to make a slit large enough to hold a square of chocolate. Widen slits and tuck a piece of chocolate into each. Place in a 9- × 13-inch (3 L) baking dish, bunching bread close together to fit. In a bowl, whisk eggs with milk, sugar, vanilla, cinnamon and salt. Pour over bread. Turn pieces so they fully soak up egg mixture. Cover and refrigerate at least 1 hour or overnight.

2. Preheat oven to 450°F (230°C). Generously brush a large, wide baking sheet with about half of the melted butter. Space soaked bread on baking sheet so pieces aren't touching. Bake in centre of preheated oven for 8 minutes. Remove from oven, brush tops of bread with remaining melted butter, then turn slices over. Continue to bake until each side is crusty and deep golden, 8 to 10 more minutes. Place toasts on plates. Serve drizzled with maple syrup.

NUTRIENTS PER PIECE 4 G PROTEIN 6 G FAT
21 G CARBOHYDRATES 1 G FIBRE 1 MG IRON
62 MG CALCIUM 279 MG SODIUM 159 CALORIES

Easy Eggs Benedict

PREPARATION TIME 30 MINUTES
COOKING TIME 12 MINUTES
MAKES 4 SERVINGS

EGGS

4 English muffins, split in half

8 slices peameal bacon or thick ham slices

8 eggs

1 tbsp (15 mL) white vinegar

SAUCE

1 cup (250 mL) unsalted butter

3 large egg yolks

2 tbsp (30 mL) freshly squeezed lemon juice or tarragon vinegar

1 tbsp (15 mL) hot water

½ tsp (2 mL) salt

2 tbsp (30 mL) finely chopped fresh tarragon (optional)

SWITCH IT UP

• Classic hollandaise sauce is made with lemon juice, but you can use tarragon vinegar (sold in most super-markets) and fresh tarragon instead to make flavourful Béarnaise sauce.

• Replace peameal bacon with smoked salmon, sautéed tomato slices or blanched asparagus.

• In place of English muffins, use hash-brown patties, crumpets or homemade scones (see our plain version of Scrumptious White Chocolate Scones, page 25).

1. Preheat oven to 200°F (90°C). For eggs, lightly toast muffin halves. Keep warm in oven on a baking sheet. (Warm plates in oven at the same time.) Coat a large frying pan with oil and set over medium heat. Add half the peameal and cook until hot and done as you like, 2 to 3 minutes per side. Place pieces on muffin halves and return to oven. Repeat with remaining bacon. Fill a wide pot with 2 inches (5 cm) water and bring to a simmer. Cover until you are ready to poach the eggs.

2. For sauce, melt butter in a small saucepan over medium-high heat, or microwave in a bowl. Skim and discard foam. Pour butter into a measuring cup, leaving white solids behind.

3. Place yolks, lemon juice, hot water and salt in a blender or food processor. Immediately whirl on high speed for 1 minute. If butter is not hot, reheat. While motor is running, slowly pour warm butter through hole in lid. Whirl until thickened, about 1 minute. Pour into an ovenproof bowl. Stir in tarragon if you wish. Keep warm in oven for up to 15 minutes.

4. Immediately prepare poached eggs. Start by adding white vinegar to simmering water. Crack an egg into a small dish, then slip into water. Repeat with 3 more eggs. You'll need to cook eggs in 2 batches. Adjust heat so water gently simmers. Cook, uncovered, until whites are set and yolks are done as you like, 2 to 6 minutes. (We like the yolks runny.)

5. Place 2 peameal-topped muffin halves on 2 plates. Using a slotted spoon, remove poached eggs. Dab whites with a paper towel to absorb water and place an egg on each muffin. Whisk hollandaise sauce and spoon overtop. Serve immediately, then repeat poaching and this step for 2 more servings.

NUTRIENTS PER SERVING 31 G PROTEIN
71 G FAT 29 G CARBOHYDRATES 2 G FIBRE 4 MG IRON
179 MG CALCIUM 1441 MG SODIUM 883 CALORIES

Spicy Baked Eggs Ranchero

PREPARATION TIME 10 MINUTES
COOKING TIME 8 MINUTES
BAKING TIME 15 MINUTES
STANDING TIME 5 MINUTES
MAKES 8 SERVINGS

4 chorizo or Italian sausages

1 red onion, chopped

1 green or yellow pepper, chopped

1 ½ cups (375 mL) bottled chunky salsa

2 cups (500 mL) grated cheddar cheese

2 tbsp (30 mL) all-purpose flour

8 eggs

2 green onions, sliced

CHATELAINE KITCHEN TIP

If you're not a hot-spice fan, just skip the chorizo sausages and use mild Italian instead.

1. Preheat oven to 375°F (190°C). Oil a large frying pan set over medium heat. Prick sausages in several places and place in pan. Turn often until browned, 4 to 6 minutes. Remove from pan. It's okay if they aren't completely cooked. Slice into thin rounds. Coat pan with more oil, then add onion and pepper. Stir often until they start to soften, about 3 minutes. Add salsa and stir until hot, 1 to 2 minutes. Stir in sausages. In a small bowl, toss half the cheese with flour. Stir into salsa mixture in pan, then spoon over bottom of a 9- × 13-inch (3 L) baking dish.

2. Crack eggs overtop salsa mixture, spacing so they don't touch. Sprinkle with remaining cheese. Bake, uncovered, in centre of preheated oven until whites of eggs are set but centres are still runny, 15 to 20 minutes. Let stand 5 minutes, then spoon onto plates. Sprinkle with green onions and serve immediately.

GET AHEAD Prepare Step 1. Cover and refrigerate overnight. When ready to bake, cover pan with foil. Bake in centre of preheated oven until mixture is hot, 15 to 20 minutes. Uncover and stir. Add eggs and continue with recipe as directed.

NUTRIENTS PER SERVING 35 G PROTEIN 47 G FAT
12 G CARBOHYDRATES 2 G FIBRE 3 MG IRON
268 MG CALCIUM 1560 MG SODIUM 611 CALORIES

Spinach and Chèvre Frittata

PREPARATION TIME 10 MINUTES
COOKING TIME 3 MINUTES
BAKING TIME 40 MINUTES
STANDING TIME 5 MINUTES
MAKES 9 PIECES

1 each small red and yellow or orange pepper

1 tsp (5 mL) butter

4 cups (1 L) baby spinach, lightly packed

1 green onion, thinly sliced

5 oz (140 g) log goat cheese

12 eggs

1 tbsp (15 mL) Dijon mustard

½ tsp (2 mL) salt

TEST KITCHEN TIP
This baked brunch
dish makes for an easy
entertaining main course.
A perfect side dish is
The Modern Cobb salad
(page 82).

1. Preheat oven to 325°F (160°C). Lightly spray with oil an 8-inch- (2 L) square baking dish. Chop peppers into 1-inch (2.5 cm) pieces. Melt butter in a large frying pan over medium-high heat. Add peppers and stir often until they start to soften, 3 to 5 minutes. Remove from heat. Stir in spinach and onion just until they start to wilt. Turn into baking dish. Crumble cheese overtop.

2. In a large bowl, whisk eggs with Dijon and salt. Pour over pepper mixture and stir to evenly coat. Bake, uncovered, in centre of preheated oven until top is golden and centre is set, 40 to 50 minutes. Remove from oven and let stand 5 minutes, then cut into pieces. Tastes great warm, or cover and refrigerate and serve cold the next day.

GET AHEAD Prepare frittata but don't bake. Cover dish with foil and refrigerate overnight. Remove from fridge and gently stir to evenly mix. Bake, uncovered, as directed. You may need to add a few extra minutes of baking time. Baked frittata will keep well in fridge for up to 1 day.

NUTRIENTS PER PIECE 12 G PROTEIN 11 G FAT
3 G CARBOHYDRATES 1 G FIBRE 2 MG IRON
94 MG CALCIUM 314 MG SODIUM 160 CALORIES

Smoked-Salmon Nachos

PREPARATION TIME 15 MINUTES
BAKING TIME 10 MINUTES
MAKES 8 TO 10 SERVINGS

3 bagels
Cooking spray
Pinches of regular or garlic salt
1 green onion
1 lemon
8 oz (250 g) block cream cheese, at room temperature
2 tbsp (30 mL) milk
8 to 10 slices smoked salmon, preferably wild
¼ red onion
1 avocado
3 tbsp (45 mL) drained capers
¼ cup (50 mL) fresh mint (optional)

SHORTCUT

If you're tight for time, skip the work of making your own bagel chips and buy some instead.

GO WILD

Any type of smoked salmon will work well in this recipe, but we prefer using wild salmon because of its fantastic flavour and bright colour.

1. Arrange racks in top and bottom thirds of oven. Preheat oven to 350°F (180°C). Carefully slice each bagel into 4 thin rounds. Lightly spray both sides with cooking spray, then sprinkle with salt. Arrange in a single layer on 2 baking sheets.

2. Bake in preheated oven until edges are lightly golden, 5 to 6 minutes per side. Switch racks halfway through baking time. Cool completely.

3. Thinly slice green onion. Finely grate ½ tsp (2 mL) peel from lemon. Place cream cheese and milk in a large bowl. Using a wooden spoon, beat until smooth. Stir in onion and lemon peel. Slice salmon into thick strips. Thinly slice red onion into strips. Slice avocado in half and discard pit. Scoop flesh from peel and coarsely chop avocado.

4. To assemble, spread bagels with cream cheese mixture. Arrange on a large platter so they don't overlap too much. Scatter smoked salmon, red onion, avocado and capers overtop. Coarsely chop or shred mint (if using) if leaves are large. Leave small leaves whole. Sprinkle overtop. Squeeze a little juice from lemon overtop if you wish.

GET AHEAD Store baked bagel rounds in an airtight container at room temperature for up to 2 days. Assemble nachos just before serving.

NUTRIENTS PER SERVING 8 G PROTEIN 14 G FAT
15 G CARBOHYDRATES 2 G FIBRE 1 MG IRON
47 MG CALCIUM 386 MG SODIUM 209 CALORIES

Fresh Fruit Salad with Lime-Ginger Drizzle

Finely grate 1 tsp (5 mL) peel and squeeze 1 tbsp (15 mL) juice from a lime. Peel, then thinly slice, a 1-inch (2.5 cm) piece of ginger. Place ginger, ¼ cup (50 mL) chopped fresh mint, ½ cup (125 mL) granulated sugar, ½ cup (125 mL) water, lime peel and juice in a small saucepan. Bring to a boil over medium-high heat, then reduce heat to medium. Simmer uncovered, without stirring, until syrupy, 2 to 3 minutes. Strain, then cool at room temperature or in refrigerator.

Prepare 6 cups (1.5 L) fresh-cut fruit, such as pineapple, raspberries and strawberries. Arrange on a platter and sprinkle with a handful of blueberries. Drizzle about 3 tbsp (45 mL) syrup over fruit just before serving.

GET AHEAD Refrigerate syrup in a sealed jar for up to 1 week. Prepare fruit up to 1 day ahead and store in the refrigerator in separate resealable plastic bags. Bring to room temperature before serving.

FRUIT 101

Pineapple: To cut a pineapple, use a large knife to slice off the top and bottom. Turn upright. Cut off tough exterior, slicing from top to bottom. Don't worry if there are small grooves remaining. Cut in half, slicing straight down through the core. Place fruit cut-side down. Using a small paring knife, cut out the grooves. This will create a pretty pattern on the pineapple. Cut out and discard core. Cut pineapple into slices or chunks.

Raspberries: The best way to make your raspberries last is to tumble them onto paper towels. Remove any with black spots, which indicates mould. Let stand a few minutes so excess moisture is absorbed. Store in a paper towel-lined container, covered, in the refrigerator.

Strawberries: Use a huller or small paring knife to remove leafy green tops. (Unless you're careful, it's easy to lose a lot of berry using a knife.)

COOKING TIP

This type of drizzle is called a simple syrup, and with its easy preparation, it certainly lives up to its name. Use the syrup with any kind of fruit — or even over ice cream for a delicious treat.

MAKES 6 TO 8 SERVINGS

Sharp-Cheddar Zucchini Bread

PREPARATION TIME 15 MINUTES
BAKING TIME 45 MINUTES
STANDING TIME 10 MINUTES
MAKES 16 SLICES

1 medium zucchini

1 ½ cups (375 mL) all-purpose flour

2 tsp (10 mL) baking powder

1 tsp (5 mL) salt

½ tsp (2 mL) each baking soda and ground nutmeg

¼ cup (50 mL) each granulated and lightly packed brown sugar

2 cups (500 mL) grated cheddar cheese, preferably old

2 eggs

⅓ cup (75 mL) vegetable oil

COOKING TIP
When zucchini are in season, this recipe is a great way to use them up.

1. Preheat oven to 350°F (180°C). Lightly coat a 9- × 5-inch (2 L) loaf pan with oil. Using large holes on a box grater, grate unpeeled zucchini. Using your hands, squeeze out as much liquid as possible. Pat dry with a kitchen towel. Zucchini should measure about 1 cup (250 mL).

2. In a large bowl, using a fork, stir flour with baking powder, salt, baking soda and nutmeg. Stir in granulated and brown sugars. Stir in zucchini and 1 ½ cups (375 mL) cheese.

3. In a small bowl, whisk eggs with oil. Pour over flour mixture and stir just until mixed. Batter will be thick. Scrape into prepared loaf pan. Smooth top as best you can, then sprinkle with remaining ½ cup (125 mL) cheese.

4. Bake in centre of preheated oven until a cake tester inserted into centre of loaf comes out clean, 45 to 50 minutes. Let stand 10 minutes. Then carefully turn loaf onto a cooling rack. Terrific warm or at room temperature.

GET AHEAD Cool loaf completely, then wrap in plastic wrap. Store at room temperature for up to 3 days, or overwrap with foil and freeze for up to 2 months.

NUTRIENTS PER SLICE 6 G PROTEIN 10 G FAT
16 G CARBOHYDRATES 1 G FIBRE 1 MG IRON
125 MG CALCIUM 309 MG SODIUM 176 CALORIES

Cranberry-Bran Muffins

PREPARATION TIME 25 MINUTES
BAKING TIME 25 MINUTES
STANDING TIME 15 MINUTES
MAKES 24 MUFFINS OR
12 MUFFINS AND 1 LOAF
(12 SLICES)

4 cups (1 L) all-purpose flour
3 cups (750 mL) natural wheat bran
2 tbsp (30 mL) baking powder
1 tsp (5 mL) each baking soda, salt, cinnamon and ground nutmeg
½ tsp (2 mL) ground allspice
5 eggs
2 ½ cups (625 mL) buttermilk
1 cup (250 mL) packed brown sugar
¾ cup (175 mL) vegetable oil
⅓ cup (75 mL) fancy molasses
1 ½ tsp (7 mL) vanilla extract
300 g pkg frozen cranberries
¾ cup (175 mL) raisins

CHATELAINE KITCHEN FREEZING TIP

Get even fresher make-ahead results by freezing unbaked batter and baking it fresh. As soon as batter is prepared, spoon into paper-lined muffin cups, filling just to rims. Freeze until firm, at least 1½ hours. Then pop frozen dough-filled paper cups into a large plastic bag. Seal and freeze for up to 1 month. To bake, place frozen dough-filled cups in a muffin tin to help them hold their shape. Bake in centre of preheated 375°F (190°C) oven until a cake tester inserted into centre of a muffin comes out clean, 25 to 35 minutes.

1. Preheat oven to 375°F (190°C). Lightly oil or spray two 12-cup muffin tins or a 12-cup muffin tin and a 9- × 5-inch (2 L) loaf pan. Place flour in a large bowl. Using a fork, stir in wheat bran, baking powder, baking soda, salt, cinnamon, nutmeg and allspice until evenly mixed.

2. In another large bowl, whisk eggs. Whisk in buttermilk, sugar, oil, molasses and vanilla. Pour over flour mixture. Stir just until mixed. Stir in cranberries and raisins to evenly distribute. Do not overmix.

3. Fill 24 muffin cups right to rims. Or, if making 12 muffins and a loaf, fill muffin cups right to rims first, then turn remaining mixture into pan.

4. Bake in centre of preheated oven until a cake tester inserted into centre of a muffin comes out clean, about 25 minutes. Remove from oven. If also baking a loaf, leave in oven and reduce temperature to 350°F (180°C). Continue baking loaf until a cake tester inserted into centre comes out clean, 35 to 45 more minutes. If top of loaf browns before it's done, cover loosely with foil. Cool on a wire rack, 15 minutes, then gently turn out.

GET AHEAD Once muffins and loaf are cooled down to room temperature, store in an airtight container at room temperature for up to 2 days, or wrap separately in plastic wrap and freeze for up to 1 month. (Or place muffins in freezer just until firm. Pop into a large plastic bag, seal and freeze. This will keep them from sticking together.)

NUTRIENTS PER MUFFIN OR SLICE 6 G PROTEIN 9 G FAT
40 G CARBOHYDRATES 5 G FIBRE 3 MG IRON
94 MG CALCIUM 255 MG SODIUM 248 CALORIES

Decadent Chocolate Brownie Muffins

PREPARATION TIME 20 MINUTES
BAKING TIME 20 MINUTES
STANDING TIME 15 MINUTES
MAKES 12 LARGE MUFFINS

2 oz (60 g) white chocolate, about 2 squares

6 oz (170 g) semi-sweet chocolate, about 6 squares

2 eggs

1 ½ cups (375 mL) granulated sugar

1 cup (250 mL) buttermilk

½ cup (125 mL) unsalted butter, melted

2 tsp (10 mL) vanilla extract

2 cups (500 mL) all-purpose flour

1 cup (250 mL) cocoa powder

2 tsp (10 mL) baking powder

1 tsp (5 mL) salt

½ tsp (2 mL) baking soda

MAKE MORE

This recipe doubles easily to make 24 muffins. Or make 12 muffins and a cake: Following directions above for adding chocolate, fill 12 muffin cups with batter, then scrape half of remaining batter into a 9- x 13-inch (3 L) baking pan. Sprinkle with chopped (not cubed) white chocolate. Scrape remaining batter overtop. Smooth top. Bake both in centre of preheated 375°F (190°C) oven until a cake tester inserted into centre comes out clean, 20 to 25 minutes for muffins and 40 minutes for cake.

1. Preheat oven to 375°F (190°C). Lightly oil a 12-cup muffin tin. Cut white chocolate into 12 small cubes (don't worry if they crumble a little). Finely chop semi-sweet chocolate.

2. In a medium bowl, whisk eggs. Whisk in sugar, buttermilk, butter and vanilla. Place flour in a very large bowl. Using a fork, stir in cocoa, baking powder, salt and baking soda, making sure no clumps of cocoa remain. Stir in semi-sweet chocolate. Pour in egg mixture and stir just until evenly mixed.

3. Spoon 1 heaping tbsp (22 mL) batter into each muffin cup. Place a cube of white chocolate into centre of each. Fill with batter to rims.

4. Bake in centre of preheated oven until a cake tester inserted into centre of a muffin comes out clean, except for any melted chocolate, 20 to 25 minutes. Remove pan to a wire rack. Cool 15 minutes, then turn out onto rack. Serve warm or cool completely on a wire rack.

GET AHEAD Store cooled muffins in an airtight container at room temperature for up to 2 days, or freeze in an airtight plastic container for up to 1 month.

NUTRIENTS PER MUFFIN 6 G PROTEIN 15 G FAT
58 G CARBOHYDRATES 4 G FIBRE 3 MG IRON
75 MG CALCIUM 322 MG SODIUM 376 CALORIES

Quick Quinoa Porridge

PREPARATION TIME 5 MINUTES
COOKING TIME 12 MINUTES
STANDING TIME 15 MINUTES
MAKES 8 SERVINGS

946 mL carton unsweetened original almond milk

1 cup (250 mL) quinoa

½ tsp (2 mL) cardamom (optional)

¼ cup (50 mL) golden raisins

¼ cup (50 mL) dried apricots, thinly sliced

¼ cup (50 mL) skin-on whole almonds, preferably toasted

Fresh berries for garnish

GOOD FOR YOU

It's a simple seed, yet hearty quinoa contains all the essential amino acids, which aid in building muscle.

1. Pour 2 cups (500 mL) almond milk into a large saucepan. Bring to a boil over high heat. In a sieve, rinse quinoa, then stir into almond milk along with cardamom. Cover and bring back to a boil. Then reduce heat and simmer for 12 minutes. Remove from heat. Using a fork, fluff. Cover and let stand until tender, about 15 minutes.

2. Stir in extra almond milk, 1 tbsp (15 mL) at a time, until mixture is as thick as you like. Stir in raisins, apricots and almonds. Spoon into bowls. Pour a little more almond milk overtop. Sprinkle with berries. Great sweetened with honey, maple syrup or brown sugar.

NUTRIENTS PER ½ CUP (125 mL) SERVING WITH 1 TBSP (15 mL)
ADDITIONAL ALMOND MILK 4 G PROTEIN 5 G FAT
22 G CARBOHYDRATES 3 G FIBRE 3 MG IRON
91 MG CALCIUM 62 MG SODIUM 141 CALORIES

Scrumptious White Chocolate Scones

PREPARATION TIME 15 MINUTES
BAKING TIME 12 MINUTES
MAKES 12 SCONES

YOGOURT CRÈME FRAÎCHE

Try this recipe in place of the usual clotted-cream scone spread: Line a sieve with a dampened cheesecloth or clean thin cloth. Place the sieve over a bowl and spread 2 cups (500 mL) Balkan-style plain yogourt (5.9% MF) over the cloth. Lightly cover and leave at room temperature for at least 2 hours, or cover with plastic wrap and refrigerate overnight. The longer the yogourt drains, the thicker it will be. Discard the liquid in the bowl.

Makes 2 cups (500 mL)

3 oz (90 g) white chocolate or ½ cup (125 mL) toasted coconut

2 cups (500 mL) all-purpose flour

2 tbsp (30 mL) granulated sugar plus extra for dusting

1 tbsp (15 mL) baking powder

½ tsp (2 mL) salt

½ cup (125 mL) unsalted butter, at room temperature

1 cup (250 mL) buttermilk or milk

2 tbsp (30 mL) milk

1. Preheat oven to 425°F (220°C). Lightly coat a rimmed baking sheet with oil or line with parchment paper. Coarsely chop chocolate. In a large bowl, stir flour with sugar, baking powder and salt to evenly mix.

2. Using your fingers, a fork or pastry blender, work in butter until crumbly. Pour in buttermilk. Using a wooden spoon, stir until almost mixed. Add chocolate and knead in, just until mixed.

3. Turn onto a floured counter. Divide dough in half. Gently pat each half into a circle about 1 inch (2.5 cm) thick. Cut each circle into 6 triangular-shaped scones, for 12 in total.

4. Place scones on baking sheet at least 1 inch (2.5 cm) apart. Lightly brush with milk. Sprinkle with a little sugar if you wish. Bake in centre of preheated oven until lightly golden, 12 to 15 minutes.

NUTRIENTS PER SCONE 4 G PROTEIN 11 G FAT
24 G CARBOHYDRATES 1 G FIBRE 1 MG IRON
85 MG CALCIUM 198 MG SODIUM 204 CALORIES

Maple and Candied-Ginger Granola

PREPARATION TIME 10 MINUTES
BAKING TIME 20 MINUTES
MAKES 6 CUPS (1.5 L) FOR
24 SERVINGS

4 cups (1 L) large-flake oats

1 cup (250 mL) natural wheat bran

¼ cup (50 mL) each slivered almonds and sunflower seeds (optional)

1 tsp (5 mL) cinnamon

¼ tsp (1 mL) salt

½ cup (125 mL) maple syrup

2 tbsp (30 mL) vegetable oil

1 tsp (5 mL) vanilla extract

1 orange

½ cup (125 mL) mix of raisins, dried cranberries and chopped
　dried apricots

2 tbsp (30 mL) finely chopped candied ginger

WHAT IS IT?

Candied ginger is fresh ginger (usually in thick slices) that has been crystallized in a sugary syrup, then tossed in sugar. Finely chopped, it makes an excellent addition to baked goods and desserts.

1. Preheat oven to 350°F (180°C). In a large bowl, stir oats with bran, almonds and sunflower seeds (if using), cinnamon and salt. In another bowl, whisk maple syrup with oil and vanilla. Finely grate 1 tsp (5 mL) peel and squeeze out 2 tbsp (30 mL) juice from orange. Stir both into syrup mixture. Pour over oat mixture and stir to mix.

2. Spread out on a large, rimmed baking sheet. Bake, uncovered, in centre of preheated oven, stirring occasionally (especially near edges of pan) to prevent burning, until oats are golden, about 20 minutes.

3. Remove pan from oven to a rack. Stir occasionally. When cool, stir in dried fruit and ginger. Spoon over yogourt and top with fresh fruit.

GET AHEAD Store granola in an airtight container at room temperature for up to 1 week, or refrigerate for up to 1 month or freeze for up to 3 months.

NUTRIENTS PER SERVING 3 G PROTEIN 2 G FAT
19 G CARBOHYDRATES 3 G FIBRE 1 MG IRON
15 MG CALCIUM 50 MG SODIUM 101 CALORIES

Best Buttermilk Pancakes

PREPARATION TIME 10 MINUTES
COOKING TIME 16 MINUTES
MAKES 12 PANCAKES

½ cup (125 mL) unsalted butter plus extra for cooking

2 cups (500 mL) buttermilk or 2 cups (500 mL) milk plus
2 tbsp (30 mL) lemon juice

2 cups (500 mL) all-purpose flour

¼ cup (50 mL) granulated sugar

2 tbsp (30 mL) poppy seeds (optional)

2 tsp (10 mL) baking powder

1 tsp (5 mL) each baking soda and salt

2 eggs

2 tsp (10 mL) vanilla extract

2 peaches, unpeeled, thinly sliced (optional)

TASTY TWEAKS

Wholesome: Substitute whole-wheat flour for all-purpose. If batter is thick, add more milk 1 tbsp (15 mL) at a time, until it's pourable.

Berry: Pour batter into pan, sprinkle each pancake with 1 heaping tbsp (22 mL) blueberries, then gently push in.

Chai-spiced: Omit poppy seeds. Stir 1 tsp (5 mL) cinnamon, ½ tsp (2 mL) ground ginger and ¼ tsp (1 mL) ground cardamom (optional) into flour mixture before adding egg mixture.

1. Melt butter in the microwave or on the stove. Set aside to cool. Measure out buttermilk, or stir milk with lemon juice, then let stand until slightly thickened, at least 5 minutes. Meanwhile, in a large bowl, using a fork, stir flour with sugar, poppy seeds (if using), baking powder, baking soda and salt. Make a well in centre.

2. In a medium bowl, whisk eggs with buttermilk, cooled melted butter and vanilla. Pour into well in flour mixture. Using a wooden spoon, stir just until blended. The batter should be a bit lumpy. For fluffy pancakes, stir as little as possible.

3. Lightly coat a large frying pan with butter and set over medium heat. (Save time by using 2 pans or a large griddle.) Pour ⅓ cup (75 mL) batter in one side of pan. Pancake will be about 6 inches (15 cm) in diameter. Add 1 or 2 more pancakes. Gently press peach slices (if using) into batter.

4. Cook until bubbles form on the top of each pancake and edges begin to brown, 2 to 4 minutes. Using a wide spatula, flip and continue cooking until the bottoms of pancakes become golden, 2 to 3 minutes. Don't press or they will become tough.

5. Serve right away or place on a plate and keep warm in a 200°F (90°C) oven while cooking remaining pancakes. Delicious drizzled with maple syrup.

NUTRIENTS PER PANCAKE 5 G PROTEIN 12 G FAT
23 G CARBOHYDRATES 1 G FIBRE 1 MG IRON
91 MG CALCIUM 411 MG SODIUM 219 CALORIES

Roasted Sugary Rum Bacon

PREPARATION TIME 5 MINUTES
ROASTING TIME 45 MINUTES
STANDING TIME 5 MINUTES
MAKES 12 THICK SLICES

2 lb (1 kg) piece peameal bacon
2 tbsp (30 mL) brown sugar
¼ cup (50 mL) rum, preferably dark, or apple or orange juice

1. Preheat oven to 350°F (180°C). For easy cleanup, line with foil a baking dish large enough to hold bacon, such as an 8-inch- (2 L) square baking dish. Place bacon, cornmeal-side up, in dish. In a small bowl, stir sugar with rum until dissolved. Spoon mixture evenly over cornmeal coating.

2. Roast, uncovered, in centre of preheated oven until bacon is warmed through and top is golden brown, 45 to 50 minutes. Remove from oven and let stand 5 minutes before slicing into 12 thick or 24 thin slices.

NUTRIENTS PER THICK SLICE 16 G PROTEIN 5 G FAT
3 G CARBOHYDRATES 0 G FIBRE 1 MG IRON
8 MG CALCIUM 994 MG SODIUM 131 CALORIES

COOKING TIP

Basting a peameal roast (best known as "Canadian bacon") with a sugar-rum coating infuses delicious flavour, and you get to skip the tedious task of frying slices of bacon by popping the full roast in the oven instead. This stress-free brunch main course is a reader favourite.

31

Cheddar, Pepper and Potato Bake

PREPARATION TIME 15 MINUTES
BAKING TIME 1 HOUR,
15 MINUTES
MAKES 8 TO 12 SERVINGS

1 cup (250 mL) sour cream

10 oz (284 mL) can undiluted condensed cream of potato or
    mushroom soup

½ cup (125 mL) butter, melted

1 tbsp (15 mL) paprika (optional)

½ tsp (2 mL) each salt and freshly ground black pepper

1 kg pkg frozen country-style hash browns

1 jalapeño pepper (optional)

1 each red and green pepper, coarsely chopped

1 large onion, chopped

1 cup (250 mL) chopped cooked ham (optional)

2 cups (500 mL) grated cheddar cheese

PERFECT SOFT-BOILED EGGS

Place eggs in a pot and cover with water. Bring to a boil. Cover and remove from heat. Let stand 5 minutes. Serve in egg cups.

1. Preheat oven to 400°F (200°C). In a very large bowl, stir sour cream with soup, butter, paprika (if using), salt and pepper. Mixture will be lumpy. Stir in frozen hash browns until evenly mixed. Seed and finely chop jalapeño. Stir into potatoes along with red and green peppers, onion, ham and 1 ½ cups (375 mL) cheddar. Mixture will be very thick. Spoon into a 9- × 13-inch (3 L) baking dish. Smooth top. Sprinkle with remaining ½ cup (125 mL) cheddar. Cover dish tightly with foil.

2. Bake in centre of preheated oven until hot, about 1 hour. Remove foil and bake until cheese is golden, 15 to 20 more minutes. Serve with soft-boiled eggs.

GET AHEAD Best eaten the day it's made, but dish will keep, covered and refrigerated, for up to 1 day. Reheat in microwave.

NUTRIENTS PER SERVING 8 G PROTEIN 19 G FAT
22 G CARBOHYDRATES 2 G FIBRE 1 MG IRON
174 MG CALCIUM 491 MG SODIUM 280 CALORIES

Creamy Bacon-and-Egg Pie

PREPARATION TIME 25 MINUTES
COOKING TIME 9 MINUTES
BAKING TIME 50 MINUTES
STANDING TIME 10 MINUTES
MAKES 8 SERVINGS

5 strips bacon

1 onion

5 oz (140 g) log goat cheese or ½ 8-oz (250 g) block cream cheese

¼ cup (50 mL) butter, melted

6 sheets frozen phyllo pastry, thawed

8 eggs

½ cup (125 mL) half-and-half cream

1 tbsp (15 mL) Dijon mustard

3 tbsp (45 mL) snipped fresh chives

½ tsp (2 mL) salt

6 cherry tomatoes, halved

WHAT IS IT?

Phyllo, meaning leaf in Greek, is an apt name for this paper-thin pastry. While preparing, cover unused phyllo with a damp kitchen towel to prevent the delicate sheets from drying out.

1. Position rack on bottom shelf of oven. Preheat oven to 325°F (160°C). In a large frying pan set over medium heat, fry bacon until crispy, 5 to 7 minutes. Meanwhile, thinly slice onion. Remove bacon to a paper towel–lined plate.

2. Add onion to fat in pan. If brown bits are stuck to pan bottom, add 1 to 2 tbsp (15 to 30 mL) water and use a wooden spoon to scrape up bits. Stir occasionally, until onion is soft and most of the liquid is absorbed, 4 to 6 minutes. Turn off heat under pan. Crumble in goat cheese and stir until melted and evenly mixed. Set pan aside.

3. Brush a 10-inch (25 cm) deep-dish pie plate with a little melted butter. Place a phyllo sheet on counter. Brush with butter. Place another sheet overtop. Brush with butter, then repeat with remaining sheets and butter. Line baking dish with phyllo, gently pressing and folding pastry edges under as needed. It's okay if some of the pastry hangs over the edge a little. Evenly spread cheese mixture on bottom of phyllo.

4. In a large bowl, whisk eggs with cream, Dijon, chives and salt until evenly mixed. Pour over cheese mixture. Bake pie on bottom rack of preheated oven for 20 minutes. Meanwhile, slice tomatoes in half. Cut bacon into chunks. After pie has baked for 20 minutes, remove to a heatproof surface. Sprinkle with tomatoes and scatter with bacon. Continue to bake until eggs are set in centre when pan is jiggled and pastry is deep golden, 30 to 35 more minutes. Let stand 10 minutes before cutting into wedges. Pie tastes best the day it's made.

NUTRIENTS PER SERVING 11 G PROTEIN 22 G FAT
13 G CARBOHYDRATES 1 G FIBRE 2 MG IRON
70 MG CALCIUM 499 MG SODIUM 296 CALORIES

snacks and appetizers

When it comes to menu planning, the first course often gets left to the last minute. But dinner becomes a party with any of these quick and easy starters, from spicy chicken satays to avocado-salmon rolls.

Quick Caprese-Style Toasts

PREPARATION TIME 10 MINUTES
BAKING TIME 7 MINUTES
BROILING TIME 5 MINUTES
MAKES 8 SLICES

1 cup (250 mL) coarsely chopped fresh basil
¼ cup (50 mL) olive oil
1 garlic clove
Pinches of salt and freshly ground black pepper
1 thick focaccia loaf
1 ½ cups (375 mL) grated mozzarella cheese
6 large balls bocconcini
5 plum tomatoes

WHAT IS IT?

The Italian cheese bocconcini, pronounced bohk-kohn-CHEE-nee, is fresh mozzarella. It is ball-shaped and comes in a variety of sizes, ranging from pearl-sized to large.

A traditional caprese salad is made with bocconcini, sliced tomatoes and fresh basil.

1. Preheat oven to 400°F (200°C). Place basil, oil, garlic, salt and pepper in a blender. Whirl to a saucy consistency. Add more oil to make it saucier if you wish. Cut focaccia into 8 thick slices. Place on a rimmed baking sheet. Spread half of basil mixture over bread, then evenly sprinkle with mozzarella. Thickly slice bocconcini and tomatoes into rounds, then arrange in overlapping slices on top of bread. Sprinkle with more salt and pepper.

2. Bake in centre of preheated oven until cheese starts to melt, 7 to 10 minutes. Broil until cheese begins to turn golden, about 5 minutes. Remove from oven and drizzle with remaining basil mixture. Cut each slice in half or serve whole. Best served warm.

GET AHEAD Cover basil mixture and refrigerate for up to 2 days. Spread on focaccia just before serving.

NUTRIENTS PER HALF SLICE 20 G PROTEIN 24 G FAT
29 G CARBOHYDRATES 3 G FIBRE 3 MG IRON
428 MG CALCIUM 655 MG SODIUM 409 CALORIES

Cheddar and Chipotle Shortbread Crisps

PREPARATION TIME 10 MINUTES
REFRIGERATION TIME 3 HOURS
BAKING TIME 8 MINUTES
PER BATCH
MAKES 7 DOZEN CRISPS

2 cups (500 mL) all-purpose flour

1 tsp (5 mL) salt

1 tsp (5 mL) ground coriander (optional)

1 chipotle chili packed in adobo sauce

1 to 2 tsp (5 to 10 mL) adobo sauce

250 g container MacLaren's Imperial cold-pack cheddar cheese, cut into chunks

1 cup (250 mL) unsalted butter, cut into cubes

CHATELAINE KITCHEN TIP

Use these crisps to make mini-sandwiches with red pepper jelly, or top with a dollop of salsa or homemade guacamole.

1. In a medium bowl, using a fork, stir flour with salt and coriander (if using). Place chipotle, 1 tsp (5 mL) adobo sauce, cheddar and butter in a food processor. Whirl until smooth, scraping down sides of bowl as necessary. Taste and add remaining 1 tsp (5 mL) adobo sauce if you like it spicier. Add flour mixture. Pulse just until mixture comes together and starts to form a ball. Mixture will be wet.

2. Lightly flour hands, then divide dough into 4 portions. Shape each portion into a log about 1 ¼ inches (3 cm) wide and 6 inches (15 cm) long. Wrap in wax paper, twisting ends to seal tightly. Refrigerate until firm, at least 3 hours.

3. To bake, position oven rack on bottom shelf of oven. Preheat oven to 400°F (200°C). Remove a log from the refrigerator and slice into ¼-inch- (5 mm) thick rounds. Place on ungreased baking sheets about 1 inch (2.5 cm) apart.

4. Bake a sheet at a time on bottom rack of preheated oven until edges are lightly browned, 8 to 10 minutes. Watch crackers carefully — once they're brown, they're done. Remove crisps to a rack to cool. Repeat with remaining logs.

GET AHEAD Store unbaked, wrapped rolls (Step 2) in a sealed plastic bag for up to 1 week, or freeze for up to 1 month. Store baked, cooled crisps in an airtight container in the refrigerator for up to 2 weeks.

NUTRIENTS PER CRISP 1 G PROTEIN 3 G FAT
3 G CARBOHYDRATES 0 G FIBRE 0 MG IRON
16 MG CALCIUM 58 MG SODIUM 40 CALORIES

Gorgonzola and Clementine Toasts

PREPARATION 20 MINUTES
MAKES 12 TOASTS

6 clementines

½ of 8 oz (250 g) pkg spreadable cream cheese, at room temperature

2 to 3 tsp (10 to 15 mL) milk

½ cup (125 mL) crumbled gorgonzola or other blue cheese

12 small thin slices toasted walnut bread or 12 Melba toasts

¼ cup (50 mL) chopped walnuts, toasted (optional)

CLEMENTINES 101

Buying

Clementines have a looser skin than other citrus fruits, so when you give them a squeeze, they should have a bit of give. Brown or green discolourations are fine, but skip fruit with bruises or soft spots. For the sweetest clementines, choose ones that are heavy for their size.

Storing

Clementines don't last as long as navel oranges, but you can extend their life by storing them in a perforated plastic bag in the refrigerator crisper. For maximum flavour, bring them to room temperature before eating.

1. Finely grate 1 tsp (5 mL) peel fro m a clementine. Place in a medium bowl along with cream cheese. Add 2 tsp (10 mL) milk. Beat mixture with a wooden spoon. Crumble in gorgonzola and stir until evenly mixed. Mixture will be lumpy. If too thick for spreading, stir in another 1 tsp (5 mL) milk.

2. Up to 1 hour before serving, peel and segment clementines. Thickly spread toasts with cheese mixture. Top each with clementine segments. Sprinkle with walnuts.

GET AHEAD Prepare cheese mixture and chop nuts. Store separately, covered, in the refrigerator for up to 3 days. Bring cheese and fruit to room temperature before assembling toasts.

NUTRIENTS PER TOAST 6 G PROTEIN 7 G FAT
18 G CARBOHYDRATES 3 G FIBRE 1 MG IRON
77 MG CALCIUM 244 MG SODIUM 157 CALORIES

Sweet Pea and Parmesan Crostini

PREPARATION TIME 15 MINUTES
COOKING TIME 7 MINUTES
MAKES 16 CROSTINI

8 thinly sliced pancetta rounds

2 cups (500 mL) shelled fresh or frozen peas

1 lemon

½ cup (125 mL) freshly grated parmesan cheese

¼ cup (50 mL) shredded fresh basil

1 tbsp (15 mL) olive oil

Generous pinches of salt

16 toasted baguette slices

EASY BAGUETTE TOASTS

For a crispy appetizer base, cut baguette into thin slices. Lightly brush both sides with olive oil. Bake on a large baking sheet at 500°F (260°C) until golden, 1 to 3 minutes per side. Cool before using.

1. Heat a large non-stick frying pan over medium-high heat. Add pancetta and cook until crisp, about 1 to 2 minutes per side. Remove to a paper towel. When cool, carefully slice in half.

2. Meanwhile, bring a partially filled pot of water to a boil. Add peas. Cook until very tender, 5 to 15 minutes. Frozen peas need only about 4 minutes. When peas are done, drain well.

3. Place peas in a food processor. Squeeze 2 tbsp (30 mL) juice from lemon and add to peas along with parmesan, basil, oil and salt. Pulse until smooth. Taste and add more oil and lemon juice if you wish. To serve, top each baguette slice with a dab of pea purée, then a piece of pancetta. Spread more purée overtop.

NUTRIENTS PER CROSTINI 3 G PROTEIN 5 G FAT
5 G CARBOHYDRATES 1 G FIBRE 1 MG IRON
44 MG CALCIUM 114 MG SODIUM 76 CALORIES

Smoky Brie with Wild Blueberry Sauce

PREPARATION TIME 5 MINUTES
GRILLING TIME 15 MINUTES
MAKES 4 TO 6 SERVINGS
WITH ⅔ CUP (150 mL) SAUCE

1 untreated cedar plank

1 shallot

1 tbsp (15 mL) butter

1 cup (250 mL) blueberries, preferably wild

Pinch of salt

⅓ cup (75 mL) orange juice

1 tbsp (15 mL) cornstarch

1 medium round or 2 small rounds of brie or camembert cheese

SWITCH IT UP

Swap sweet summer strawberries for blueberries.

1. Place cedar plank in kitchen sink, large bucket or dish. Cover with water. Weigh plank down with a couple of heavy cans so it stays submerged. Soak at least 1 hour, and preferably overnight. (See sidebar, page 124.)

2. Thinly slice shallot and cut butter into cubes. Place both in a foil pie plate along with blueberries. Sprinkle with salt. In a bowl, stir orange juice with cornstarch until dissolved. Stir into blueberry mixture. Tightly cover pie plate with foil.

3. When ready to grill, heat barbecue to medium-high, then reduce heat on one side of barbecue to medium. Place plank on side that is set to medium, and pie plate with blueberries on side that is set to medium-high. Barbecue, lid closed, until plank starts to smoke, about 5 minutes. Place cheese on plank. Continue grilling, lid closed, until cheese starts to soften and berries are saucy, about 10 minutes. You don't need to stir berries. Check plank often. If it catches fire, immediately spray with water and reduce heat under plank.

4. Turn off grill and carefully remove plate with blueberry sauce. Using a wide barbecue spatula and tongs, carefully remove plank with cheese. Place on a heatproof surface. Spoon blueberry sauce over cheese. Serve with crackers, flatbread or slices of baguette.

NUTRIENTS PER SERVING WITH 1 TBSP (15 mL) SAUCE
8 G PROTEIN 13 G FAT 7 G CARBOHYDRATES 1 G FIBRE
0 MG IRON 74 MG CALCIUM 257 MG SODIUM 171 CALORIES

Spicy and Sweet Nuts

Preheat oven to 325°F (160°C). In a large bowl, whisk 1 egg white with 1 tsp (5 mL) granulated sugar and ½ tsp (2 mL) salt. Whisk in generous pinches of cinnamon and hot chili powder or smoked paprika. Stir in 3 cups (750 mL) unsalted nuts. Line a baking sheet with parchment paper. Spread nuts overtop. Roast, stirring occasionally, until dry, about 15 minutes. Cool completely.

MAKES 3 CUPS (750 ML)

SWITCH IT UP

Use honey in place of sugar and curry in place of chili powder. Omit cinnamon.

GIFT IDEA

Nuts will keep well stored in the freezer for up to 1 month — ideal for packing in pretty containers for hostess or birthday presents.

LUNCH SUGGESTION

Spiced nuts make a great snack during the day. Opt for the healthiest nuts — almonds, walnuts, Brazil nuts or pistachios are all good choices.

Golden Hummus

PREPARATION TIME 15 MINUTES
MAKES 2 CUPS (500 mL)

1 medium sweet potato

19 oz (540 mL) can chickpeas

1 large lemon

1 tbsp (15 mL) dark sesame oil

2 garlic cloves

Generous pinches of salt and freshly ground black pepper

CHATELAINE KITCHEN TIP

Traditionally, hummus is made with tahini (sesame paste). In its place we added sesame oil, since it's a more versatile ingredient to have on hand — it's great in stir-fries and dressings, too.

GOOD FOR YOU

The sweet potato gives this popular dip a healthy boost. You can serve it with pita, crackers or breadsticks, but we love it served with fresh veggies..

1. Pierce potato with a fork, then place in microwave on a piece of paper towel. Microwave on high until very soft, 4 to 6 minutes. When cool enough to handle, cut in half. Using a spoon, scrape flesh into a food processor.

2. Rinse and drain chickpeas. Add to potato. Squeeze 3 tbsp (45 mL) juice from lemon. Add to potato along with sesame oil, garlic, salt and pepper. Purée until smooth. Spoon into a serving bowl. Serve with cucumber rounds, steamed fiddleheads or crackers.

GET AHEAD Cover dip and refrigerate for up to 2 days.

NUTRIENTS PER TBSP (15 mL) 1 G PROTEIN 1 G FAT
3 G CARBOHYDRATES 1 G FIBRE 0 MG IRON
7 MG CALCIUM 37 MG SODIUM 24 CALORIES

Genovese Pesto Dip

PREPARATION TIME 5 MINUTES
MAKES 2 ¾ CUPS (675 mL)

5 sun-dried tomatoes, packed in oil

8 oz (250 g) block cream cheese, at room temperature

10 oz (300 g) log goat cheese

½ cup (125 mL) toasted pine nuts

⅓ cup (75 mL) pesto, store-bought or homemade (sidebar, page 76; preferably use Genovese basil for its spicy taste)

SERVING SUGGESTION

Fabulous served warm too. Microwave on medium, stirring occasionally, until warm.

1. Thinly slice sun-dried tomatoes and place three-quarters of them in a food processor. Add cream and goat cheeses. Whirl to mix, then whirl in nuts and two-thirds of the pesto. Scrape into a serving bowl. Spoon remaining pesto overtop and scatter with remaining sun-dried tomatoes. Serve with bread sticks or cut vegetables.

GET AHEAD Cover dip and refrigerate for up to 2 days. Bring to room temperature before serving.

NUTRIENTS PER 1 TBSP (15 mL) 2 G PROTEIN 5 G FAT
1 G CARBOHYDRATES 0 G FIBRE 0 MG IRON
18 MG CALCIUM 65 MG SODIUM 57 CALORIES

Vietnamese-Style Beef Skewers

PREPARATION TIME 15 MINUTES
FREEZING TIME 30 MINUTES
BROILING TIME 5 MINUTES
MAKES 30 SKEWERS

30 small wooden skewers

1 lb (500 g) top sirloin steak, about 1 inch (2.5 cm) thick

1 lemon

2 tbsp (30 mL) vegetable oil

5 garlic cloves, minced, or 1 tbsp (15 mL) bottled minced garlic

1 tbsp (15 mL) finely grated fresh ginger or 2 ½ tsp (12 mL) bottled minced ginger

1 tsp (5 mL) each ground coriander and cinnamon

2 tbsp (30 mL) soy sauce

¼ cup (50 mL) finely chopped fresh mint (optional)

THE BEST CUT

Slicing beef across its natural grain results in a more tender piece than if sliced *along* the grain.

COOKING TIP

A delicious Vietnamese lemon grass dish inspired this recipe. Since lemon grass isn't always easy to find, use a mix of lemon peel and grated fresh ginger.

1. Soak skewers in water for 20 minutes (see sidebar, page 124). To make steak easier to slice, place in freezer for about 30 minutes. Meanwhile, line a shallow-rimmed baking sheet with foil.

2. Finely grate 1 tbsp (15 mL) peel from lemon into a medium bowl. Stir in oil, garlic, ginger, coriander and cinnamon. Mixture will form a paste. After steak has chilled, slice across the grain into very thin strips. Add beef to garlic mixture and stir to evenly coat. Refrigerate if not cooking immediately.

3. When ready to cook, position oven rack in top third of oven. Preheat broiler. Tightly thread 1 strip of beef onto each skewer. If strips are small, thread 2 or 3 strips onto a skewer.

4. Place skewers on baking sheet. (It will be a tight fit.) Brush with soy sauce. Broil until meat loses its pink colour, 5 to 7 minutes. You don't need to turn skewers. Remove from oven and arrange on a platter. Sprinkle with mint if you wish. Serve with lime or lemon wedges.

NUTRIENTS PER SKEWER 3 G PROTEIN 2 G FAT
1 G CARBOHYDRATES 0 G FIBRE 0 MG IRON
4 MG CALCIUM 74 MG SODIUM 28 CALORIES

Fresh Mint and Shrimp Salad Rolls

PREPARATION TIME 40 MINUTES
SOAKING TIME 15 MINUTES
MAKES 15 ROLLS

340 g pkg frozen cooked medium shrimp, peeled
½ of 227 g pkg thin rice vermicelli
½ head bibb or Boston lettuce
1 bunch fresh mint
1 cup (250 mL) coarsely chopped fresh cilantro
½ cup (125 mL) finely grated carrots
15 rice-paper rounds, about 6 inches (15 cm) in diameter

TANGY DIPPING SAUCE

Stir ¾ cup (175 mL) rice vinegar with ¼ cup (50 mL) fish sauce, 4 tsp (20 mL) granulated sugar, 2 tbsp (30 mL) finely grated carrots and 2 tsp (10 mL) finely chopped jalapeño pepper. Use right away or cover and refrigerate overnight.

Makes 1 ¼ cups (300 mL)

1. Thaw shrimp according to package directions (or see sidebar, page 246). Pat dry with paper towels. Place noodles in a large bowl and cover with very hot water. Soak 15 minutes. Drain well. Meanwhile, separate lettuce leaves and slice in half. Remove mint leaves from stems. Cut larger leaves in half. Stir cilantro and carrots into drained soaked noodles.

2. Cover a cutting board with a damp kitchen towel. Fill a large bowl or pie plate with hot water and place beside board. Line salad roll fillings up near board. Working with 1 sheet of rice paper at a time, soak in the hot water until very pliable, about 10 seconds. Gently lay wet round on towel. Line up 3 shrimp along bottom third of round. Top with a lettuce half and a tiny mound of noodles. Place a couple of mint leaves on top. Make sure not to overfill or sheets will be difficult to roll up.

3. Lift the sheet edge nearest you and pull tightly over filling, rolling toward the centre. When you reach centre, fold in sides to partially cover filling. Continue to tightly roll up sheet to form a log. To seal, dip your finger in water and rub over seam. Set roll, seam-side down, on a platter. Repeat with remaining ingredients. If rice-paper rounds curl before being soaked, don't worry. As soaking water cools, replace with hot water. Just before serving, slice rolls in half diagonally. Serve with Tangy Dipping Sauce (see sidebar, left).

GET AHEAD Cover rolls and refrigerate for up to 4 hours. Cut just before serving.

NUTRIENTS PER ROLL WITH 1 TBSP (15 mL) DIPPING SAUCE
6 G PROTEIN 1 G FAT 12 G CARBOHYDRATES 1 G FIBRE
1 MG IRON 22 MG CALCIUM 336 MG SODIUM 76 CALORIES

Spicy Chicken Satays

PREPARATION TIME 25 MINUTES
BROILING TIME 7 MINUTES
MAKES 20 SKEWERS

20 small wooden skewers

2 limes

⅓ cup (75 mL) finely chopped fresh cilantro

2 tbsp (30 mL) vegetable oil

2 tsp (10 mL) bottled chopped garlic or 3 small garlic cloves, minced

2 tsp (10 mL) hot chili-garlic sauce

½ tsp (2 mL) salt

4 skinless, boneless chicken breasts

4 tbsp (60 mL) soy sauce

½ tsp (2 mL) dark sesame oil

DINNER TONIGHT

These juicy satays double as a terrific main for a weeknight meal.

1. Soak skewers in water for 20 minutes (see sidebar, page 124). Finely grate 1 tbsp (15 mL) peel from limes into a large bowl. Stir in cilantro, vegetable oil, garlic, chili-garlic sauce and salt.

2. Cut chicken lengthwise into ½-inch- (1 cm) thick strips. Stir into cilantro mixture to coat. Refrigerate if not using right away.

3. When ready to cook, position oven rack in top third of oven. Preheat broiler. Line a rimmed baking sheet with foil and brush with vegetable oil or coat with cooking spray. Then thread 1 strip of chicken onto each skewer. Place on baking sheet. (It will be a tight fit.)

4. Broil until meat is lightly golden and firm to the touch, 7 to 9 minutes. You don't need to turn skewers. Sprinkle with more cilantro if you wish. In a small bowl, stir soy sauce with sesame oil for dipping. Arrange skewers and dipping sauce on a platter. Add lime wedges for squeezing over satays if you wish.

GET AHEAD Prepare chicken up to 2 days ahead and thread onto skewers. Keep covered and refrigerated until ready to cook.

NUTRIENTS PER SKEWER WITH 1 TSP (5 mL) SAUCE
6 G PROTEIN 2 G FAT 1 G CARBOHYDRATES 0 G FIBRE
0 MG IRON 3 MG CALCIUM 280 MG SODIUM 45 CALORIES

Avocado and Salmon Rolls

PREPARATION TIME 20 MINUTES
REFRIGERATION TIME 4 HOURS
MAKES 20 ROLLS

AVOCADO TRICK

Adding lemon to cut avocado helps prevent it from browning, but lime does an even better job. We found that with the addition of lime juice, avocado keeps its colour overnight.

8 oz (250 g) block cream cheese

2 tbsp (30 mL) snipped fresh chives

1 lime

½ very ripe avocado, peeled

5 oz (150 g) pkg wild smoked salmon, about 12 slices

2 tbsp (30 mL) sesame seeds (optional)

1. In a bowl, stir cream cheese with chives. Squeeze 2 tsp (10 mL) juice from lime and add to cream cheese along with avocado. Using a fork, mash to mix. Lay a large sheet of plastic wrap on counter. Arrange 6 salmon slices in centre, overlapping slightly, to form a rectangle. Spread half of avocado mixture over salmon almost to edges.

2. Starting from long edge, gently roll salmon, lifting plastic wrap to help form a log. Don't wrap plastic into roll. Sprinkle with half of sesame seeds (if using), rolling to coat. Wrap in plastic wrap. Twist ends to tighten roll. Repeat with remaining ingredients. Refrigerate rolls until firm, 4 hours or preferably overnight. With a serrated knife, gently slice into thick rounds. Serve on rice chips, rice crackers or thin cucumber slices, and top with more chives if you wish.

NUTRIENTS PER 2 ROLLS 4 G PROTEIN 6 G FAT
1 G CARBOHYDRATES 1 G FIBRE 0 MG IRON
12 MG CALCIUM 152 MG SODIUM 74 CALORIES

Smoked Trout and Mango Bites

PREPARATION TIME 20 MINUTES
MAKES 36 ROLLS

1 ripe mango
1 green onion
1 lime
½ tsp (2 mL) dark sesame oil
¼ tsp (1 mL) each salt and hot chili flakes
8 oz (250 g) smoked trout or a smoked or cooked salmon fillet
1 large English cucumber, unpeeled

MAKING THE CUT

Even though most cuts can be done with a knife, using a Japanese mandoline is quicker. This kitchen tool (that's pronounced the same as the string instrument MAN-duh-lihn) is ideal for making thin slices and julienne pieces (as in this recipe). It comes with different blades for each cut. Using the guard, hold the ingredient in place, then slide it back and forth over the mandoline and blade. Be sure to use the safety guard.

1. Slice mango into long, thin strips (see sidebar). Thinly slice onion on the diagonal. Place both in a bowl. Squeeze 1 tbsp (15 mL) juice from lime overtop. Add oil, salt, chili flakes and lime juice. Toss to evenly coat. Break or cut fish into long, thin pieces, about the length of mango slices.

2. Using a vegetable peeler, peel long strips from one side of cucumber until you hit the seeds, then turn over and peel strips from other side. Or using a mandoline, thinly slice cucumbers lengthwise. Working with 1 strip at a time, lay a few strips of mango (make sure to get some onion on it) parallel to the short bottom edge of cucumber. It should overhang both sides of cucumber. Top with 1 or 2 pieces of fish. Roll up in cucumber. Repeat with remaining ingredients. Slice rolls in half, then arrange cut-side down on a platter.

GET AHEAD Prepare mango mixture and peel cucumber strips. Wrap separately and refrigerate overnight. Prepare rolls but don't cut. Cover and refrigerate for up to 5 hours. Slice just before serving.

NUTRIENTS PER ROLL 2 G PROTEIN 1 G FAT
1 G CARBOHYDRATES 0 G FIBRE 0 MG IRON
3 MG CALCIUM 142 MG SODIUM 18 CALORIES

Thai Turkey Meatballs

PREPARATION TIME 15 MINUTES
BAKING TIME 15 MINUTES
MAKES 36 MEATBALLS

1 lemon or lime

2 green onions

2 garlic cloves

1 egg

2 tbsp (30 mL) hot chili-garlic sauce

2 tsp (10 mL) fish sauce

1 lb (500 g) ground turkey or chicken

3 tbsp (45 mL) cornstarch

2 tbsp (30 mL) finely chopped fresh cilantro

CHATELAINE KITCHEN TIP

No dipping sauce required — these tasty bites are moist and bursting with flavour without any glaze.

1. Arrange oven racks in top and bottom thirds of oven. Preheat oven to 350°F (180°C). Spray 2 foil-lined baking sheets with oil. Finely grate peel from lemon. Thinly slice onions and mince garlic. Place all in bowl. Whisk in egg, chili-garlic sauce and fish sauce. Crumble in meat. Sprinkle with cornstarch and cilantro. Mix together (the mixture will be wet). Form into 1-inch (2.5 cm) balls.

2. Bake on baking sheets in preheated oven until firm to the touch, 15 to 20 minutes. You don't need to turn meatballs. Transfer to a serving dish. Serve with toothpicks for spearing.

GET AHEAD Prepare meatballs, but don't bake. Freeze on waxed paper on baking sheets until firm, then freeze in plastic bags for up to 1 month. Bake from frozen, according to directions, adding an extra 5 to 7 minutes of baking time.

NUTRIENTS PER 3 MEATBALLS 7 G PROTEIN 4 G FAT
3 G CARBOHYDRATES 0 G FIBRE 0 MG IRON
12 MG CALCIUM 131 MG SODIUM 73 CALORIES

salads

Tired of the same old salad mix? Find inspiration in simple sides like coleslaw with apple and fennel, or tomatoes with mint. And if salad is on the dinner menu, a cobb with avocado and asparagus is both fresh and satisfying.

Roasted Plum and Spinach Salad

6 plums

⅔ cup (150 mL) olive oil, plus extra for coating

5 strips bacon

8 large fresh sage leaves or 2 tsp (10 mL) dried sage leaves

½ small red onion

3 large garlic cloves

2 tbsp (30 mL) honey Dijon or regular Dijon mustard

⅓ cup (75 mL) red wine vinegar

1 tsp (5 mL) salt

2 tbsp (30 mL) maple syrup

2 5-oz (140 g) pkgs baby spinach, about 16 cups (4 L)

EVERYDAY COOKING SUGGESTION

For fewer servings, cut the recipe in half. You may need to reduce the roasting time.

1. Preheat oven to 450°F (230°C). Cut plums in half and discard pits. Slice plums into wedges and place in a bowl. Drizzle with enough oil to coat, then toss. Lightly oil a large baking sheet. Or, for easier cleanup, line with foil and lightly spray with oil. Place bacon and plums on baking sheet. If ingredients are cramped, use 2 baking sheets. If using fresh sage, spread over a separate small piece of parchment or foil. Fold into a packet and place on baking sheet. Roast in preheated oven, turning once, until fruit is tender and bacon and sage are crisp, about 12 minutes.

2. Meanwhile, thinly slice onion and mince garlic. In a small bowl, whisk Dijon with vinegar, garlic and salt. If using dried sage instead of fresh, add to mixture. Gradually whisk in ⅔ cup (150 mL) olive oil.

3. Transfer bacon to paper towels to drain. Set roasted sage aside. Slice bacon into pieces. Toss plums in a bowl with maple syrup.

4. Place spinach in a very large bowl. Add bacon, plums and onion. Crumble roasted sage overtop. Stir dressing and drizzle in just enough to lightly coat.

NUTRIENTS PER SERVING 2 G PROTEIN 15 G FAT
9 G CARBOHYDRATES 1 G FIBRE 1 MG IRON
33 MG CALCIUM 303 MG SODIUM 173 CALORIES

Classic Caesar Salad

PREPARATION TIME 15 MINUTES
COOKING TIME 3 MINUTES
MAKES 4 TO 6 SERVINGS

4 slices white bread

3 tbsp (45 mL) butter

2 garlic cloves

3 anchovy fillets or 1 tsp (5 mL) anchovy paste

1 lemon

1 tsp (5 mL) Dijon or ¼ tsp (1 mL) dry mustard

½ tsp (2 mL) Worcestershire sauce

¼ tsp (1 mL) each salt and freshly ground black pepper

⅓ cup (75 mL) olive oil

2 tbsp (30 mL) mayonnaise or 1 egg

½ cup (125 mL) freshly grated parmesan cheese

1 large head or 2 hearts romaine lettuce

4 to 5 strips cooked bacon, crumbled (optional)

HEALTH TIP

Traditionally, Caesar salad gets its creamy dressing made with raw egg. But that's not for everyone. If serving this dressing to children, pregnant women, and elderly or immuno-compromised persons (for whom raw perishable foods are not suggested), use mayonnaise rather than egg.

TASTY TWEAK

Create a vegetarian version by using capers instead of anchovies, and roasted red pepper instead of bacon.

1. For croutons, trim and discard crusts from bread. Cut bread into ½-inch (1 cm) cubes. Heat butter in a frying pan over medium heat. Add bread, tossing to coat. Stir and turn until golden, 3 to 5 minutes. If the bread is browning too quickly, reduce heat. Turn onto paper towels.

2. For dressing, finely chop garlic and anchovies and place in a large bowl. If using a garlic press, push anchovies through the press as well. Squeeze in 2 tbsp (30 mL) juice from lemon. Add Dijon, Worcestershire sauce, salt and pepper. Whisk to mix. Gradually whisk oil into mixture, pouring very slowly to emulsify. Whisk in mayonnaise or egg (see sidebar, top left). Whisk in about half of the parmesan.

3. For salad, tear or slice lettuce into pieces and add to dressing. Sprinkle with bacon if you wish, and remaining parmesan. Toss to evenly coat and scatter with croutons. Serve with lemon wedges for those who like a tangier dressing.

GET AHEAD If using mayonnaise, dressing will keep well, covered and refrigerated, for up to 3 days. (If using egg, use dressing right away.)

NUTRIENTS PER SERVING 6 G PROTEIN 24 G FAT
14 G CARBOHYDRATES 3 G FIBRE 2 MG IRON
152 MG CALCIUM 461 MG SODIUM 292 CALORIES

California-Sushi-Roll Salad

PREPARATION TIME 15 MINUTES
COOKING TIME 7 MINUTES
MAKES 4 TO 6 SERVINGS

½ of 450 g pkg orzo, about 1 ½ cups (375 mL)

1 lime

2 garlic cloves, minced

2 tbsp (30 mL) granulated sugar

2 tbsp (30 mL) each fish sauce and soy sauce

½ tsp (2 mL) hot chili flakes

½ English cucumber

1 green onion

1 avocado

8 oz (250 g) imitation crab or 1 cup (250 mL) shredded cooked crabmeat

1 tbsp (15 mL) coarsely chopped pickled ginger

1 tbsp (15 mL) sesame seeds (optional)

WHAT IS IT?

Orzo is a quick-cooking rice-shaped pasta perfect for using in dishes that call for rice. Make sure to cook orzo following package directions.

1. Fill a large pot with water, add salt, then bring to a boil over high heat. Add orzo. Stir to separate. Boil, uncovered and stirring occasionally, until al dente, about 7 minutes. Drain well. Do not rinse.

2. Meanwhile, squeeze 2 tbsp (30 mL) juice from lime into a small bowl. Stir in garlic, sugar, fish sauce, soy sauce and chili flakes. Slice cucumber in half lengthwise. Using a small spoon, scrape out and discard seeds. Thinly slice cucumber and onion. Slice avocado in half and discard pit. Scoop flesh from peel. Coarsely chop avocado and crab.

3. Place drained orzo in a large bowl. Pour dressing overtop, tossing to coat. Add cucumber, onion, avocado, crab and ginger. Gently toss until evenly mixed. Sprinkle with sesame seeds if you wish. Great served warm or cold.

GET AHEAD Cover salad and refrigerate for up to 1 day. Add avocado just before serving.

NUTRIENTS PER SERVING 11 G PROTEIN 6 G FAT
45 G CARBOHYDRATES 5 G FIBRE 1 MG IRON
31 MG CALCIUM 1196 MG SODIUM 279 CALORIES

Minted Summer Tomatoes

PREPARATION TIME 5 MINUTES
STANDING TIME 30 MINUTES
MAKES 6 TO 8 SERVINGS

2 tbsp (30 mL) balsamic vinegar

1 tbsp (15 mL) olive oil

1 tsp (5 mL) granulated sugar

½ tsp (2 mL) salt

¼ small red onion, thinly sliced

1 jalapeño pepper, seeded and finely chopped

4 to 6 large tomatoes, preferably a mix of red and yellow

¼ cup (50 mL) shredded fresh mint

¼ cup (50 mL) crumbled goat cheese

JALAPEÑO TIP

Jalapeño peppers vary in heat. Always taste them and add more or less depending on how much spice you like. For extra kick, keep their membrane and seeds — that's where most of the heat is.

1. In a medium bowl, whisk vinegar with oil, sugar and salt. Stir in onion and jalapeño.

2. Thickly slice tomatoes. Arrange on a platter. Pour dressing evenly overtop. Let stand 30 minutes, allowing flavours to infuse. Sprinkle with mint and cheese. Serve with a crusty baguette to soak up extra dressing.

NUTRIENTS PER SERVING 3 G PROTEIN 4 G FAT
6 G CARBOHYDRATES 1 G FIBRE 1 MG IRON
27 MG CALCIUM 201 MG SODIUM 71 CALORIES

Warm Curried-Potato Salad

PREPARATION TIME 10 MINUTES
COOKING TIME 20 MINUTES
MAKES 8 SERVINGS

4 medium potatoes, preferably Yukon gold

3 to 4 small sweet potatoes

½ tsp (2 mL) salt

3 tbsp (45 mL) white wine vinegar

1 tbsp (15 mL) Indian curry paste

Generous pinches of granulated sugar

⅓ cup (75 mL) olive oil

1 cup (250 mL) coarsely chopped fresh cilantro

4 green onions

CURRY TIP

Indian curry paste is precooked, so it's not as harsh as curry powder, which means you can add it to no-cook recipes (like the vinaigrette in this recipe).

1. Peel all potatoes, then cut into 1-inch (2.5 cm) chunks, keeping the Yukon gold and sweet potatoes separate. Place the Yukon gold in a large pot. Cover with water and add salt. Bring to a boil, covered, over high heat, then boil gently for 5 minutes. Carefully stir in sweet potatoes. Cover and continue boiling gently until very tender, 15 to 20 more minutes. Drain and transfer to a large bowl.

2. Meanwhile, in a small bowl, stir vinegar with curry paste and sugar. Slowly whisk in oil. Prepare cilantro and thinly slice onions. Drizzle dressing over potatoes. Sprinkle with cilantro and onions. Stir to evenly coat. Taste and add salt if you wish. Delicious warm, at room temperature or cold.

GET AHEAD Cover salad and refrigerate for up to 2 days.

NUTRIENTS PER SERVING 2 G PROTEIN 10 G FAT
23 G CARBOHYDRATES 3 G FIBRE 1 MG IRON
25 MG CALCIUM 162 MG SODIUM 189 CALORIES

Triple Red Potato Salad

PREPARATION TIME 15 MINUTES
COOKING TIME 8 MINUTES
MAKES 12 CUPS (3 L)

3 lb (1.5 kg) baby potatoes, red-skinned, unpeeled

4 green onions

2 red peppers

½ small red onion

¾ cup (175 mL) mayonnaise, preferably light

3 tbsp (45 mL) finely chopped dill pickles or sweet pickle relish

1 tbsp (15 mL) Dijon mustard

1 cup (250 mL) coarsely chopped fresh dill

TEST KITCHEN TIP

To mellow the strong flavour of red onions, we added them to the simmering potatoes for the last couple of minutes of cooking.

1. Cut potatoes into thick rounds and place in a very large pot. Add enough cold water to cover potatoes. Cover and bring to a boil over high heat, then reduce heat to medium. Partially cover and simmer until fork-tender, 8 to 10 minutes.

2. Meanwhile, thinly slice green onions and peppers. Place red onion, cut-side down, on a cutting board. Thinly slice, then separate. In a large bowl, stir mayonnaise with pickles and Dijon.

3. Stir peppers and red onion into boiling water for the last 2 minutes of potato cooking time. When potatoes are fork-tender, drain well. Add hot potatoes, peppers and onions to bowl with dressing. Sprinkle with dill. Toss until evenly coated. Delicious warm, at room temperature or chilled.

GET AHEAD Cover salad and refrigerate for up to 3 days. Before serving, taste and stir in more mayonnaise or dill if you wish — the potatoes will soak up the dressing as they stand.

NUTRIENTS PER 1 CUP (250 mL) 3 G PROTEIN 5 G FAT
22 G CARBOHYDRATES 3 G FIBRE 1 MG IRON
23 MG CALCIUM 162 MG SODIUM 141 CALORIES

Light and Creamy Coleslaw

PREPARATION TIME 15 MINUTES
REFRIGERATION TIME 2 HOURS
MAKES 8 SERVINGS

2 apples, preferably Granny Smith, unpeeled

2 lemons

½ napa or ¼ red cabbage, shredded

2 colourful peppers or ½ fennel bulb

1 cup (250 mL) light or regular mayonnaise

½ cup (125 mL) plain yogourt or sour cream

1 tbsp (15 mL) celery seeds

¼ tsp (1 mL) salt

FENNEL

The feathery tops of fennel are called fronds. They make a pretty and delicate-flavoured garnish for dishes with fennel.

1. Core apples, then julienne. Place in a very large bowl. Squeeze a little lemon juice overtop and toss to coat. Thinly shred cabbage with a sharp knife and add to apples.

2. Thinly slice peppers. If using fennel, remove fronds and set aside for garnish. Cut out and discard core. Place cut-side down on cutting board, then thinly slice. Add to cabbage and apples.

3. Squeeze ¼ cup (50 mL) juice from lemons into a small bowl. Stir in mayonnaise, yogourt, celery seeds and salt. Drizzle over coleslaw and toss to coat. Cover and refrigerate until cold, at least 2 hours. If salad becomes watery, simply drain. Before serving, top with fennel fronds if you wish.

GET AHEAD Cover salad and refrigerate for up to 12 hours.

NUTRIENTS PER SERVING 2 G PROTEIN 11 G FAT
14 G CARBOHYDRATES 2 G FIBRE 1 MG IRON
95 MG CALCIUM 290 MG SODIUM 152 CALORIES

Mediterranean Tomato and Bean Salad

PREPARATION TIME 15 MINUTES
COOKING TIME 2 MINUTES
MAKES 6 CUPS (1.5 L)

3 cups (750 mL) green beans

½ fennel bulb

½ cup (125 mL) marinated artichoke hearts, drained

19 oz (540 mL) can beans, such as white navy or black

1 pint grape tomatoes

⅓ cup (75 mL) pesto, preferably homemade (sidebar, page 76)

Generous pinches of salt (optional)

1 lemon

10-MINUTE TIP

To make homemade pesto in a blender or food processor, whirl 1 cup (250 mL) packed basil leaves with ¼ cup (50 mL) toasted pine nuts, 1 tbsp (15 mL) freshly squeezed lemon juice, 2 coarsely chopped garlic cloves and pinches of salt and freshly ground black pepper until fairly smooth. While the motor is running, gradually add ½ cup (125 mL) olive oil. Continue to blend until emulsified

Get ahead:

Cover and refrigerate pesto for up to 3 days.

Makes 1 cup (250 mL)

1. Partially fill a large frying pan with water and bring to a boil over high heat. Meanwhile, trim green beans and cut in half. When water is boiling, add beans and cook until tender-crisp, 2 to 3 minutes. Drain, then plunge into a bowl of ice water and drain again. Dry well with a kitchen towel.

2. Cut out and discard core and most of the feathery fronds from fennel. Slice into thin strips. Coarsely chop artichokes. Rinse and drain canned beans. Place fennel, artichokes and canned beans in a large bowl. Add green beans, tomatoes and pesto. Stir to evenly coat. Taste and add salt if needed. Squeeze about 1 tbsp (15 mL) juice from lemon overtop and toss to coat. Garnish with feathery fennel fronds if you wish.

GET AHEAD Cover and refrigerate salad for up to 3 days. Flavour improves as it sits, but if salad is dry, stir in a little more pesto.

NUTRIENTS PER 1 CUP (250 mL) 7 G PROTEIN 6 G FAT
22 G CARBOHYDRATES 9 G FIBRE 2 MG IRON
87 MG CALCIUM 418 MG SODIUM 162 CALORIES

Three Homemade Dressings

GINGER-SESAME DRIZZLE

MAKES 1 ½ CUPS (375 mL)

Finely grate 4 tsp (20 mL) fresh ginger into a medium bowl. Add ½ cup (125 mL) each rice vinegar and hoisin or teriyaki sauce. Slowly whisk in ½ cup (125 mL) vegetable oil and 2 tbsp (30 mL) dark sesame oil until evenly mixed. If using teriyaki, taste and add 2 tbsp (30 mL) honey if you wish. Stir in ½ tsp (2 mL) hot chili flakes. Stir in minced fresh garlic if you wish.

GET AHEAD If making ahead, prepare dressing as directed but don't add the garlic. Cover dressing and refrigerate for up to 1 week. Just before using, add garlic if you wish, then whisk or shake.

TASTY TWEAKS Give your next salad a twist by adding: Wasabi peas and broken crispy chow mein noodles or shrimp chips; toasted coconut, sesame seeds or salted pumpkin seeds; grated apple and carrot.

PROVENÇAL VINAIGRETTE

MAKES 1 CUP (250 mL)

In a medium bowl, whisk 1 tbsp (15 mL) Dijon mustard with 4 tsp (20 mL) white wine vinegar, ½ tsp (2 mL) dried tarragon leaves and salt to taste. Slowly whisk in 1 cup (250 mL) olive oil.

GET AHEAD Cover dressing and refrigerate for up to 1 week. Whisk or shake just before using.

SHORTCUT The secret to an oil-based dressing is to emulsify it. Traditionally, you do this by slowly whisking and incorporating the oil into the other dressing ingredients. Or you can use this shortcut: Place all dressing ingredients (including the oil) in a jar, then seal with a lid. Shake until dressing is evenly mixed and thick.

BUTTERMILK DRESSING

MAKES 1 ¼ CUPS (300 mL)

In a medium bowl, stir ¾ cup (175 mL) buttermilk with ¼ cup (50 mL) snipped chives or chopped parsley or cilantro. Add ½ cup (125 mL) crumbled goat cheese or a blue cheese such as gorgonzola or stilton. Mash with a fork. Stir in generous pinches of salt and freshly ground black pepper.

GET AHEAD Cover dressing and refrigerate for up to 3 days. Stir just before using.

COOKING TIP You can also use this dressing as a base for bread crumb coatings for baked chicken.

Mexican Pasta Salad

PREPARATION TIME 15 MINUTES
COOKING TIME 8 MINUTES
MAKES 4 SERVINGS

½ of 450 g pkg small pasta, such as tubetti or shells

1 plum tomato

1 yellow pepper

½ small red onion

½ cup (125 mL) mayonnaise

2 tbsp (30 mL) salsa

1 tsp (5 mL) finely chopped chipotle chili (optional)

1 tsp (5 mL) chili powder

½ tsp (2 mL) each ground cumin and salt

1 ripe avocado

½ cup (125 mL) chopped fresh cilantro

COOKING TIP

For a more modern look, use small-sized tubetti pasta in place of the usual elbow macaroni.

1. Bring a large pot of water to a boil. Add pasta and cook according to package directions until al dente, 8 to 10 minutes. Drain well. Meanwhile, chop tomato and thinly slice pepper and onion into bite-sized strips. Place in a large bowl. In a small bowl, stir mayonnaise with salsa, chipotle, chili powder, cumin and salt. Add pasta to vegetables. Drizzle with mayonnaise dressing, tossing to evenly coat. Cover and refrigerate until cold if you wish. (It's great both chilled and at room temperature.)

2. Just before serving, slice avocado in half and discard pit. Scoop flesh from peel, then thinly slice into semicircles. Gently toss with salad, along with cilantro. Taste and add more mayonnaise if needed.

GET AHEAD Prepare Step 1. Cover dressed salad and refrigerate for up to 1 day. Add avocado and cilantro just before serving.

NUTRIENTS PER SERVING 9 G PROTEIN 30 G FAT
52 G CARBOHYDRATES 7 G FIBRE 3 MG IRON
38 MG CALCIUM 654 MG SODIUM 508 CALORIES

Spicy Tabbouleh

PREPARATION TIME 10 MINUTES
COOKING TIME 15 MINUTES
STANDING TIME 5 MINUTES
MAKES 5 CUPS (1.25 L)

GOOD FOR YOU

Bulgur is loaded with nutrients, including fibre, folate and manganese — to name just a few. These steamed and dried wheat kernels are most commonly used in Middle Eastern salads and rice dishes.

SALAD

1 cup (250 mL) bulgur

2 large ripe tomatoes, chopped

1 cup (250 mL) finely chopped fresh cilantro or parsley

2 tbsp (30 mL) chopped drained pickled hot peppers

¼ cup (50 mL) pine nuts, preferably toasted (optional)

DRESSING

1 lemon

⅓ cup (75 mL) olive oil

2 garlic cloves, minced

1 tsp (5 mL) toasted cumin seeds or ½ tsp (2 mL) ground cumin

¼ tsp (1 mL) salt

Freshly ground black pepper

1. For salad, in a large saucepan, bring 2 cups (500 mL) water to a boil over high heat. Stir in bulgur. Reduce heat to low and simmer, covered, until most of the water is absorbed, 15 to 20 minutes. Remove from heat. Let stand, covered, 5 minutes. Then drain off any excess water and set aside, uncovered, to cool. Meanwhile, chop tomatoes and finely chop cilantro and hot peppers. Place in a large bowl along with pine nuts. Fluff bulgur with a fork, then stir into tomato mixture.

2. For dressing, squeeze 2 tbsp (30 mL) juice from lemon into a small bowl. Whisk in oil, garlic, cumin, salt and pepper. Stir into salad. Taste and add a bit more salt or lemon juice if needed. Excellent served with Fiery Asian Burgers (page 143).

GET AHEAD Cover tabbouleh and refrigerate for up to 2 days.

NUTRIENTS PER CUP (250 mL) 6 G PROTEIN 19 G FAT
32 G CARBOHYDRATES 5 G FIBRE 2 MG IRON
36 MG CALCIUM 195 MG SODIUM 304 CALORIES

The Modern Cobb

PREPARATION TIME 15 MINUTES
COOKING TIME 18 MINUTES
MAKES 4 SERVINGS

3 skinless, boneless chicken breasts

8 slices pancetta

1 bunch asparagus

1 avocado

8 cups (2 L) baby arugula or spinach

1 cup (250 mL) grape tomatoes, about ½ pint

Buttermilk Dressing (page 79)

HISTORY OF THE COBB

The cherished American classic cobb (created in Hollywood) is made with bacon, slices of hard-boiled egg, iceberg lettuce, chopped tomatoes and cooked turkey or chicken, and topped with crumbled blue cheese.

We've replaced the standard iceberg lettuce with peppery arugula, subbed pancetta (Italian cured bacon) for bacon and added tender-crisp asparagus spears to update this classic dinner salad.

1. Lightly coat a frying pan with oil and set over medium heat. Add chicken and cook until light golden, 3 to 4 minutes per side. Reduce heat to medium-low. Cover and cook, turning occasionally, until chicken is springy when pressed, 6 to 8 more minutes. Remove to a plate. Add pancetta to pan, in batches if necessary so that it's not crowded. Increase heat to medium. Cook until crisp, 2 to 3 minutes per side. Remove to paper towels. Repeat with remaining pancetta, if necessary.

2. Meanwhile, partially fill a large frying pan with water and bring to a boil over high heat. Snap tough ends from asparagus and discard. Boil asparagus until tender-crisp, about 2 to 3 minutes. Drain and rinse under cold water to stop cooking. Pat dry with a kitchen towel.

3. Slice chicken. Cut avocado in half and discard pit. Scoop flesh from peel, then thinly slice. Divide arugula between 4 individual plates. Top with chicken, pancetta, asparagus spears, avocado and tomatoes. Drizzle with Buttermilk Dressing.

NUTRIENTS PER SERVING 37 G PROTEIN 21 G FAT
15 G CARBOHYDRATES 7 G FIBRE 3 MG IRON
382 MG CALCIUM 655 MG SODIUM 383 CALORIES

Coconut Rice Salad with Shrimp

PREPARATION TIME 10 MINUTES
SOAKING TIME 20 MINUTES
COOKING TIME 20 MINUTES
GRILLING TIME 4 MINUTES
MAKES 4 SERVINGS

8 small wooden skewers

400 mL can unsweetened coconut milk, preferably light

1 cup (250 mL) basmati or long-grain rice

1 tsp (5 mL) ground cardamom (optional)

1 cinnamon stick

½ tsp (2 mL) salt

¼ tsp (1 mL) hot chili flakes

½ lb (250 g) green beans

2 green onions

1 ripe mango

½ English cucumber

¾ lb (350 g) fresh or frozen uncooked, preferably large or medium shrimp, peeled

1 tbsp (15 mL) vegetable oil

1 tsp (5 mL) each ground coriander and garlic salt

COCONUT MILK 101

Sweetened coconut milk is often reserved for baking recipes, while unsweetened is most commonly used in soups and curries. Be sure to check the recipe and the label when you're purchasing coconut milk. Before opening, give the can of coconut milk a good shake to mix the solid and liquid together.

1. Soak skewers in water for 20 minutes (see sidebar, page 124). Pour coconut milk into a large measuring cup. Add water to make 2 ½ cups (625 mL). Pour into a large saucepan. Stir in rice, cardamom (if using), cinnamon stick, salt and chili flakes. Cover and bring to a boil over high heat. Stir and reduce heat to low. Simmer, covered, 10 minutes. Trim beans, then cut in half. After rice has cooked 10 minutes, scatter beans overtop. Cover and cook until liquid is absorbed, about 10 minutes. Meanwhile, thinly slice onions. When rice is done, turn into a large bowl. Discard cinnamon stick. Stir in onions. Set aside.

2. Slice mango into thin bite-sized strips (see sidebar, page 136). Slice cucumber in half lengthwise. Scrape out and discard seeds. Coarsely chop. Stir mango and cucumber into rice mixture.

3. Oil grill and heat barbecue to medium. If using frozen shrimp, thaw according to package directions (or see sidebar, page 246). Pat shrimp dry with paper towels. Place in a bowl. Add oil, coriander and garlic salt, tossing to coat. Thread 4 to 5 shrimp on a skewer. For easy turning, thread a second skewer through shrimp. Repeat. Grill until shrimp are pink, about 2 minutes per side. Serve kebabs over coconut rice salad.

NUTRIENTS PER SERVING 23 G PROTEIN 10 G FAT
57 G CARBOHYDRATES 4 G FIBRE 3 MG IRON
0 MG CALCIUM 744 MG SODIUM 404 CALORIES

Easy Arugula and Hazelnut Salad

PREPARATION TIME 15 MINUTES
MAKES 6 SERVINGS

1 garlic clove

2 tbsp (30 mL) white wine vinegar or champagne vinegar

1 tsp (5 mL) Dijon mustard

¼ tsp (1 mL) each dried thyme leaves and salt

Pinch of granulated sugar

¼ cup (50 mL) olive oil

¼ cup (50 mL) snipped fresh chives

3 pink grapefruits or tangerines

1 fennel bulb

12 cups (3 L) baby arugula

6 slices prosciutto (optional)

¾ cup (175 mL) toasted hazelnuts

SWITCH IT UP

Feel free to use any citrus fruit and nuts you like. Mandarins and other types of oranges work well in place of grapefruit or tangerines. Instead of hazelnuts, try almonds or cashews.

1. Mince garlic and place in a small bowl. Whisk in vinegar, Dijon, thyme, salt and sugar. Slowly whisk in oil until evenly mixed. Stir in chives.

2. Cut off the top and bottom of grapefruits. Slice off and discard remaining peel, including all white pith, so flesh is showing. Carefully slice segments out, leaving membrane that separates them behind. Set segments aside and discard membrane. Trim the feathery fronds from fennel, cut in half and discard the core. Slice into thin strips.

3. Just before serving, place arugula, grapefruit segments and fennel in a large bowl. Drizzle with dressing and toss to mix. Divide among individual plates. Tear and scatter prosciutto overtop if you wish. Sprinkle with hazelnuts.

GET AHEAD Prepare Steps 1 and 2. Cover dressing and refrigerate for up to 1 week. Cover grapefruit and fennel and refrigerate for up to 1 day. Store nuts in an airtight container for up to 1 week.

NUTRIENTS PER SERVING 7 G PROTEIN 20 G FAT
20 G CARBOHYDRATES 7 G FIBRE 3 MG IRON
233 MG CALCIUM 157 MG SODIUM 265 CALORIES

Warm Balsamic-Soaked Mushroom and Spinach Salad

PREPARATION TIME 5 MINUTES
GRILLING TIME 8 MINUTES
MAKES 4 SERVINGS

2 green onions
½ red onion
8 cups (2 L) baby spinach, arugula or mixed greens
½ cup (125 mL) grated mozzarella cheese
8 oz (250 g) pkg sliced button mushrooms
2 tbsp (30 mL) balsamic vinegar
1 tbsp (15 mL) olive oil
1 garlic clove, minced, or 1 tsp (5 mL) bottled chopped garlic
¼ tsp (1 mL) each salt and freshly ground black pepper

DRESS IT UP

Use a mix of mushrooms, such as oyster and shiitake, for a more upscale, modern look.

1. Thinly slice green onions. Place red onion, cut-side down, on a cutting board. Thinly slice, then separate. Place both in a large bowl and toss with spinach and mozzarella.

2. Heat barbecue to medium. Place mushrooms in a foil pie plate (a packet made of foil doesn't work well because mushrooms give off a lot of juice). Drizzle with 1 tbsp (15 mL) each vinegar and oil. Add garlic, salt and pepper, stirring to evenly mix. Cover pie plate tightly with foil.

3. Place on grill and cook with lid closed until mushrooms are soft, 8 to 10 minutes. You don't need to stir. Carefully remove pie plate from grill and remove foil. Pour mushrooms and liquid over spinach, tossing to evenly coat. Taste and add remaining 1 tbsp (15 mL) vinegar if you wish.

NUTRIENTS PER SERVING 8 G PROTEIN 8 G FAT
11 G CARBOHYDRATES 5 G FIBRE 4 MG IRON
210 MG CALCIUM 294 MG SODIUM 132 CALORIES

soups

Every season needs a soup, from squash with bacon in the fall to vodka-spiked gazpacho in the summer. These 14 easy recipes are hearty enough for family meals, and pretty enough for entertaining.

Homemade Chicken Broth

PREPARATION TIME 15 MINUTES
ROASTING TIME 30 MINUTES
COOKING TIME 1 HOUR
MAKES 12 CUPS (3 L)

5 lb (2.5 kg) mix of chicken bones, such as necks and backs (can be purchased at butcher)

Vegetable oil

2 leeks or 1 large sweet onion

2 carrots

2 celery stalks

2 tbsp (30 mL) butter

¼ cup (50 mL) coarsely chopped parsley stems

2 sprigs each fresh thyme and rosemary

2 bay leaves

2 garlic cloves, crushed

1 tbsp (15 mL) whole black peppercorns

CHATELAINE KITCHEN TIP

Take some of your most treasured recipes — soups, stews and risottos — up a notch by using your own homemade chicken broth. Don't add salt. This way you can season the dishes you include the broth in to your liking.

1. Preheat oven to 475°F (240°C). If chicken bones are large, use a cleaver to chop into smaller pieces. Place in a shallow roasting pan. Drizzle with a little oil and toss to coat. Roast in preheated oven, turning occasionally, until bones are fragrant and dark, 30 to 40 minutes.

2. Meanwhile, cut off and discard root ends of leeks. Cut leeks in half lengthwise. Fan out under cold running water to remove grit. Chop leeks, carrots and celery. Melt butter in a large stockpot over medium-low heat. Add vegetables, parsley stems, thyme, rosemary, bay leaves, garlic and peppercorns. Stir often until lightly browned, 15 to 20 minutes. After chicken has roasted for 30 minutes, drain fat from pan and discard. Add bones to pot with vegetable mixture. Pour a little water into roasting pan. Using a wooden spoon, scrape up any brown bits and add to pot. Pour in enough water to completely cover bones, about 16 cups (4 L).

3. Bring to a boil over high heat, stirring often. Reduce heat and simmer for 45 to 60 minutes to develop flavour. Skim off any foam that rises to the surface. Stir occasionally. Then spoon out and discard bones. Strain broth through a large mesh sieve into another pot. To concentrate flavour, boil broth to reduce by half.

GET AHEAD Cover broth and refrigerate overnight. Then skim off and discard any fat that has risen to the surface. Broth will keep well, covered and refrigerated, for up to 5 days, or divide into smaller portions and freeze for up to 4 months.

NUTRIENTS PER CUP (250 mL) 5 G PROTEIN 1 G FAT
1 G CARBOHYDRATES 0 G FIBRE 1 MG IRON
10 MG CALCIUM 32 MG SODIUM 39 CALORIES

Fabulous French Onion Soup

PREPARATION TIME 25 MINUTES
COOKING TIME 45 MINUTES
BROILING TIME 6 MINUTES
MAKES 4 SERVINGS

2 medium white or red onions or 6 small white onions,
    about 1 ½ lb (750 g)

2 tbsp (30 mL) butter

1 tbsp (15 mL) oil

1 tsp (5 mL) granulated sugar

3 ⅔ cups (900 mL) beef broth, good-quality store-bought or homemade,
    or 2 284-mL cans undiluted beef broth

½ cup (125 mL) dry white or red wine

1 tbsp (15 mL) Dijon mustard

6 sprigs fresh thyme or 1 tsp (5 mL) dried thyme leaves

1 bay leaf

1 small baguette

1 tbsp (15 mL) butter, at room temperature

1 to 2 cups (250 to 500 mL) grated gruyère or emmenthal cheese

SWITCH IT UP

Broth: For a milder flavour, replace beef broth with chicken broth (if using from a carton, omit water). Or boost taste by adding 2 tbsp (30 mL) brandy or a ½ oz (14 g) package of dried mushrooms to broth before simmering.

Cheese: Try a stronger, nippier cheese such as grated asiago, or a crumbled blue cheese such as gorgonzola or stilton.

Serving: No heatproof soup bowls? Use an oven-safe pot. Create a raft of cheese-topped toasts on the surface of the soup right in the pot. Place in oven and broil until toasts are golden, about 5 minutes.

1. Peel onions. Cut each in half lengthwise, slicing through root end. Place onions, cut-side down, on a chopping board, then thinly slice into semicircles. Sliced onions should measure about 5 cups (1.25 L).

2. Heat butter and oil in a large pot over medium heat. Add onions, then sprinkle with sugar. Cook, uncovered and stirring often, until very soft and caramelized, about 15 minutes. Reduce heat if they brown too quickly.

3. Add broth, wine, Dijon, thyme and bay leaf. If using a carton of broth, add ½ cup (125 mL) water. For canned, add 3 cups (750 mL) water. If using homemade broth, do not add water. Scrape up and stir in any brown bits from pot bottom. Bring mixture to a boil over high heat. Cover and reduce heat to medium-low. Simmer for 30 minutes to develop flavour. Discard bay leaf and thyme sprigs.

4. Place oven rack in top half of oven. Preheat broiler. Cut bread into 8 slices, each ½-inch (1 cm) thick. Butter both sides of each. Toast on a baking sheet until lightly golden, about 2 minutes per side.

5. Place oven-safe soup bowls on a baking sheet. Ladle in soup. Top each with 2 toasts. Sprinkle with cheese. Place baking sheet in oven. Broil until cheese is bubbly, 2 to 4 minutes. Serve immediately.

GET AHEAD Cover soup (without toasts) and refrigerate for up to 3 days, or freeze for up to 2 months. The flavour improves as it stands.

NUTRIENTS PER SERVING 15 G PROTEIN 23 G FAT
36 G CARBOHYDRATES 3 G FIBRE 2 MG IRON
362 MG CALCIUM 1649 MG SODIUM 407 CALORIES

Squash Soup with Smoky Bacon

PREPARATION TIME 20 MINUTES
COOKING TIME 29 MINUTES
MAKES 8 CUPS (2 L)

1 large butternut squash or 5 cups (1.25 L) precut squash pieces
4 garlic cloves
2 plum tomatoes
1 large onion
5 slices bacon, preferably thick-cut
½ tsp (2 mL) each dried sage leaves, oregano leaves and salt
900 mL carton chicken broth or 2 284-mL cans undiluted chicken broth
Handful of fresh sage leaves, chopped (optional)

SQUASH TRICK

To easily peel squash or pumpkin, make a large slit through skin with a knife, then microwave on high to soften the skin a little, 2 to 3 minutes. When cool enough to handle, peel with a knife or vegetable peeler.

COOKING TIP

For a vegetarian version, use vegetable broth in place of chicken and skip the bacon.

1. Peel squash (see sidebar). Cut in half, scoop out and discard pulp and seeds, then chop into small pieces. Coarsely chop garlic, tomatoes and onion.

2. Set a large pot over medium-low heat. Add bacon. Cook until crispy, 8 to 10 minutes. Transfer to a paper towel–lined plate. Leave about 2 tbsp (30 mL) bacon fat in pot. If you are not using bacon, add 2 tbsp (30 mL) vegetable oil to pot. Increase heat to medium. Add garlic and onion. Stir often until onion starts to soften, about 3 minutes. Add tomatoes. Sprinkle with sage, oregano and salt. Stir occasionally until tomatoes break down, 3 to 5 more minutes.

3. Pour in broth. If using canned, add 2 cans of water. Using a wooden spoon, scrape up and stir in any brown bits from pot bottom. Add squash and bring to a boil. Reduce heat and simmer, covered and stirring occasionally, until squash is very tender, 15 to 25 minutes. Meanwhile, coarsely chop bacon.

4. Working in batches, whirl soup in a blender or food processor, then pour into a large measuring cup or another pot. (Alternatively, use a hand blender.) Taste and add more herbs to taste. Ladle soup into bowls. Top with bacon, and sprinkle with chopped fresh sage leaves if you wish.

GET AHEAD Cover soup and refrigerate for up to 5 days, or freeze for up to 3 months.

NUTRIENTS PER CUP (250 mL) 4 G PROTEIN 7 G FAT
14 G CARBOHYDRATES 2 G FIBRE 1 MG IRON
57 MG CALCIUM 698 MG SODIUM 131 CALORIES

Sweet Potato and Leek Soup with Aged Cheddar

Cut off and discard root ends and dark green tops of 3 thin leeks. Cut leeks in half lengthwise. Fan out under cold running water to remove grit. Thinly slice. Melt 2 tbsp (30 mL) butter in a large pot and set over medium heat. Add leeks. Sauté, stirring often, until softened slightly, about 5 minutes.

Meanwhile, peel and coarsely chop 6 medium sweet potatoes and 2 carrots. When leeks have softened, add potatoes, carrots and a generous sprinkling of fresh thyme or pinches of dried thyme leaves. Stir in two 900 mL cartons of chicken or vegetable broth. Cover and bring to a boil over high heat, then reduce heat to medium. Cover and gently boil, stirring occasionally, until very tender, about 30 minutes.

Ladle half into a food processor and purée until smooth. Stir in 1 ½ cups (375 mL) grated old cheddar until melted. Ladle soup into bowls and garnish with more grated cheddar, if you wish. Garnish with fried leeks or crumbled cooked bacon and snipped fresh chives.

GET AHEAD Store soup in a covered container and refrigerate for up to 5 days, or freeze for up to 3 months.

MAKES 4 TO 6 SERVINGS

FLAVOUR BOOST

For a more robust taste, roast your potatoes and carrots. Preheat oven to 400°F (200°C). Prick potatoes all over. Lightly oil peeled carrots. Place both on a baking sheet. Roast until tender, 40 to 60 minutes. If carrots are fork-tender before potatoes, remove and set aside. Remove cooked potatoes from oven and let cool. When potatoes are cool enough to handle, scoop flesh from skins. Add to the soup as directed. The cooking time will be reduced thanks to the precooked potatoes. Or serve as a side dish, sprinkled with salt and pepper.

Honey-Laced Carrot and Thyme Soup

PREPARATION TIME 8 MINUTES
COOKING TIME 20 MINUTES
MAKES 5 CUPS (1.25 L)

2 lb (1 kg) bag carrots, peeled and thickly sliced

2 10-oz (284 mL) cans undiluted chicken broth or 4 cups (1 L) chicken bouillon

1 large onion, chopped

2 tbsp (30 mL) honey

3 garlic cloves, chopped, or 2 tsp (10 mL) bottled chopped garlic

4 large sprigs fresh thyme or 1 tbsp (15 mL) dried thyme leaves

Fresh mint sprigs (optional)

¼ cup (50 mL) crumbled blue cheese (optional)

SERVING SUGGESTION

For an appetizer, serve warm soup in heatproof rock glasses or small espresso cups.

1. Place carrots, broth, onion, honey, garlic, and thyme in a large pot. If using canned broth, add 2 cans of water. Cover and bring to a boil over high heat, then reduce heat to medium. Gently boil until carrots are tender, 20 to 25 minutes.

2. Discard thyme sprigs. To create a smooth texture, ladle half of soup into a food processor. Whirl until smooth. Strain soup through a sieve into another pot or saucepan. Repeat with remaining soup. Reheat over medium-low heat, stirring often. Stir in a little water if soup is too thick. Ladle into soup bowls, and top each with a small sprig of mint or crumble a little blue cheese overtop, if you wish.

GET AHEAD Strain soup in food processor into a refrigerator container. Cover and refrigerate for up to 5 days, or freeze for up to 3 months. When ready to serve, reheat in the microwave or a saucepan. Garnish with mint or blue cheese.

NUTRIENTS PER CUP (250 mL) 4 G PROTEIN 0 G FAT
28 G CARBOHYDRATES 4 G FIBRE 4 MG IRON
80 MG CALCIUM 888 MG SODIUM 132 CALORIES

Spiked Pepper Gazpacho

PREPARATION TIME 15 MINUTES
REFRIGERATION TIME 2 HOURS
MAKES 7 CUPS (1.75 L)

8 ripe plum tomatoes or 4 large tomatoes

1 English cucumber

4 roasted red peppers, store-bought or homemade (sidebar, page 107)

1 green pepper

1 large jalapeño pepper, seeded

4 garlic cloves

2 tbsp (30 mL) each olive oil and red wine vinegar

1 tsp (5 mL) ground cumin

½ tsp (2 mL) salt

340 mL can vegetable cocktail

¼ cup (50 mL) vodka (optional)

GAZPACHO

This chilled soup is one of Spain's most celebrated warm-weather dishes.

1. Chop tomatoes, then place in a food processor. Peel cucumber, then slice in half lengthwise. Using a small spoon, scrape out and discard seeds. Coarsely chop cucumber and red, green and jalapeño peppers. Mince garlic. Add to tomatoes along with peppers, oil, vinegar, cumin and salt.

2. Pulse just until coarsely chopped. Pour in vegetable juice and vodka (if using). Refrigerate in sealed jars until cold, at least 2 hours, and preferably overnight. Serve with a swirl of sour cream and a cilantro leaf.

NUTRIENTS PER ½ CUP (125 mL) 1 G PROTEIN 2 G FAT
6 G CARBOHYDRATES 1 G FIBRE 1 MG IRON
23 MG CALCIUM 262 MG SODIUM 44 CALORIES

Thai Lime-Vegetable Soup

PREPARATION TIME 20 MINUTES
COOKING TIME 19 MINUTES
MAKES 14 CUPS (3.5 L)

4 garlic cloves or 2 ½ tsp (12 mL) bottled chopped garlic

2 onions

½ small butternut squash or ½ lb (250 g) pkg peeled and chopped fresh butternut squash pieces

4 carrots

900 mL carton vegetable broth

2 400-mL cans unsweetened coconut milk

2 tsp (10 mL) hot chili-garlic sauce

1 each yellow and orange pepper

3 celery stalks

1 large lime

1 cup (250 mL) coarsely chopped fresh cilantro

CUT CALORIES
Reduce the calorie count by using light coconut milk in place of regular.

1. Mince garlic. Coarsely chop onions. Lightly coat a large pot with oil and set over medium-low heat. Add garlic and onions. Stir often until onions soften, 6 to 8 minutes. Meanwhile, if using half a butternut squash, peel (see sidebar, page 97), scoop out and discard pulp and seeds, then cut into 1-inch (2.5 cm) cubes. If using packaged squash, cut larger pieces into 1-inch (2.5 cm) cubes. Thinly slice carrots.

2. When onions are soft, pour in broth. If using canned broth, add 2 cans of water. Stir in coconut milk, chili-garlic sauce, squash and carrots. Bring to a boil over high heat, stirring often. Reduce heat to medium and simmer, uncovered and stirring often, until squash and carrots are almost tender, 8 to 10 minutes.

3. Meanwhile, core and seed peppers. Coarsely chop. Thinly slice celery. When squash is almost done, add peppers and celery. Bring to a boil, then simmer, uncovered and stirring often, until vegetables are done as you like, 5 to 8 more minutes. Stir in juice of half a lime. Add cilantro. Taste and add more lime juice if you wish.

GET AHEAD Cover soup and refrigerate for up to 4 days, or freeze for up to 2 months. To serve, defrost and reheat in the microwave. If soup separates, stir or whisk until mixed. Or reheat in a pot over medium-low heat, stirring often.

NUTRIENTS PER CUP (250 mL) 3 G PROTEIN 13 G FAT
9 G CARBOHYDRATES 1 G FIBRE 2 MG IRON
37 MG CALCIUM 244 MG SODIUM 151 CALORIES

Ginger-Scented Shrimp and Mushroom Soup

PREPARATION TIME 5 MINUTES
COOKING TIME 7 MINUTES
MAKES 6 CUPS (1.5 L)

8 oz (250 g) mixed mushrooms, such as button, oyster and portobello, about 2 cups (500 mL)

1-inch (2.5 cm) piece ginger, peeled

900 mL carton chicken broth or 3 ½ cups (875 mL) chicken bouillon

3 tbsp (45 mL) white vinegar

2 tsp (10 mL) granulated sugar

2 tsp (10 mL) soy sauce

½ tsp (2 mL) hot chili-garlic sauce

340 g pkg frozen (unthawed) uncooked, medium or large shrimp, peeled

8 oz (227 mL) can sliced bamboo shoots, drained (optional)

1 green onion

1 tsp (5 mL) dark sesame oil

1. Slice mushrooms. Lightly coat a large pot with oil and set over medium-high heat. Cook the mushrooms in the pot, stirring often, until lightly browned around edges, 2 to 3 minutes. Meanwhile, thinly slice ginger. When mushrooms are browned, pour in broth. Stir in ginger, vinegar, sugar, soy sauce and chili-garlic sauce. Bring to a boil over medium-high heat. Boil to develop flavour, about 3 minutes.

2. Add shrimp and bamboo shoots (if using). Stir occasionally until shrimp turn pink, 2 to 3 minutes. Meanwhile, thinly slice onion. Remove from heat and stir onion and sesame oil into broth. Taste and add more chili-garlic sauce and sesame oil, if you wish.

GET AHEAD Prepare Step 1. Cover cooled mixture and refrigerate for up to 1 day, or freeze for up to 1 month. Just before serving, reheat in a large saucepan. When mixture is boiling, continue with Step 2.

NUTRIENTS PER CUP (250 mL) 13 G PROTEIN 2 G FAT
4 G CARBOHYDRATES 0 G FIBRE 2 MG IRON
42 MG CALCIUM 772 MG SODIUM 93 CALORIES

Spiced Harvest Pumpkin and Pepper Stew

PREPARATION TIME 15 MINUTES
COOKING TIME 26 MINUTES
MAKES 8 CUPS (2 L)

½ small sugar pumpkin

2 leeks

2 tbsp (30 mL) butter

4 garlic cloves, minced

1 to 2 jalapeño peppers, seeded and chopped

2 tbsp (30 mL) freshly grated ginger

2 sweet peppers, preferably red and yellow

1 tbsp (15 mL) curry powder or 2 tsp (10 mL) Indian curry paste

¼ tsp (1 mL) each ground allspice and cinnamon

2 10-oz (284-mL) cans undiluted chicken broth

400 mL can unsweetened coconut milk

14 oz (398 mL) can tomato sauce, about 1 ⅔ cups (400 mL)

4 to 6 skinless, boneless chicken breasts (optional)

SWITCH IT UP

Can't find pumpkin? Use butternut squash instead.

SAFE STORAGE

The best way to cool a stew? Partially covered, in the fridge. Leaving it out at room temperature can cause spoilage.

1. Peel pumpkin (see sidebar, page 97), cut into quarters, then scoop out and discard pulp and seeds. Cut pumpkin into small cubes. Cut off and discard dark green part of leeks. Slice leeks in half lengthwise. Fan out under cold running water to remove grit. Thinly slice.

2. Melt butter in a large pot over medium-low heat. Add leeks, garlic, jalapeños and ginger. Stir often until leeks begin to soften, about 5 minutes.

3. Meanwhile, coarsely chop peppers. Once leeks are soft, add curry powder, allspice and cinnamon. Stir constantly until fragrant, 1 minute. Pour in broth, coconut milk and tomato sauce. Bring to a boil over high heat. Then add pumpkin and peppers. Cover, reduce heat and simmer, stirring often, until pumpkin is fork-tender, about 15 minutes. Meanwhile, cut chicken (if using) into bite-sized pieces. When pumpkin is almost fork-tender, stir in chicken. Cover and simmer, stirring occasionally, until chicken is cooked through, 5 to 7 minutes.

NUTRIENTS PER CUP (250 mL) 22 G PROTEIN 15 G FAT
17 G CARBOHYDRATES 3 G FIBRE 4 MG IRON
60 MG CALCIUM 812 MG SODIUM 282 CALORIES

Roasted Red Pepper and Corn Chowder

PREPARATION TIME 15 MINUTES
COOKING TIME 20 MINUTES
MAKES 11 CUPS (2.75 L)

HOME-ROASTED PEPPERS

Position rack in top third of oven. Preheat oven to 475°F (240°C). Line a baking sheet with foil. Lightly coat whole peppers with vegetable oil. Roast until their skins begin to char, about 20 minutes. When done, remove baking sheet to a heatproof surface. Tightly cover peppers with another piece of foil. Let stand until cool enough to handle. Peel and discard skins. Halve or quarter peppers, then remove and discard seeds.

4 garlic cloves

2 small onions

2 large potatoes

3 tbsp (45 mL) butter

4 cups (1 L) chicken bouillon or 900 mL carton chicken broth

1 tsp (5 mL) dried tarragon leaves

½ tsp (2 mL) each salt and freshly ground black pepper

6 large roasted red peppers, preferably homemade (see sidebar)

1 cup (250 mL) frozen or canned corn niblets

1. Mince garlic and chop onions. Peel then chop potatoes into small cubes. Melt butter in a large pot over medium heat. Add garlic and onions. Cook, stirring often, until onions are soft, about 5 minutes. Add potatoes, bouillon, tarragon, salt and pepper. Bring to a boil, then reduce heat. Cover and simmer, stirring occasionally, until potatoes are fork-tender, about 12 minutes.

2. Meanwhile, whirl peppers in a food processor until puréed. When potatoes are done, stir in puréed peppers and corn. Bring to a boil, then reduce heat. Cover and simmer until corn is warmed through, about 3 minutes. Ladle into bowls.

GET AHEAD Cover soup and refrigerate for up to 3 days.

NUTRIENTS PER 1 CUP (250 mL) 3 G PROTEIN 4 G FAT
17 G CARBOHYDRATES 2 G FIBRE 1 MG IRON
21 MG CALCIUM 459 MG SODIUM 106 CALORIES

The Ultimate Split Pea and Ham

PREPARATION TIME 10 MINUTES
SLOW-COOKING TIME 4 HOURS
MAKES 11 CUPS (2.75 L)

450 g pkg dried split green peas, about 2 ⅓ cups (575 mL)

900 mL carton chicken broth or 4 cups (1 L) Homemade Chicken Broth (page 92)

3 celery stalks, thickly sliced

3 carrots, sliced

1 onion, finely chopped

2 tsp (10 mL) dried Italian seasoning

2 bay leaves

1 lb (500 g) smoked pork hock

2 tsp (10 mL) chipotle Tabasco sauce (optional)

STOVETOP DIRECTIONS

Combine ingredients in a large pot. Cover and bring to a boil. Reduce heat and simmer until peas and pork are tender, 1½ to 2 hours. Continue with recipe as directed.

TEST KITCHEN TIP

Boost the flavour of many long-simmering recipes, such as soups and stews, by adding smoked pork hock to the pot. You'll find this in the meat section at your local grocery store.

1. Pick through peas and remove any stones. Rinse peas with water. Drain well, then place in bowl of slow cooker (or see sidebar for stovetop directions). Pour in broth and 3 cups (750 mL) water. Stir in celery, carrots, onion, Italian seasoning and bay leaves. Add pork hock.

2. Cover and cook until pork is tender and falling off the bone, 4 hours on high or 6 hours on low. Discard bay leaves. Place pork on a cutting board. Remove and discard skin, fat and bones. Cut meat into chunks.

3. To thicken soup, whirl one-third in a food processor, then return to slow cooker. Add pork and stir to evenly mix. Taste and stir in Tabasco sauce (if using).

GET AHEAD Cover soup and refrigerate for up to 3 days, or freeze for up to 3 months.

NUTRIENTS PER 1 CUP (250 mL) 16 G PROTEIN 2 G FAT
29 G CARBOHYDRATES 4 G FIBRE 2 MG IRON
39 MG CALCIUM 619 MG SODIUM 194 CALORIES

Creamy Broccoli Soup

PREPARATION TIME 20 MINUTES
COOKING TIME 15 MINUTES
MAKES 4 SERVINGS

10-MINUTE TIP
Lacy parmesan crisps
Preheat oven to 350°F (180°C). Line a baking sheet with parchment paper or coat with vegetable oil or cooking spray. In a small bowl, stir ¾ cup (175 mL) finely grated fresh parmesan with 1 tsp (5 mL) all-purpose flour. Spoon 1 heaping tsp (7 mL) cheese mixture onto baking sheet. Gently spread to form a small circle about 2 inches (5 cm) in diameter. Fill baking sheet with 4 or 5 more circles, making sure to spread them out evenly and leaving at least 2 inches (5 cm) in between. Bake in centre of preheated oven until golden, 5 to 7 minutes. Cool crisps completely on baking sheet before removing. Repeat until all cheese mixture is used.

1 large bunch broccoli

5 garlic cloves

1 large onion

2 tsp (10 mL) vegetable oil

10 oz (284 mL) can undiluted chicken broth

3 cups (750 mL) milk, preferably 2%

1 cup (250 mL) coarsely chopped fresh cilantro, loosely packed

¼ cup (50 mL) freshly grated parmesan cheese

1. Trim florets from broccoli stalks. Finely chop florets. Peel stalks, then finely chop. Slice garlic cloves in half. Coarsely chop onion. Heat oil in a large pot over medium heat. Add garlic and onion. Stir often until onion has softened, about 5 minutes. Add broccoli stalks. Stir in broth. Bring mixture to a boil, then cover and reduce heat to medium-low. Simmer, stirring occasionally, until stalks are tender, 6 to 8 minutes. Pour in milk. Bring mixture to a boil, stirring often. Add broccoli florets. Boil just until tender, 2 to 3 minutes. Remove from heat and stir in cilantro.

2. Pour half of soup into a food processor fitted with a metal blade. Whirl until mixture is puréed, scraping down sides of bowl as necessary. Press through a sieve into another pot. Mash as much broccoli pulp as possible through sieve using the bottom of a soup ladle in a circular motion. This may seem time-consuming but it creates a nice texture. Discard any pulp that doesn't pass through sieve. Purée remaining soup, then pour back into mixture. Heat soup over medium-high heat. Stir often until hot, about 1 minute. Remove from heat. Stir in parmesan until melted. Ladle soup into bowls and serve immediately with Lacy Parmesan Crisps (see sidebar).

GET AHEAD Cover soup with plastic wrap or pour into an airtight container and refrigerate for up to 4 days.

NUTRIENTS PER SERVING WITHOUT PARMESAN CRISPS
16 G PROTEIN 9 G FAT 18 G CARBOHYDRATES 2 G FIBRE
2 MG IRON 381 MG CALCIUM 712 MG SODIUM 210 CALORIES

French Country Chicken Soup

PREPARATION TIME 10 MINUTES
SLOW-COOKING TIME 3 HOURS
OR COOKING TIME 45 MINUTES
MAKES 10 CUPS (2.5 L)

6 bone-in chicken thighs or 1 whole chicken, cut into pieces

2 900-mL cartons chicken broth or 8 cups (2 L) chicken bouillon

1 tbsp (15 mL) Dijon mustard

2 tsp (10 mL) dried tarragon leaves

½ tsp (2 mL) each ground nutmeg and white pepper

6 baby potatoes

4 carrots

2 celery stalks

3 leeks

COOKING TIP

This recipe works well using Homemade Chicken Broth (page 92).

1. Discard skin from chicken and trim any fat. Pour broth into bowl of slow cooker or a large pot. Whisk in Dijon, tarragon, nutmeg and pepper. Add chicken. Cut potatoes, carrots and celery into thick chunks and add to pot.

2. Slice off and discard tough dark green tops of leeks. Slice leeks in half lengthwise. Fan out under cold running water to remove grit. Slice into thick pieces, then stir into chicken mixture.

3. If cooking in slow cooker, cover and cook until vegetables and chicken are tender and cooked through, 3 hours on high or 6 hours on low. If cooking on stovetop, cover and bring to a boil. Reduce heat so broth is gently simmering. Cook covered, stirring occasionally, until vegetables are tender and chicken is cooked through, about 45 minutes.

4. When done, remove chicken to a cutting board. When cool enough to handle, remove and discard bones, then cut chicken into chunks. Stir into soup. Serve with thick slices of baguette for dunking.

GET AHEAD Cover soup and refrigerate for up to 3 days, or freeze for up to 3 months.

NUTRIENTS PER 1 CUP (250 mL) 9 G PROTEIN 2 G FAT
10 G CARBOHYDRATES 2 G FIBRE 1 MG IRON
41 MG CALCIUM 780 MG SODIUM 102 CALORIES

Silky Crab Bisque

PREPARATION TIME 10 MINUTES
COOKING TIME 21 MINUTES
MAKES 2 ½ CUPS (625 mL)

2 tbsp (30 mL) butter

1 garlic clove, minced

1 small onion, chopped

½ tsp (2 mL) fennel seeds (optional)

1 small potato, peeled

2 tbsp (30 mL) tomato paste

½ cup (125 mL) each dry sherry and half-and-half cream

240 mL bottle clam juice

½ cup (125 mL) frozen or tinned crabmeat or diced imitation crab, plus crab for garnishing (optional)

1 green onion, thinly sliced

SERVING SUGGESTION

For a change from the usual presentation, ladle soup into small bowls. Rest a soup spoon over each bowl. Sprinkle crab into spoon.

1. Melt butter in a large saucepan over medium heat. Add garlic, onion and fennel seeds (if using). Stir often, until onion is soft, 5 to 6 minutes. Meanwhile, chop potato.

2. Stir tomato paste into softened onion and stir until fragrant, 1 to 2 minutes. Pour in sherry. Using a wooden spoon, scrape up and stir in any brown bits from pan bottom. Stir in cream, clam juice and potato. Bring to a boil, then reduce heat. Cover and simmer, stirring occasionally, until potato is very tender, 15 to 20 minutes.

3. Pour soup into a food processor and purée until fairly smooth. Return to pan and add crab. If soup is thicker than you like, thin with a little water or milk. Stir often until heated through. Ladle into bowls. Top with a few pieces of crab if you wish, and onion.

NUTRIENTS PER ½ CUP (125 mL) 4 G PROTEIN 7 G FAT
13 G CARBOHYDRATES 1 G FIBRE 1 MG IRON
52 MG CALCIUM 253 MG SODIUM 137 CALORIES

poultry

Perfect roasts, burgers, stir-fries and casseroles — here are Chatelaine's most requested chicken dishes, plus ideas for turkey and duck when it's time to switch it up.

Butterflied Chili-Lime Chicken with Roasted Garlic

PREPARATION TIME 15 MINUTES
ROASTING TIME 1 HOUR
STANDING TIME 10 MINUTES
MAKES 4 SERVINGS

3 lb (1.5 kg) whole chicken

2 limes

1 tbsp (15 mL) butter, at room temperature

½ tsp (2 mL) each salt and freshly ground black pepper

¼ tsp (1 mL) hot chili flakes

2 whole garlic heads, unpeeled

Olive oil

GARLIC TIP
Roasting brings out garlic's sweetness. Roasted garlic (follow instructions in recipe) can also be added to soups, salads and pizza, or even cheese and crackers.

1. Preheat oven to 375°F (190°C). To flatten chicken, place on cutting board, breast-side down. Using kitchen shears or a sharp knife, starting at the neck, cut through bones on both sides of the backbone. Remove back and discard or use for Homemade Chicken Broth (page 92). Turn chicken breast-side up. Use your hands to push breast downward and flatten. If wet, pat dry with paper towels.

2. Grate peel from 1 lime into a small bowl. Stir in butter, salt, pepper and chili flakes. Rub over chicken skin. Cut limes into thick slices. Place close together in the centre of a large baking sheet with shallow sides. Set chicken, breast-side up, on lime slices. Slice off and discard top third of each garlic head. Lightly coat garlic with a little oil. Place beside chicken. To prevent burning, cover garlic tops with small pieces of foil.

3. Roast, uncovered, in centre of preheated oven, 30 minutes. Continue to roast for 20 more minutes, basting occasionally. Increase heat to 400°F (200°C) and continue to roast until skin is deep golden and crispy, and an instant-read thermometer inserted into thickest part of thigh reads 170°F (77°C), about 10 more minutes. Remove to a cutting board and let stand, loosely covered with foil, 10 minutes before slicing. Slice each head of garlic in half. Serve chicken with roasted garlic on the side or squish cloves out of their papery skins and rub all over the chicken.

NUTRIENTS PER SERVING 26 G PROTEIN 20 G FAT
5 G CARBOHYDRATES 0 G FIBRE 1 MG IRON
33 MG CALCIUM 387 MG SODIUM 300 CALORIES

Crispy Coconut Chicken Drumsticks

PREPARATION TIME 10 MINUTES
MARINATING TIME AT LEAST
8 HOURS
BAKING TIME 50 MINUTES
MAKES 12 DRUMSTICKS

12 chicken drumsticks
½ cup (125 mL) finely chopped fresh cilantro
1 ½ tsp (7 mL) hot chili flakes
1 cup (250 mL) pineapple juice
1 cup (250 mL) panko (see sidebar, page 189) or 1 pkg coating mix
½ cup (125 mL) unsweetened desiccated coconut

CHATELAINE KITCHEN TIP

These chicken drumsticks make excellent picnic fare. Simply store cold chicken in plastic bags or plastic containers with tight-fitting lids. Keep cool. Wrap a few extra sprigs of cilantro in a damp paper towel, then plastic. Scatter over chicken before serving.

1. Using a paper towel for grip, pull off skin from chicken and discard. Using a knife, make a few small shallow slashes in each drumstick. Place in a large plastic bag. Add cilantro to bag. Sprinkle in chili flakes. Pour in pineapple juice. Push chicken down into marinade, then squeeze out as much air as possible from bag. Seal with an elastic band as close to chicken as you can. Place bag in a bowl. Refrigerate at least 8 hours or overnight.

2. Just before baking, preheat oven to 400°F (200°C). Line a rimmed baking sheet with foil. Place a wire rack on top. Place crumbs and coconut in a resealable plastic bag. Seal and shake to mix. Remove chicken from marinade. Discard marinade. Working with 1 drumstick at a time, add to bag with coating mix. Reseal and shake to evenly coat. Place drumstick on rack. Repeat with remaining chicken. Discard remaining coating. If using panko, lightly spray drumsticks with oil. If using coating mix, there's no need to spray.

3. Bake in centre of preheated oven until golden and crispy, 50 to 55 minutes.

GET AHEAD Cover cooked chicken and refrigerate for up to 1 day.

NUTRIENTS PER 2 DRUMSTICKS (USING COATING MIX VERSION)
25 G PROTEIN 11 G FAT 14 G CARBOHYDRATES 1 G FIBRE 2 MG IRON
26 MG CALCIUM 435 MG SODIUM 257 CALORIES

BBQ Chicken with Piri Piri Sauce

PREPARATION TIME 5 MINUTES
REFRIGERATION TIME 10 MINUTES
COOKING TIME 4 MINUTES
GRILLING TIME 12 MINUTES
MAKES 4 SERVINGS,
PLUS EXTRA SAUCE

LEFTOVERS?
Leftover sauce can
be used on pork
chops or steak.

5 garlic cloves
1 sweet red pepper
1 jalapeño pepper
½ cup (125 mL) olive oil
2 tbsp (30 mL) white, cider or red wine vinegar
1 tsp (5 mL) salt
½ tsp (2 mL) hot chili flakes
4 bone-in chicken breasts or legs

1. Cut garlic cloves in half. Coarsely chop red pepper. Coarsely chop jalapeño, including seeds. Place all in a medium saucepan set over medium heat. Add oil, vinegar, salt and chili flakes. Stir often until peppers sizzle and soften, about 4 minutes. Pour into a large bowl. Refrigerate for 10 minutes to cool. Pour into a food processor or blender and pulse until puréed.

2. When ready to barbecue, oil grill and heat barbecue to medium. Place chicken in a large bowl. Pour in ⅓ cup (75 mL) sauce and turn to evenly coat. Cover and refrigerate remaining sauce for up to 1 week. Place chicken on grill. Barbecue, lid closed, 6 minutes, then brush on any sauce left in bowl. Turn chicken and continue to barbecue, lid closed, until chicken feels springy when pressed and is cooked through, 6 to 8 minutes.

NUTRIENTS PER SERVING 31 G PROTEIN 9 G FAT
1 G CARBOHYDRATES 0 G FIBRE 1 MG IRON
8 MG CALCIUM 211 MG SODIUM 210 CALORIES

Perfect Roast Chicken

PREPARATION 15 MINUTES
ROASTING TIME 1 HOUR,
15 MINUTES
STANDING TIME 10 MINUTES
MAKES 4 TO 6 SERVINGS

COOKING TIP

Citrus stuffing, such as lemon, lime or orange placed in the cavity of a chicken, creates a juicier bird. It also gives off fragrant steam as it heats.

CARVING A CHICKEN

First, let chicken stand for 10 minutes — this allows juices to redistribute; if sliced right away, the juices pour out. Standing also allows the meat to firm up, which makes slicing easier. Once the chicken has rested, pull each leg back until it pops at the joint. Slice off the legs at joint. Hold each wing down and slice along the bottom of the breast, removing the wings. To cut the breast into slices, begin at the outside and slice parallel to the breastbone. Or for whole breasts, slice down the breast bone, starting at the neck, and pull the breast meat away from the bone.

3 ½ lb (1.75 kg) whole chicken
1 large lemon
4 garlic cloves, peeled
Generous pinches of coarse salt
2 tbsp (30 mL) butter, at room temperature

1. Preheat oven to 375°F (190°C). Remove neck and giblets from body cavity of chicken. Set aside and use for gravy if you wish. Place rack in shallow-sided roasting pan. Lightly spray with oil and set both aside.

2. Cut lemon into 4 wedges. Coarsely chop garlic. Sprinkle garlic and salt over the inside of cavity. Stuff in lemon wedges.

3. Place chicken breast-side up on rack in roasting pan. Rub butter over skin. Sprinkle all over with salt. If you want chicken to hold its shape, tie legs together. But when testing, we got a more evenly cooked bird with crispier leg skin when we didn't do this. Tuck wings underneath bird.

4. Roast, uncovered, in centre of preheated oven, basting once or twice with pan juices, until an instant-read thermometer inserted into thickest part of thigh reads 170°F (77°C) and leg moves easily and its juices run clear, about 1 ¼ to 1 ¾ hours.

5. Remove cooked chicken to a cutting board. Loosely cover with foil and let stand 10 minutes before carving.

NUTRIENTS PER SERVING 43 G PROTEIN 25 G FAT
5 G CARBOHYDRATES 1 G FIBRE 2 MG IRON
36 MG CALCIUM 196 MG SODIUM 430 CALORIES

Stuffed Greek Chicken

PREPARATION TIME 10 MINUTES
GRILLING TIME 16 MINUTES OR
COOKING TIME 45 MINUTES
MAKES 4 SERVINGS

1 roasted red pepper, store-bought or homemade (page 107)

2 green onions

½ cup (125 mL) crumbled feta cheese

4 large skinless, boneless chicken breasts

Toothpicks (optional)

Vegetable oil

1 tsp (5 mL) each dried oregano leaves and garlic salt

1 lemon (optional)

SOAKING WOOD

It's always best to soak wood, such as toothpicks, skewers and (untreated) cedar planks, in water before using for cooking. They absorb water, which prevents them from burning when heated. Soak toothpicks and skewers for 20 minutes or so, and planks for at least 1 hour, and preferably overnight.

1. Oil grill and heat barbecue to medium. If roasting, preheat oven to 400°F (200°C). Chop pepper and thinly slice onions. Mash cheese with roasted pepper in a bowl. Stir in onions. Working with 1 breast at a time, form a pocket in thickest side by making a horizontal cut about 2 ½ inches (6 cm) long and 1 ½ inches (4 cm) deep.

2. Gently open and stuff in cheese mixture, pushing as close to centre of breast as possible. Wet inside edges of opening and press down to seal. If using tooth-picks, insert through edge opening to hold together.

3. Lightly oil outside of chicken and generously sprinkle with oregano and garlic salt. Place chicken on grill. Barbecue, lid closed, until chicken is cooked through, 8 to 10 minutes per side. If roasting, bake, uncovered, on a large rimmed baking sheet in preheated oven until chicken is cooked through, 45 to 55 minutes. Don't turn. If cheese leaks out during roasting, scoop up and serve with chicken. Squeeze lemon juice overtop before serving if you wish.

NUTRIENTS PER SERVING 41 G PROTEIN 7 G FAT
3 G CARBOHYDRATES 1 G FIBRE 1 MG IRON
115 MG CALCIUM 615 MG SODIUM 241 CALORIES

Herb-Coated Chicken with Roasted Cauliflower

Place 2 cups (500 mL) loosely packed fresh herbs, such as a mix of basil, mint, dill and rosemary, in a food processor. (If using rosemary, use the leaves from only a sprig or two as a part of the mix, since its flavour is quite strong.) Add 1 tsp (5 mL) salt. Pulse until coarsely chopped. While motor is running, whirl in 3 tbsp (45 mL) olive oil. Using a sharp knife, make shallow slits over 8 chicken thighs or 4 chicken breasts. Pour herbed oil overtop. Turn to coat. Cover and refrigerate for 1 hour. Approximately 20 minutes before chicken is done marinating, arrange racks in top and bottom thirds of oven. Preheat oven to 375°F (190°C).

Meanwhile, cut half of cauliflower into florets and coarsely chop 2 red peppers. Place all in a large bowl. Drizzle with a little olive oil and sprinkle with salt, preferably coarse. Toss to mix. Spread out vegetables on a baking sheet. When oven is preheated, turn chicken onto a foil-lined baking sheet. Roast cauliflower and peppers until tender, about 30 minutes. Remove and loosely cover with foil. Roast chicken (at the same time as vegetables) until springy when pressed and cooked through, 35 to 60 minutes, depending on type of chicken (see below for roasting time guidelines). Serve vegetables alongside chicken.

MAKES 4 SERVINGS

THERMOMETER

Rely on your instant-read thermometer to decide when meat is done. Insert into the thickest part of the meat without touching the bone. It should read 170°F (77°C) for chicken pieces and for whole unstuffed chicken.

Chicken roasting times

Chicken roasts best in a preheated 375°F (190°C) oven. Follow these cooking times:

Skinless, boneless chicken thighs: 30 to 35 minutes

Skinless, boneless chicken breasts: 35 to 45 minutes

Skin-on, bone-in chicken thighs: 35 to 50 minutes

Skin-on, bone-in chicken breasts: 40 to 60 minutes

Cheesy Layered Chicken and Vegetable Roast

PREPARATION TIME 10 MINUTES
ROASTING TIME 25 MINUTES
MAKES 2 SERVINGS

1 small red onion

1 large pepper, preferably red, yellow or orange

2 skinless, boneless chicken breasts

¼ cup (50 mL) pitted kalamata or pimento-stuffed olives

2 tbsp (30 mL) olive oil

½ tsp (2 mL) dried oregano leaves

¼ tsp (1 mL) each paprika, salt and pepper

1 cup (250 mL) grated mozzarella or cheddar cheese

DINNER TONIGHT
Try this easy-to-assemble and yummy meal on a busy weeknight.

1. Preheat oven to 375°F (190°C). Thickly slice onion into rounds, then separate into rings. Place in a large bowl. Halve pepper, then core and seed. Cut each half into quarters. Add pepper, chicken and olives to onion. Drizzle with oil and sprinkle with oregano, paprika, salt and pepper. Stir to coat. Push chicken to side of bowl.

2. Evenly spread onion, pepper and olives in an 8-inch- (2 L) square baking dish. Evenly sprinkle with ½ cup (125 mL) cheese. Place chicken on top. Sprinkle with remaining ½ cup (125 mL) cheese. Roast, uncovered, in centre of preheated oven until chicken is cooked through and cheese is melted, 25 to 35 minutes.

NUTRIENTS PER SERVING 44 G PROTEIN 36 G FAT
14 G CARBOHYDRATES 3 G FIBRE 2 MG IRON
369 MG CALCIUM 1154 MG SODIUM 552 CALORIES

Country Pot Pie

PREPARATION TIME 25 MINUTES
COOKING TIME 8 MINUTES
BAKING TIME 30 MINUTES
STANDING TIME 10 MINUTES
MAKES 4 TO 6 SERVINGS

3 skinless, boneless chicken breasts

1 carrot

1 celery stalk

1 red or green pepper

½ onion

3 tbsp (45 mL) butter

¼ cup (50 mL) all-purpose flour

1 ½ cups (375 mL) milk

2 cups (500 mL) small broccoli florets

½ cup (125 mL) frozen peas

3 tbsp (45 mL) finely chopped fresh thyme or rosemary or 1 tbsp (15 mL) dried thyme or rosemary leaves

1 tsp (5 mL) salt

½ of 397 g pkg frozen puff pastry, thawed, or 450 g pkg pre-rolled puff pastry 10 × 10 inches (25 × 25 cm)

1 egg, beaten

GET AHEAD

Prepare recipe as directed, but use ⅓ cup (75 mL) all-purpose flour to thicken cream sauce. Vegetables exude water as pie sits, so extra flour will help to keep the sauce thick. Brush pastry top with egg. Cover with plastic wrap and refrigerate for up to 1 day. Preheat oven to 375°F (190°C). Remove plastic wrap. Bake straight from fridge until filling is bubbly, about 70 minutes. If pastry is darkening too much around edges, loosely cover edges with foil.

1. Preheat oven to 400°F (200°C). Cut chicken into 1-inch (2.5 cm) pieces. Thinly slice carrot and celery. Chop pepper and onion. Lightly coat a large frying pan with oil and set over medium-high heat. Cook chicken in pan, stirring often, until lightly golden, 3 to 4 minutes. Add carrot, celery, pepper and onion. Stir often until onion begins to soften, 2 to 3 minutes. Transfer chicken and vegetables to a bowl.

2. Return pan to the burner and reduce heat to medium. Melt butter in the pan, then gradually whisk in flour until evenly mixed and bubbly, 1 minute. Slowly whisk in milk. Whisk until thickened, 2 to 3 minutes. Remove from heat. Add broccoli, peas, 1 tbsp (15 mL) fresh or 1 tsp (5 mL) dried thyme and salt. Return chicken and onion mixture to pan. Stir to evenly coat. Mixture will be very thick. Turn into an 8-inch- (2 L) square baking dish or dish that holds 8 cups (2 L) and place on a rimmed baking sheet.

3. Cut pastry in half. To cover 8-inch- (2 L) square dish, on a lightly floured surface roll each piece into a 10-inch (25 cm) square. It's okay if edges are uneven. Brush 1 square with egg, then sprinkle remaining 2 tbsp (30 mL) fresh or 2 tsp (10 mL) dried thyme overtop. Cover with remaining square of pastry. Press together.

4. Carefully pick up pastry and lay over filling. Tuck in any overhanging edges, then press edges of pastry onto rim of dish. With a knife tip, pierce middle of pastry in 3 or 4 places to allow steam to escape. Lightly brush top with egg. Bake in centre of preheated oven until pastry is golden and filling is bubbly, 30 to 35 minutes. Let stand 10 minutes before serving. Sauce will thicken as it sits.

NUTRIENTS PER SERVING 23 G PROTEIN 22 G FAT
28 G CARBOHYDRATES 3 G FIBRE 3 MG IRON
115 MG CALCIUM 629 MG SODIUM 405 CALORIES

Butter Chicken

PREPARATION TIME 15 MINUTES
COOKING TIME 36 MINUTES
MAKES 10 TO 12 SERVINGS

2 tbsp (30 mL) ground cumin

1 tbsp (15 mL) ground coriander

1 tsp (5 mL) salt

10 skinless, boneless chicken breasts or 20 skinless, boneless thighs

¼ cup (50 mL) butter

8 garlic cloves

3 to 4 hot peppers, such as jalapeño or serrano

1 large onion

1 cup (250 mL) chopped fresh cilantro

¼ cup (50 mL) finely grated fresh ginger

2 cups (500 mL) whipping cream

2 14-oz (398 mL) cans tomato sauce

2 cups (500 mL) frozen peas

COOKING TIP

This incredibly flavourful creamy dish is spiced with a trio of Indian flavours: cumin, coriander and ginger. Don't hesitate to make it in advance; its taste and texture improve as it sits.

1. Place cumin, coriander and salt in a small bowl. Stir to evenly mix. Slice each chicken breast into 3 or 4 long pieces. Melt half of the butter in the largest, widest pot you have, over medium-high heat. Add half of the chicken. Sprinkle with half of cumin mixture. Turn often until chicken is a light golden colour, 5 to 6 minutes. Remove to a large bowl. Repeat with remaining butter, chicken and cumin mixture.

2. Meanwhile, mince garlic. Finely chop peppers, including seeds. (If you shy away from fiery-hot dishes, remove and discard seeds before chopping.) After chopping, the peppers should measure about ½ cup (125 mL). Coarsely chop onion. Prepare cilantro and ginger. Set aside.

3. When chicken is removed from pot, reduce heat to medium. Add garlic and onion. Sauté until slightly softened, 3 to 4 minutes. Pour in cream. Using a wooden spoon, scrape up and stir in any brown bits from pot bottom. Stir in tomato sauce, peppers and ginger. Simmer 10 minutes to develop flavours.

4. Return chicken and juices to pot. If you don't think this will all fit in the pot, pour half the sauce into another large pot and add half the chicken to each. When mixture starts to boil, reduce heat to medium-low. Cover and simmer, stirring chicken occasionally, until cooked through, 10 to 15 minutes. Stir in peas and cilantro. Cook until peas are hot, about 3 minutes. Remove from heat. Taste and add more cilantro if you wish.

GET AHEAD Prepare butter chicken but don't add cilantro and peas. Refrigerate, covered, for up to 2 days, or freeze for up to 2 months. After reheating on medium heat for about 15 minutes, stir in cilantro and peas. Great served with Coconut Milk–Infused Rice (page 303).

NUTRIENTS PER SERVING 29 G PROTEIN 21 G FAT
13 G CARBOHYDRATES 3 G FIBRE 2 MG IRON
70 MG CALCIUM 689 MG SODIUM 354 CALORIES

Cheater Coq au Vin

PREPARATION TIME 15 MINUTES
COOKING TIME 44 MINUTES
MAKES 6 SERVINGS

4 bacon slices

12 oz (350 g) pkg whole button or shiitake mushrooms or a mix of mushrooms

12 skinless, boneless chicken thighs or 6 chicken breasts

1 red onion or 4 shallots or 8 pearl onions (see sidebar)

2 tbsp (30 mL) butter

2 tbsp (30 mL) all-purpose flour

2 cups (500 mL) dry white or red wine

10 oz (284 mL) can undiluted chicken broth

¼ cup (50 mL) cognac or brandy

2 tsp (10 mL) Dijon mustard

2 tsp (10 mL) dried thyme leaves

½ cup (125 mL) chopped fresh parsley

COOKING TIPS

• Coq au vin is often made with pearl onions, but they're a pain to peel, so we've provided options. If using pearl, boil in water for 3 minutes. Then plunge into cold water and leave for 2 minutes. Slice off root ends and peel off skins.

• Red wine is traditionally used in this recipe, but white works just as well. Use whichever you like to drink.

• French chefs begin this dish by cutting up a whole chicken. The skin adds flavour, but it also adds lots of fat and softens during cooking. Save time and calories by using skinless, boneless chicken.

1. Stack bacon and slice crosswise into thin strips. Set a large pot over medium heat. Add bacon and cook, uncovered and stirring occasionally, until crispy, 5 to 7 minutes. As pieces are done, remove to a large bowl.

2. Meanwhile, wipe mushrooms clean with a damp paper towel (see sidebar, page 314). Slice large ones in half; leave small ones whole. Add to bacon fat in pan. Stir often until brown around edges, 3 minutes. Add mushrooms to bowl with bacon.

3. Lightly coat pan with oil. Add half of chicken. Cook until lightly golden, about 3 minutes per side. Remove to bowl with mushrooms and bacon. Repeat with remaining chicken. Meanwhile, cut onion in half, then slice each half into quarters. If using shallots, slice into quarters; leave pearl onions whole.

4. Melt butter in pan. Add onion. Sauté 2 minutes. Add flour and stir constantly for 2 minutes. Pour in a little bit of the wine. Scrape up and stir in any brown bits from pot bottom. Stir in remaining wine, broth, cognac, Dijon and thyme. Return bacon, mushrooms and chicken to pot. Bring to a boil over high heat, then reduce heat to medium-low. Simmer, partially covered and stirring often, until chicken is cooked through and liquid thickens a little, 20 to 25 minutes. Taste and add salt and pepper, if needed. Stir in parsley. Serve alongside roasted potatoes and cooked green beans. Serve with crusty bread for soaking up all the flavourful sauce.

GET AHEAD Cover and refrigerate for up to 2 days or freeze for up to 1 month.

NUTRIENTS PER SERVING 26 G PROTEIN 18 G FAT
11 G CARBOHYDRATES 2 G FIBRE 3 MG IRON
50 MG CALCIUM 624 MG SODIUM 334 CALORIES

Buffalo Wing Chicken

PREPARATION TIME 5 MINUTES
COOKING TIME 12 MINUTES
MAKES 4 TO 6 SERVINGS

LEFTOVERS?
Chop up any leftovers
and toss into a
crisp salad.

12 skinless, boneless chicken thighs

½ cup (125 mL) barbecue sauce

1 tsp (5 mL) Tabasco sauce

⅓ cup (75 mL) crumbled blue cheese

1 green onion, thinly sliced

1. Lightly coat a large frying pan with vegetable oil and set over medium-high heat. Add chicken. (Leave thighs rolled up; don't flatten them out.) Cook until golden, 2 to 3 minutes per side. Meanwhile, in a small bowl, stir barbecue sauce with Tabasco sauce.

2. When chicken is golden, remove to a large plate. Pour ¼ cup (50 mL) water into pan. Using a wooden spoon, scrape up and stir in any brown bits from pan bottom. Stir in barbecue sauce mixture, then return chicken to pan. Turn pieces to coat with sauce. Reduce heat to medium-low. Cover and simmer, turning chicken occasionally until cooked through, 8 to 12 minutes. Place on plates and pour sauce overtop. Sprinkle with cheese and onions. Don't forget the celery and carrots sticks!

NUTRIENTS PER SERVING 24 G PROTEIN 9 G FAT
3 G CARBOHYDRATES 0 G FIBRE 1 MG IRON
57 MG CALCIUM 378 MG SODIUM 196 CALORIES

Saucy French-Style Chicken with Peaches

PREPARATION TIME 10 MINUTES
COOKING TIME 15 MINUTES
MAKES 4 SERVINGS

1 tbsp (15 mL) olive oil

4 skinless, boneless chicken breasts

Generous pinches of salt

3 peaches, unpeeled

1 shallot

½ cup (125 mL) white wine or dry vermouth

2 tbsp (30 mL) grainy mustard or 1 tbsp (15 mL) Dijon mustard

½ cup (125 mL) whipping cream or sour cream

⅓ cup (75 mL) snipped fresh chives or chopped fresh dill

TEST KITCHEN TIP

Take advantage of peach season by preparing this creamy chicken dinner when peaches are at their peak.

1. Coat a large frying pan with oil and set over medium-high heat. Lightly sprinkle both sides of chicken with salt, then place in pan. Cook, turning occasionally, until golden and springy when pressed, 12 to 14 minutes. Remove to a plate.

2. Meanwhile, cut peaches in half and discard pits. Cut peaches into wedges. Finely chop shallot. After removing chicken from pan, reduce heat to medium. Add wine, then scrape up and stir in any brown bits from pan bottom. Add peaches and shallot. Stir often, until peaches soften slightly and wine is reduced, 2 to 4 minutes.

3. Stir in mustard, then whipping cream. (If using sour cream, add after chicken is reheated.) Return chicken and any juices to pan and boil gently, uncovered, turning chicken occasionally, until sauce thickens slightly and chicken is hot, 1 to 2 minutes. Taste and add salt if needed. Sprinkle with chives. Lovely with rice and green beans.

NUTRIENTS PER SERVING 32 G PROTEIN 17 G FAT
9 G CARBOHYDRATES 2 G FIBRE 1 MG IRON
47 MG CALCIUM 187 MG SODIUM 331 CALORIES

Chicken on Cilantro-Ginger Noodles

PREPARATION TIME 20 MINUTES
COOKING TIME 8 MINUTES
MAKES 4 SERVINGS

⅓ of 450 g pkg rice-stick noodles, at least ¼ inch (5 mm) wide

2 handfuls of snow peas, about 7 oz (200 g), trimmed

3 tbsp (45 mL) white wine vinegar

2 tbsp (30 mL) grated fresh ginger

1 tbsp (15 mL) dark sesame oil

1 tbsp (15 mL) granulated sugar

1 tsp (5 mL) Dijon mustard

Generous pinches of salt

3 tbsp (45 mL) vegetable oil

½ English cucumber, unpeeled

6 small radishes

1 ripe mango

1 cup (250 mL) coarsely chopped fresh cilantro

4 thin chicken or turkey cutlets, about ¾ lb (350 g)

Generous pinches of freshly ground black pepper

Sesame seeds (optional)

MANGO TRICK

The easiest way to use the succulent flesh of a mango is to start by slicing both "cheeks" from the pit. Then score the flesh, without cutting through the skin, into strips or cubes. Push on the skin, flipping the flesh outward. It should look like a porcupine. Cut strips or cubes from the skin. Slice any remaining flesh from the pit as best you can.

1. Cook noodles according to package directions, 2 to 3 minutes. Or soak noodles by separating and placing in a large bowl. Cover completely with very hot water. Let stand until tender, 5 to 15 minutes. Stir frequently. Add snow peas for the last 2 minutes of cooking or soaking.

2. Meanwhile, in a medium bowl, whisk vinegar with ginger, sesame oil, sugar, Dijon and pinches of salt. Slowly whisk in 2 tbsp (30 mL) vegetable oil.

3. Cut cucumber in half lengthwise, then thinly slice into semicircles. Slice radishes into thin rounds. Slice mango into bite-sized strips (see sidebar). Combine cucumbers, radishes and mango with cilantro in a large bowl. Drain noodles and snow peas and add to bowl. Drizzle with three-quarters of the dressing and toss to coat.

4. Heat remaining 1 tbsp (15 mL) vegetable oil in a large frying pan over medium heat. Sprinkle chicken with pinches of salt and pepper. Sauté until light golden and springy when pressed, 3 to 4 minutes per side. Remove to a cutting board and slice into thick strips. Place noodle mixture on individual plates. Lay chicken on top. Drizzle chicken with remaining dressing. Sprinkle with sesame seeds if you wish.

NUTRIENTS PER SERVING 23 G PROTEIN 16 G FAT
50 G CARBOHYDRATES 4 G FIBRE 2 MG IRON
47 MG CALCIUM 94 MG SODIUM 433 CALORIES

Ginger Chicken Stir-Fry with Greens

PREPARATION TIME 10 MINUTES
COOKING TIME 6 MINUTES
MAKES 3 SERVINGS

4 baby bok choy or 4 to 5 large bok choy stalks

3 skinless, boneless chicken breasts or 6 skinless, boneless chicken thighs

½ cup (125 mL) teriyaki sauce

3 tbsp (45 mL) cornstarch

1 garlic clove

1 tsp (5 mL) grated fresh ginger

1 tbsp (15 mL) vegetable oil

1 cup (250 mL) chicken broth, preferably low-sodium

4 cups (1 L) baby spinach

GINGER TRICK

The easiest way to peel ginger is to press the edge of a spoon just underneath the skin of a knob of ginger. Pull down and away in long pieces.

1. If using baby bok choy, slice in half lengthwise. If using large bok choy, slice into pieces, about 1 inch (2.5 cm) wide. Cut chicken into bite-sized strips. In a bowl, stir teriyaki sauce with cornstarch until dissolved. Mince garlic and prepare ginger, then stir into teriyaki mixture.

2. Heat oil in a large frying pan or wok over medium-high heat. Add chicken and stir-fry until no longer pink, about 3 minutes. Add broth, teriyaki mixture and bok choy. Pan will be full, but the greens will wilt quickly. Stir constantly until chicken is cooked through, 3 to 4 minutes. Stir in spinach and allow to wilt. Serve over rice or noodles.

NUTRIENTS PER SERVING 37 G PROTEIN 7 G FAT
19 G CARBOHYDRATES 2 G FIBRE 4 MG IRON
175 MG CALCIUM 2286 MG SODIUM 289 CALORIES

Citrus, Chicken and Spinach Toss

PREPARATION TIME 10 MINUTES
MAKES 4 SERVINGS

1 garlic clove

1 tbsp (15 mL) white wine vinegar

1 tsp (5 mL) Dijon mustard

1 tsp (5 mL) honey

1 tsp (5 mL) ground cumin

Generous pinches of salt

2 tbsp (30 mL) olive oil

2 oranges

1 small zucchini

6 cups (1.5 L) baby spinach

3 cups (750 mL) bite-sized pieces cooked chicken

SWITCH IT UP

Switch up the protein by adding chunks of tofu or slices of cooked beef in place of the chicken.

1. Mince garlic. In a bowl, stir vinegar with Dijon, honey, garlic, cumin and salt. Slowly whisk in oil.

2. Slice a small piece off top and bottom of oranges. Cut off and discard remaining peel, including white pith. Thinly slice into rounds. Cut rounds in half if you wish. Thinly slice zucchini into rounds. Add ingredients to a large bowl and toss with spinach and chicken. Just before serving, drizzle with dressing, tossing to coat.

NUTRIENTS PER SERVING 38 G PROTEIN 15 G FAT
12 G CARBOHYDRATES 3 G FIBRE 3 MG IRON
100 MG CALCIUM 145 MG SODIUM 316 CALORIES

Fiery Asian Burgers

PREPARATION TIME 10 MINUTES
GRILLING TIME 12 MINUTES
MAKES 4 BURGERS

1 lime
1 green onion, thinly sliced
2 tbsp (30 mL) soy sauce
1 tbsp (15 mL) hot chili-garlic sauce
1 tsp (5 mL) dark sesame oil
½ tsp (2 mL) ground ginger
1 lb (500 g) ground chicken

SWITCH IT UP

This recipe also works well with beef, pork or lamb in place of chicken, and even with veggie ground round.

SERVING SUGGESTION

For extra Asian flavour, serve with pickled ginger.

1. Oil grill and heat barbecue to medium. Finely grate 1 tsp (5 mL) peel from lime into a large bowl. Squeeze in 1 tbsp (15 mL) juice from lime. Stir in onion, soy sauce, chili-garlic sauce, sesame oil and ginger. Crumble in chicken. Using a fork or your hands, gently mix together. Shape into 4 burgers, about ½ inch (1 cm) thick.

2. Place on grill. Barbecue, lid closed, until burgers are cooked through, 6 to 8 minutes per side. Tuck into toasted sesame buns with your favourite fixings.

NUTRIENTS PER BURGER 20 G PROTEIN 13 G FAT
2 G CARBOHYDRATES 0 G FIBRE 2 MG IRON
29 MG CALCIUM 596 MG SODIUM 205 CALORIES

Latin-Style Turkey Roll

PREPARATION TIME 25 MINUTES
ROASTING TIME 55 MINUTES
STANDING TIME 10 MINUTES
MAKES 6 TO 8 SERVINGS

2 cups (500 mL) grated mozzarella or monterey Jack cheese

3 green onions

3 whole roasted red peppers, store-bought or homemade (page 107)

½ cup (125 mL) coarsely chopped fresh cilantro or ¼ cup (50 mL) shredded fresh basil

3 tbsp (45 mL) finely chopped pickled jalapeño peppers

1 ½ to 2 lb (750 g to 1 kg) boneless, rolled turkey breast (see sidebar)

Butcher's string

1 tsp (5 mL) olive oil

½ tsp (2 mL) dried oregano leaves

Generous pinches of salt and freshly ground black pepper

½ cup (125 mL) sour cream

½ tsp (2 mL) ground cumin

SHOPPING TIP

If you can't find a 2 lb (1 kg) boneless, rolled turkey breast at the grocery store, ask at the meat counter if one can be cut for you, or use two 1 to 1½ lb (500 to 750 g) boneless turkey breasts instead.

1. Preheat oven to 350°F (180°C). Line a rimmed baking sheet with foil. Place cheese in a medium bowl. Thinly slice onions. Pat roasted peppers dry with paper towels, then slice into thick strips. Add onions, roasted peppers, cilantro and jalapeños to bowl and stir to evenly mix.

2. If there is netting around turkey, discard. Place turkey, skin-side down, on a cutting board or piece of waxed paper and unroll. For turkey to be rerolled easily, it should be roughly rectangular and of even thickness. To even out thickness, cut slits into thick parts of turkey, then open up like a book. Cover with a piece of plastic wrap, then lightly pound thick parts with a meat mallet or bottom of a heavy pan until about the same thickness. Excessive pounding will toughen turkey.

3. Mound cheese mixture close to a short edge of the breast. Starting with short end, tightly roll turkey into a log. It's okay if some of filling spills out — just gently pack back into openings at each end. Tie turkey roll with string. Place seam-side down on baking sheet. Brush with oil, then sprinkle with oregano, salt and pepper.

4. Roast, uncovered, in centre of preheated oven until an instant-read thermometer inserted into thickest part of meat reads 170°F (77°C), 55 to 65 minutes, depending on thickness of roll. Meanwhile, for dipping sauce, in a small bowl, stir sour cream with cumin. When turkey is done, remove from oven. Let stand at least 10 minutes, covered loosely with foil. Remove string. Thickly slice. Delicious warm or at room temperature. Serve with dipping sauce and slices of tomato and avocado.

NUTRIENTS PER SERVING 33 G PROTEIN 16 G FAT
3 G CARBOHYDRATES 1 G FIBRE 2 MG IRON
237 MG CALCIUM 297 MG SODIUM 282 CALORIES

Crispy Duck with Ginger-Clementine Sauce

PREPARATION TIME 15 MINUTES
COOKING TIME 18 MINUTES
MAKES 4 SERVINGS

2 duck breasts, about ¾ lb (350 g) each, or 4 skin-on, boneless chicken breasts, any size
½ tsp (2 mL) ground nutmeg
Pinches of salt and freshly ground black pepper
4 clementines
2 green onions
1 shallot
1 cup (250 mL) orange-tangerine or regular orange juice
½ cup (125 mL) sherry
6 slices peeled fresh ginger
1 tbsp (15 mL) granulated sugar
Pinches of salt and freshly ground black pepper

PARTY WORTHY
Turn this dish into a salad starter by thinly slicing cooked duck. Divide lightly dressed salad greens among plates. Add toasted nuts and cheese. Top each salad with fanned duck slices. Drizzle with clementine sauce.

1. Preheat oven to 225°F (110°C). Place duck, skin-side up, on a cutting board. Using a sharp knife, score skin in a diamond pattern, spacing each cut about ¼ inch (5 mm) apart, as best you can. (If using chicken, don't score skin.) Turn meat-side up and sprinkle with nutmeg, salt and pepper. Rub into meat.

2. Set a large frying pan (not non-stick) over medium heat. There's no need to add oil. If using chicken, see cooking instructions below. Place duck, skin-side down, in hot pan. Cook until skin is deep golden brown and crispy, 8 to 12 minutes. If it starts to burn, reduce heat. Drain off fat frequently. Turn duck and continue to cook, uncovered, 2 to 4 more minutes for rare or 6 to 8 minutes for medium-rare, depending on size of breasts. We prefer duck pink. Loosely cover with foil and place in oven to keep warm while preparing sauce. To cook chicken, lightly coat pan with oil. Cook, uncovered and turning occasionally, until skin is golden, 3 to 4 minutes. Cover and cook until springy when pressed, 10 to 12 more minutes. Loosely cover with foil and place in oven to keep warm while preparing sauce.

3. Meanwhile, peel and segment clementines. Thinly slice onions diagonally. Thinly slice shallot. When duck is removed from pan, pour in juice and sherry. Using a wooden spoon, scrape up and stir in any brown bits from pan bottom. Add shallot, ginger, sugar, salt and pepper. Increase heat to high and bring mixture to a boil. Stir occasionally, uncovered, until thickened, 8 to 10 minutes. Remove and discard ginger. Stir in clementine segments.

4. Place duck on a cutting board. Thickly slice breasts diagonally. Pour any duck juices into sauce and stir in. Spoon sauce and clementines onto warm dinner plates. Fan out duck slices on top of sauce. Or if serving chicken, place on plates and spoon sauce overtop. Sprinkle with green onions.

NUTRIENTS PER SERVING 21 G PROTEIN 22 G FAT
24 G CARBOHYDRATES 2 G FIBRE 5 MG IRON
58 MG CALCIUM 113 MG SODIUM 395 CALORIES

meat

Some nights nothing else will do but a juicy steak or perfect prime rib. From everyday favourites to entertaining classics, there's a recipe here for every occasion.

Boldly Spiced Big-Batch Beef

PREPARATION TIME 10 MINUTES
MAKES 10 CUPS (2.5 L)

2 green onions

4 lb (2 kg) medium ground beef

3 eggs

1 cup (250 mL) regular sour cream

1 cup (250 mL) store-bought dry bread crumbs

3 tbsp (45 mL) fresh thyme or ½ tsp (2 mL) dried thyme leaves

1 tbsp (15 mL) dried oregano leaves

2 tsp (10 mL) salt

BEEF IT UP

Italian: Add chopped sun-dried tomatoes and fresh basil, minced garlic and a handful of freshly grated parmesan or asiago cheese.

Greek: Add chopped roasted red peppers, sliced black olives and crumbled feta cheese.

Asian: Add a splash of teriyaki sauce, pinches of hot chili flakes, chopped fresh cilantro, grated fresh ginger and chopped water chestnuts.

1. Thinly slice onions. Crumble beef into a large bowl. Add remaining ingredients. Using your hands, work until mixed. Don't overmix or meat will toughen. Cook now (see below for specific dish instructions) or freeze for later.

GET AHEAD Freeze beef mixture for up to 1 month.

NUTRIENTS PER ½ CUP (125 mL) 19 G PROTEIN 13 G FAT
5 G CARBOHYDRATES 0 G FIBRE 2 MG IRON
40 MG CALCIUM 336 MG SODIUM 230 CALORIES

HOW TO COOK . . .

Meatloaf

Form meat mixture into free-form loaves, about 9 x 5 inches (23 x 13 cm), on a foil-lined baking sheet. Top with slice of white or red onion if you wish — they'll caramelize as meatloaf bakes. Bake at 350°F (180°C) until an instant-read thermometer inserted into centre of meatloaf reads 160°F (70°C), 70 to 80 minutes.

Meatballs

Lightly coat a large frying pan with oil and set over medium heat. Slightly dampen your hands and roll meat mixture into 1-inch (2.5 cm) balls, adding to the oil as each is formed. Don't crowd pan — meatballs will need to be cooked in batches. Turn often until lightly browned, 5 to 7 minutes. Remove each to a large plate when done. Repeat with remaining meatballs, adding more oil to pan if needed. Add to pasta sauce or toss in a sticky sauce and use as an appetizer.

Stuffed Peppers

Stir meat (preferably Mediterranean-flavoured) with quick-cooking rice, about 1 cup (250 mL) for every 1 lb (500 g) beef. Core peppers, then stuff with meat mixture. Bake, covered, at 375°F (190°C) for 30 minutes, then uncover and continue baking for 20 to 30 more minutes.

CHATELAINE KITCHEN TIP

This perfectly seasoned meat makes an excellent base for meatloaf, meatballs and stuffed peppers.

Barbecued Steaks with Argentinean Sauce

PREPARATION TIME 20 MINUTES
GRILLING TIME 6 MINUTES
MAKES 6 SERVINGS

QUICK ARGENTINEAN-STYLE SALAD

Finely chop ½ a jalapeño pepper. Mince 2 garlic cloves. Place both in a small bowl, then whisk in 2 tbsp (30 mL) olive oil, 1 tbsp (15 mL) red wine vinegar, ¼ tsp (1 mL) salt and a pinch of granulated sugar. Arrange slices of cooked baby potatoes, wedges of hard-boiled eggs and tomatoes, and slices of avocado and sweet onion on salad plates. Drizzle with dressing and sprinkle with pinches of ground cumin.

½ **jalapeño pepper**
3 **green onions**
2 **shallots**
1 **cup (250 mL) coarsely chopped fresh cilantro**
½ **cup (125 mL) coarsely chopped fresh parsley**
1 **tbsp (15 mL) dried oregano leaves**
¼ **tsp (1 mL) salt**
¾ **cup (175 mL) olive oil, plus extra for drizzling**
¼ **cup (50 mL) red wine vinegar**
6 **sirloin steaks, at least 1 inch (2.5 cm) thick**
Generous pinches of coarse salt and freshly ground black pepper

1. If you prefer a milder spiced sauce, remove seeds from jalapeño. Coarsely chop jalapeño, onions and shallots. Pulse in a food processor or blender along with cilantro, parsley, oregano and salt until finely chopped. While motor is running, slowly pour in ¾ cup (175 mL) oil and the vinegar. Sauce should still have a bit of texture.

2. Oil grill and heat barbecue to medium-high. Drizzle steak with oil and sprinkle with salt and pepper, then rub in. Barbecue, lid open, 3 to 4 minutes per side for medium-rare. Serve sauce alongside steaks.

NUTRIENTS PER SERVING 60 G PROTEIN 42 G FAT
3 G CARBOHYDRATES 1 G FIBRE 7 MG IRON
41 MG CALCIUM 223 MG SODIUM 634 CALORIES

Shared Steak with Shiitake Mushroom Sauce

PREPARATION TIME 5 MINUTES
COOKING TIME 7 MINUTES
BROILING TIME 8 MINUTES
STANDING TIME 5 MINUTES
MAKES 2 SERVINGS

12 oz (350 g) rib-eye or top sirloin steak, about 1 inch (2.5 cm) thick
Vegetable oil
½ tsp (2 mL) five-spice powder (optional)
Pinches of salt and coarsely ground black pepper
12 oz (350 g) mixed fresh mushrooms, such as shiitake, cremini and oyster
2 tbsp (30 mL) butter
3 tbsp (45 mL) brandy
1 tbsp (15 mL) hoisin or 2 tbsp (30 mL) teriyaki sauce
1 green onion, thinly sliced

1. Bring steak to room temperature. Place oven rack about 3 inches (8 cm) from broiler. Preheat broiler. Set a wire rack on a rimmed baking sheet. Brush steak all over with oil. Sprinkle both sides with five-spice powder (if using), salt and pepper, then rub in. Place steak on wire rack.

2. If using shiitake mushrooms, discard stems and thickly slice caps. Thickly slice cremini and oyster mushrooms. Melt butter in a frying pan over medium heat. Add shiitake and cremini mushrooms. Stir often until softened around edges, 5 to 7 minutes. Stir in oyster mushrooms, brandy, hoisin sauce and onion. Stir often until very bubbly, about 2 minutes. Remove from heat and cover.

3. After you start cooking mushrooms, place steak under broiler. For medium-rare, broil until beef gives slight resistance when pressed with your finger, about 4 minutes per side. Remove to a cutting board. Let stand 5 minutes before slicing and arranging on 2 warmed plates. Spoon mushrooms and sauce overtop.

NUTRIENTS PER SERVING 35 G PROTEIN 36 G FAT
10 G CARBOHYDRATES 3 G FIBRE 5 MG IRON
36 MG CALCIUM 299 MG SODIUM 537 CALORIES

Mushroom-Stuffed Sirloin Steak Rolls

PREPARATION TIME 15 MINUTES
SOAKING TIME 15 MINUTES
COOKING TIME 9 MINUTES
GRILLING TIME 15 MINUTES
STANDING TIME 5 MINUTES
MAKES 4 SERVINGS

STUFFING

2 pkgs dried shiitake mushrooms, each about ½ oz (14 g)

2 tbsp (30 mL) butter

2 garlic cloves, minced, or 1 ½ tsp (7 mL) bottled chopped garlic

1 small sweet onion, chopped

½ cup (125 mL) Madeira or port

½ tsp (2 mL) dried thyme leaves

½ cup (125 mL) freshly grated parmesan cheese

Pinches of salt

STEAKS

2 top sirloin steaks, at least 1 lb (500 g) each and 1 inch (2.5 cm) thick

Butcher's string

4 tbsp (60 mL) butter, melted

3 tbsp (45 mL) chopped fresh tarragon or 1 tsp (5 mL) dried tarragon leaves

1 garlic clove, minced

1 tsp (5 mL) cracked black peppercorns

1 tsp (5 mL) Dijon mustard

1. For stuffing, place dried mushrooms in a bowl. Add enough boiling water to cover and leave until soft, 15 to 20 minutes. Melt butter in a frying pan set over medium heat. Add garlic and onion and stir often until soft, about 5 minutes. As soon as mushrooms are soft, drain and squeeze out excess liquid. Finely chop. Add to onion mixture along with Madeira and thyme. Stir often until most of the liquid has evaporated, 4 to 8 minutes. Turn into a bowl and stir in parmesan. Taste and add salt or more parmesan if needed.

2. For steaks, trim excess fat from each piece. Run the point of a sharp knife horizontally through one side of a steak, cutting just until it will open up like a book. Repeat with remaining steak. Place a piece of wax paper over open steaks. Use a rolling pin to pound meat to as even a thickness as possible. Spread half of cooled stuffing over each steak, leaving a ½-inch (1 cm) border uncovered. Gently roll up, in jelly-roll fashion, and tie in several places with butcher's string to keep stuffing in.

SHORTCUT

Prepare stuffing (Step 1). Run the point of a sharp knife horizontally through one side of a steak, cutting just until you have made a pocket. Repeat with remaining steak. Press half the stuffing into each. Push toothpicks diagonally through the top and bottom edges. Barbecue, covered, turning steaks once, until an instant-read thermometer inserted into thickest part of meat reads 130°F (54°C) for medium-rare, 12 to 15 minutes.

3. When ready to barbecue, oil grill and heat to medium. Brush outside of rolls with 1 tbsp (15 mL) melted butter. Place on grill. Barbecue with lid closed, turning often, until meat gives a little resistance when pressed, 15 to 20 minutes for medium-rare.

4. Meanwhile, stir remaining 3 tbsp (45 mL) melted butter with tarragon, garlic, peppercorns and Dijon. When rolls are done, remove to a cutting board. Cut string, remove and discard. Drizzle some butter sauce overtop. Let stand 5 minutes, then thickly slice. Place on plates and spoon remaining sauce overtop.

GET AHEAD Cover cooled stuffing (Step 1) and refrigerate for up to 2 days. Bring to room temperature before using. Uncooked stuffed rolls (Step 2) will keep well, wrapped, in refrigerator for up to 2 days. Bring to room temperature before grilling.

NUTRIENTS PER SERVING 51 G PROTEIN 30 G FAT
15 G CARBOHYDRATES 2 G FIBRE 5 MG IRON
181 MG CALCIUM 429 MG SODIUM 429 CALORIES

Shaking Beef Salad with Mango

PREPARATION TIME 15 MINUTES
STANDING TIME 20 MINUTES
COOKING TIME 5 MINUTES
MAKES 6 SERVINGS

3 garlic cloves

¼ cup (50 mL) dry sherry

1 tbsp (15 mL) soy sauce

1 ½ lb (750 g) top sirloin steak, at least 1 inch (2.5 cm) thick

2 limes

2 tsp (10 mL) each fish sauce, granulated sugar and hot chili-garlic sauce

1 firm ripe mango

½ English cucumber, unpeeled

1 cup (250 mL) fresh basil or mint leaves

6 oz (170 g) pkg baby spinach, about 7 cups (1.75 L)

SLICING RAW BEEF

Chill steak for a few minutes in the freezer before cutting. Once the beef firms up a bit, it's easier to slice thinly.

1. Mince garlic and place in a large bowl. Stir in sherry and soy sauce. Thinly slice steak across the grain. Add to sauce and turn to coat. Let stand at room temperature for 20 minutes, stirring occasionally, or cover and refrigerate for up to 2 hours.

2. Meanwhile, squeeze 3 tbsp (45 mL) juice from limes into a small bowl. Stir in fish sauce, sugar and chili-garlic sauce. Set aside. Slice mango into long, thin bite-sized strips (see sidebar, page 136). Cut cucumber in half lengthwise. Scrape out and discard seeds. Thinly slice. Tear any large basil or mint leaves in half. In a large salad bowl, toss spinach with mango, cucumber and basil to evenly mix.

3. Drain meat and save marinade. Lightly coat a large frying pan or wok with oil and set over high heat. When pan is hot, add one-third or half of the meat, being careful not to crowd pan. Stir-fry until meat loses its pink colour and edges begin to brown, 2 to 4 minutes. It's okay if brown bits stick to pan bottom. Remove meat to a plate. Repeat with remaining beef in 1 or 2 more batches. Pour saved meat marinade into pan. Scrape up and stir in any brown bits from pan bottom. Boil marinade for 1 minute. Return meat and any juices to pan. Stir to coat meat, then remove from heat.

4. Add lime mixture to spinach, tossing to coat. Arrange on a large platter. Spoon beef and any juices overtop. Serve immediately.

NUTRIENTS PER SERVING 26 G PROTEIN 5 G FAT
11 G CARBOHYDRATES 2 G FIBRE 4 MG IRON
73 MG CALCIUM 430 MG SODIUM 206 CALORIES

Five-Spice Beef Stir-Fry

PREPARATION TIME 10 MINUTES
COOKING TIME 7 MINUTES
MAKES 4 SERVINGS

1 bunch broccoli

1 red pepper

1 lb (500 g) top sirloin steak or stir-fry strips

⅓ cup (75 mL) each hoisin sauce and soy sauce

2 tsp (10 mL) cornstarch

1 to 1 ½ tsp (5 to 7 mL) five-spice powder

1 tbsp (15 mL) vegetable oil

8 oz (250 g) pkg sliced button mushrooms, about 4 cups (1 L)

FIVE-SPICE POWDER

This mix usually includes ground star anise, cloves, fennel seeds, cinnamon and Szechuan peppercorns and is available in the spice section of grocery stores and Asian food markets.

1. Cut stems from broccoli. Peel, then slice into thin rounds. Slice florets into small pieces. Slice pepper into strips. If using steak, cut off excess fat. Slice meat into thin strips. In a small bowl, stir hoisin sauce with soy sauce, cornstarch and five-spice powder.

2. Heat oil in a large frying pan or wok over medium-high heat. Add beef and stir-fry just until it loses its pink colour, 2 to 3 minutes. Add mushrooms, broccoli and pepper. Stir-fry until vegetables begin to soften, 2 to 3 minutes. Stir hoisin mixture and add to beef and vegetables. Stir constantly until sauce thickens, about 3 minutes. Serve over rice or noodles.

NUTRIENTS PER SERVING 32 G PROTEIN 9 G FAT
24 G CARBOHYDRATES 5 G FIBRE 5 MG IRON
73 MG CALCIUM 1661 MG SODIUM 305 CALORIES

Catalan Beef Stew

PREPARATION TIME 8 MINUTES
SLOW COOKING TIME 4 HOURS
MAKES 4 TO 6 SERVINGS

1 ½ to 2 lb (750 g to 1 kg) outside round steak, at least 1 ½ inches (4 cm) thick

1 onion

28 oz (796 mL) can diced or whole tomatoes

1 cup (250 mL) pitted kalamata olives (see sidebar, left)

2 tbsp (30 mL) capers, drained

6 large garlic cloves, coarsely chopped, or 2 tbsp (30 mL) bottled chopped garlic

2 tsp (10 mL) dried thyme leaves

Pinches of salt and freshly ground black pepper

Chopped fresh parsley or cilantro (optional)

PITTING OLIVES

To easily pit kalamata olives, place them on a cutting board, then smash with the flat edge of a knife. Olives will split open. Remove pits and discard, then coarsely chop the flesh.

LEFTOVERS?

Shred the meat in this dish for a hearty sauce to serve over pasta.

1. Trim fat from beef. Slice beef into large cubes. Cut onion into wedges. Place both in bowl of slow cooker. Stir in tomatoes. If using whole tomatoes, break up. Stir in olives, capers, garlic, thyme, salt and pepper.

2. Cover and cook until beef is tender, 4 to 5 hours on high or 8 to 10 hours on low. Add a sprinkling of chopped fresh parsley if you wish. Spoon over rice or noodles.

GET AHEAD Cool stew completely (see sidebar, page 106), then cover and refrigerate for up to 3 days, or freeze for up to 3 months.

NUTRIENTS PER SERVING 27 G PROTEIN 14 G FAT
11 G CARBOHYDRATES 3 G FIBRE 4 MG IRON
81 MG CALCIUM 1094 MG SODIUM 274 CALORIES

Quick Roast with Garlicky Cherry Tomatoes

PREPARATION TIME 10 MINUTES
ROASTING TIME 1 HOUR
STANDING TIME 10 MINUTES
MAKES 3 TO 4 SERVINGS

2 lb (1 kg) quick-cooking roast, such as strip loin, inside round or top sirloin

2 tbsp (30 mL) Dijon mustard

1 tsp (5 mL) each dried thyme leaves and coarsely ground black pepper

1 pint cherry tomatoes

2 garlic cloves, chopped, or 1 tsp (5 mL) bottled chopped garlic

1 tbsp (15 mL) olive oil

1 tsp (5 mL) Italian seasoning

Pinches of salt and freshly ground black pepper

1 tbsp (15 mL) balsamic vinegar

¼ cup (50 mL) chopped fresh parsley

DINNER TONIGHT

A roast isn't just for special occasions — try this quick dish for weeknight dinners too.

1. Bring roast to room temperature. Preheat oven to 325°F (160°C). Place beef in a roasting or broiler pan. Stir Dijon with thyme and 1 tsp (5 mL) pepper and spread evenly all over beef. Roast, uncovered, in centre of preheated oven, 20 minutes.

2. Meanwhile, place tomatoes and garlic in a bowl. Drizzle with oil and sprinkle with seasoning, salt and pepper. Toss to coat. After meat has roasted 20 minutes, scatter tomatoes around beef. Continue roasting until an instant-read thermometer inserted into thickest part of meat reads 130°F (54°C) for medium-rare, 40 to 45 more minutes.

3. Remove beef to a cutting board. Cover with foil and let stand 10 minutes before slicing. Drizzle tomatoes with vinegar, stirring to coat, and sprinkle with parsley before serving.

NUTRIENTS PER SERVING 52 G PROTEIN 16 G FAT
6 G CARBOHYDRATES 2 G FIBRE 6 MG IRON
49 MG CALCIUM 198 MG SODIUM 387 CALORIES

Curried Roast Beef with Coconut Gravy

PREPARATION TIME 10 MINUTES
ROASTING TIME 1 HOUR
STANDING TIME 5 MINUTES
COOKING TIME 5 MINUTES
MAKES 6 TO 8 SERVINGS

1 tbsp (15 mL) Thai curry paste, preferably red

1 tbsp (15 mL) olive oil

3 lb (1.5 kg) sirloin roast

400 mL can unsweetened coconut milk

1 tbsp (15 mL) cornstarch

½ cup (125 mL) shredded fresh basil or coarsely chopped fresh cilantro

3 green onions

Salt (optional)

1 lime (optional)

1. Preheat oven to 325°F (160°C). In a small bowl, stir curry paste with oil. Place beef in a large ovenproof frying pan or pot just large enough to hold it. Rub curry mixture all over meat. Roast, uncovered, in preheated oven for 30 minutes. Add ¼ cup (50 mL) water to pan, then continue to roast until an instant-read thermometer inserted into thickest part of meat reads 140°F (60°C), about 30 more minutes. Remove beef to a cutting board. Loosely cover with foil and let stand 5 minutes. Do not wash pan.

2. In a medium bowl, whisk coconut milk with cornstarch until cornstarch is dissolved. Pour into beef pan and set over medium heat. Using a wooden spoon, scrape up and stir in any brown bits from pan bottom. Stir frequently until thickened, 5 to 7 minutes. If mixture sticks to pan bottom, reduce heat.

3. Meanwhile, prepare basil and thinly slice onions. When gravy is thickened, stir in basil and onions. Season to taste with salt or a squeeze of lime juice if you wish. Slice beef. Divide among individual plates and drizzle with gravy. Or arrange on a platter and pour some of the gravy overtop. Serve remaining gravy in a gravy boat.

NUTRIENTS PER SERVING 37 G PROTEIN 24 G FAT
3 G CARBOHYDRATES 1 G FIBRE 6 MG IRON
29 MG CALCIUM 104 MG SODIUM 385 CALORIES

Perfect Prime Rib

PREPARATION TIME 5 MINUTES
STANDING TIME 2 HOURS,
15 MINUTES
ROASTING TIME 2 HOURS
MAKES 16 SERVINGS

RED WINE PAN GRAVY

While meat is standing, make gravy: Spoon out and discard all but 3 tbsp (45 mL) fat; leave all pan juices. Place roasting pan holding juices and fat over 2 burners or pour liquids into a large pot. Heat over medium heat. When gently boiling, sift in 3 tbsp (45 mL) all-purpose flour, stirring constantly. Gradually whisk in 1 cup (250 mL) dry red or white wine, then 2 cups (500 mL) beef broth. Stir constantly until gravy comes to a boil. Reduce heat and simmer, stirring often, until thickened, about 5 minutes. Taste and add salt and pepper if needed. Makes 3½ cups (875 mL)

6 to 8 lb (3 to 4 kg) beef prime rib
¼ cup (50 mL) Dijon mustard
1 tbsp (15 mL) vegetable oil
2 tsp (10 mL) each dried thyme leaves and coarsely ground black pepper
½ tsp (2 mL) salt, preferably coarse

1. Place roast, fat-side up, on a rack in a roasting pan. In a bowl, stir Dijon with oil, thyme, pepper and salt. Brush over meat, coating ends lightly. Don't coat bottom. Let stand, uncovered, until meat comes to room temperature, about 2 hours.

2. Preheat oven to 350°F (180°C). Place beef in centre of oven. Roast, uncovered, until an instant-read thermometer inserted into thickest part of meat reads 125°F (52°C) for rare, 130°F (54°C) for medium-rare or 140°F (60°C) for medium. This will take 2 to 3 hours, depending on size of roast and how you like it cooked.

3. Remove to a carving board and loosely cover with a tent of foil. Let stand 15 minutes before carving. During this time, the internal temperature will continue to rise by 5 to 10 degrees, and the juices will become more evenly distributed.

4. To carve, remove strings. Hold roast with a carving fork. Using a long, sharp knife, slice roast along the rack of bones so you can lift it off in one large piece. Slice bones into individual ribs and serve or refrigerate for another day.

5. Place meat, fat-side up, on the board. Hold it steady, then slice vertically across the grain to achieve the best tender texture. Excellent served with Shortcut Scalloped Potatoes (page 306) and Chili-Garlic Beans (page 313).

NUTRIENTS PER SERVING 26 G PROTEIN 16 G FAT
1 G CARBOHYDRATES 0 G FIBRE 2 MG IRON
18 MG CALCIUM 184 MG SODIUM 264 CALORIES

Spicy Mexican-Style Brisket

PREPARATION TIME 15 MINUTES
COOKING TIME 2 HOURS,
18 MINUTES
STANDING TIME 5 MINUTES
MAKES 8 SERVINGS

2 ½ to 3 lb (1.25 to 1.5 kg) piece of brisket

Salt and freshly ground black pepper

4 garlic cloves

1 onion

2 tsp (10 mL) finely chopped chipotle chili packed in adobo sauce

28 oz (796 mL) can diced tomatoes

1 tbsp (15 mL) each dried oregano leaves, chili powder and brown sugar

1 tbsp (15 mL) red wine vinegar

1 tsp (5 mL) each ground cumin and dried thyme leaves

2 tbsp (30 mL) cornstarch (optional)

2 green onions, sliced

SHOPPING TIP

Chipotle chilies (smoked jalapeños) packed in adobo sauce are sold in small cans, usually in the salsa section of supermarkets.

1. Lightly coat a large pot with oil and set over medium heat. Generously sprinkle brisket with salt and pepper. Place in pot and brown, 4 to 6 minutes per side. Meanwhile, mince garlic. Cut onion in half, then thinly slice. Chop chipotle.

2. Remove browned meat to a plate. Add garlic and onion to fat in pot. Stir often until onion starts to soften, 2 to 3 minutes. Add tomatoes. Using a wooden spoon, scrape up and stir in brown bits from pot bottom. Stir in chipotle, oregano, chili powder, sugar, vinegar, cumin and thyme. Return meat and any juices to pot. Bring to a boil, then cover and reduce heat to medium-low. Simmer, turning meat occasionally, until fork-tender, 2 to 2 ½ hours.

3. Remove meat to a cutting board and let stand 5 minutes before slicing. If sauce is too thin, stir cornstarch with 3 tbsp (45 mL) cold water until dissolved. Bring sauce to a boil over high heat. Stir in cornstarch mixture. Boil, stirring constantly, until thickened, 2 to 3 minutes. Spoon some sauce onto a platter. Arrange slices overtop. Drizzle with more sauce and scatter with onions. Serve remaining sauce in gravy boat.

GET AHEAD Cover brisket and sauce and refrigerate for up to 3 days. Reheat in a large pot over medium-low heat.

NUTRIENTS PER SERVING WITH ¼ CUP (50 mL) SAUCE
27 G PROTEIN 14 G FAT 5 G CARBOHYDRATES 1 G FIBRE
3 MG IRON 36 MG CALCIUM 138 MG SODIUM 258 CALORIES

Cuban Beef with Cilantro Salsa

PREPARATION TIME 20 MINUTES
ROASTING TIME 2 HOURS
STANDING TIME 10 MINUTES
COOKING TIME 8 MINUTES
MAKES 6 TO 8 SERVINGS

BEEF

20 garlic cloves

3 jalapeño peppers or ⅓ cup (75 mL) pickled jalapeños

⅓ cup (75 mL) olive oil

2 tbsp (30 mL) ground cumin

1 tsp (5 mL) each salt and freshly ground black pepper

½ cup (125 mL) red wine vinegar

2 cups (500 mL) orange juice

4 lb (2 kg) top sirloin or strip loin roast

SALSA

2 large tomatoes

½ red onion

1 cup (250 mL) coarsely chopped fresh cilantro

2 tbsp (30 mL) olive oil

¼ tsp (1 mL) salt

TEST KITCHEN TIP

If you're looking for extra heat in a dish with jalapeño, make sure to add the seeds — they're the spiciest part of these peppers.

1. Preheat oven to 350°F (180°C). For beef, coarsely chop garlic and jalapeños. Pour oil into a microwave-safe measuring cup. Microwave on high until warm, 40 to 50 seconds. Purée garlic, jalapeños, cumin, salt and pepper in a food processor until smooth. Add warm oil and vinegar, then orange juice, whirling to combine.

2. Place beef in a 9- × 13-inch (3 L) baking dish. Pour juice mixture overtop and turn to coat, rubbing into beef. Roast in centre of preheated oven, occasionally basting with pan juices, until an instant-read thermometer inserted into thickest part of meat reads 130°F (54°C) for medium-rare, 2 to 2 ¼ hours.

3. Meanwhile, prepare salsa. Cut tomatoes in half. Remove seeds. Chop tomatoes. Finely chop onion and coarsely chop cilantro. Place all in a large bowl. Stir in oil and salt until evenly mixed.

4. When beef is done, remove from oven. Place meat on cutting board. Loosely tent with foil and let stand 10 minutes before slicing. Meanwhile, skim and discard fat from pan juices. Pour juices into a wide saucepan. Boil over high heat, stirring occasionally, until reduced by half, 8 to 10 minutes. Slice beef. Arrange on platter. Drizzle sauce overtop. Serve salsa on the side.

NUTRIENTS PER SERVING 50 G PROTEIN 20 G FAT
15 G CARBOHYDRATES 2 G FIBRE 7 MG IRON
85 MG CALCIUM 509 MG SODIUM 438 CALORIES

Barely Jerked BBQ Pork

PREPARATION TIME 10 MINUTES
REFRIGERATION TIME 1 HOUR
GRILLING TIME 18 MINUTES
STANDING TIME 5 MINUTES
MAKES 4 TO 6 SERVINGS

2 large garlic cloves or 1 ½ tsp (7 mL) bottled chopped garlic

1 jalapeño pepper or 1 tsp (5 mL) minced pickled jalapeño

1 green onion

1 lime

2 tbsp (30 mL) coarsely chopped fresh cilantro

1 tbsp (15 mL) paprika

2 tsp (10 mL) each brown sugar, ground ginger and cinnamon

1 tsp (2 mL) each salt and freshly ground black pepper

¼ tsp (1 mL) each ground coriander, allspice and nutmeg

2 pork tenderloins, each about ¾ lb (375 g)

CLASSIC JERK CHICKEN

Use chicken legs in place of pork to make the classic Jamaican recipe. Grill until chicken is cooked through.

1. Slice garlic cloves in half. Halve jalapeño, core and seed, then coarsely chop. Slice onion. Place jalapeño and onion in a food processor. Squeeze in 1 tbsp (15 mL) juice from lime. Add cilantro, paprika, sugar and seasonings. Pulse until a paste forms, scraping down sides of bowl as necessary. Rub evenly over pork. Place on a plate. Cover with a bowl so coating won't be disturbed. Refrigerate at least 1 hour and preferably overnight.

2. Lightly oil grill and heat barbecue to medium. Tuck thin end of tenderloins underneath meat. Grill with lid closed, turning meat occasionally, until springy when pressed and an instant-read thermometer inserted into thickest part of pork reads 160°F (70°C), 18 to 20 minutes. Remove from grill. Let stand 5 minutes before slicing.

GET AHEAD Cover cooked pork and refrigerate for up to 2 days.

NUTRIENTS PER SERVING 28 G PROTEIN 4 G FAT
4 G CARBOHYDRATES 1 G FIBRE 2 MG IRON
26 MG CALCIUM 435 MG SODIUM 164 CALORIES

Smoky White-Bean Chili

PREPARATION TIME 15 MINUTES
COOKING TIME 30 MINUTES
MAKES 4 SERVINGS

1 lb (500 g) extra-lean ground beef, pork or turkey

4 garlic cloves, minced

1 tbsp (15 mL) each chili powder and dried oregano leaves

3 chipotle chilies packed in adobo sauce

1 green or red pepper or zucchini

1 large onion

19 oz (540 mL) can white kidney or navy beans, drained and rinsed

28 oz (796 mL) can diced tomatoes, preferably without added salt

1 tbsp (15 mL) tomato paste

GOOD FOR YOU

This version is high in fibre, and lower in fat than your average chili.

1. Lightly coat a large pot with vegetable oil and set over medium-high heat. Add meat, garlic, chili powder and oregano. Stirring frequently with a fork to break meat up, cook until meat loses its pink colour, 5 to 7 minutes. Meanwhile, finely chop chipotles and chop pepper and onion. Once meat is cooked, stir in all other ingredients.

2. Bring to a boil, then reduce heat to medium-low. Cover and simmer, stirring occasionally, until vegetables are tender and flavours have developed, 25 to 40 minutes. Great served with a dollop of plain low-fat yogourt and snipped fresh chives.

NUTRIENTS PER SERVING 25 G PROTEIN 7 G FAT
33 G CARBOHYDRATES 9 G FIBRE 5 MG IRON
79 MG CALCIUM 350 MG SODIUM 294 CALORIES

Succulent and Smoky Ribs

PREPARATION TIME 10 MINUTES
COOKING TIME 1 HOUR
GRILLING TIME 15 MINUTES
MAKES 4 SERVINGS

3 lb (1.5 kg) pork baby back ribs

355 mL bottle beer

½ cup (125 mL) hoisin sauce

2 garlic cloves, minced, or 1 ½ tsp (7 mL) bottled chopped garlic

1 tbsp (15 mL) each grated fresh ginger and granulated sugar

1 tbsp (15 mL) vegetable oil

2 tbsp (30 mL) sherry

1 to 2 tsp (5 to 10 mL) hot chili-garlic sauce or ½ tsp (2 mL) hot chili flakes

BRING IT INDOORS

If you don't want to barbecue, broil ribs on a large baking sheet. Baste occasionally with sauce until ribs are thickly glazed, about 15 to 20 minutes.

1. Slice each rack of ribs in half. Place in a large pot. Add beer and enough water to cover ribs. Bring to a boil. Reduce heat so the liquid boils gently. Cover and cook until ribs are fork-tender, 60 to 75 minutes.

2. Meanwhile, in a small bowl, stir hoisin with garlic, ginger, sugar and oil until sugar is dissolved. Stir in sherry and chili-garlic sauce.

3. When ribs are tender, drain well.

4. When ready to barbecue, oil grill and heat to medium. Brush ribs with sauce and place on the grill. Barbecue, turning and basting often with sauce, until well glazed and hot through, about 15 minutes. When ribs are done, remove to a cutting board. Slice into individual ribs or 4 rib portions and serve.

GET AHEAD Cover boiled ribs and refrigerate for up to 3 days, or freeze for up to 1 month. Brush with sauce just before grilling.

NUTRIENTS PER SERVING 35 G PROTEIN 40 G FAT
19 G CARBOHYDRATES 1 G FIBRE 2 MG IRON
28 MG CALCIUM 585 MG SODIUM 582 CALORIES

Char Siu with Grilled Pork

PREPARATION TIME 5 MINUTES
GRILLING TIME 12 MINUTES
MAKES 4 SERVINGS

4 pork loin chops

Vegetable oil

Freshly ground black pepper

½ cup (125 mL) char siu sauce

¾ tsp (4 mL) minced chipotle chili packed in adobo sauce, or a dash of Tabasco sauce

1 orange, thickly sliced

4 green onions

SHOPPING TIP

Char siu (pronounced char-SYOO) sauce is sold in the Asian section of most supermarkets, and in Asian food markets.

1. Oil grill and heat barbecue to high. Lightly rub chops with oil. Sprinkle both sides with pepper. In a small bowl, stir char siu sauce with chipotle. Set 2 tbsp (30 mL) aside for brushing on cooked chops.

2. Place meat on grill and reduce heat to medium. Cover and grill pork 2 minutes per side, then brush both sides with sauce. Continue turning and brushing chops with sauce for 2 more minutes. Continue grilling until chops give slightly when pressed, 3 to 5 more minutes per side.

3. After chops have cooked a few minutes, add orange slices and whole onions to grill. Turn occasionally until lightly charred, removing each as it is done. Thickly slice onions.

4. Place chops on plates. Spoon reserved sauce overtop. Arrange orange slices overtop, then scatter with onions. Add rice and a salad and dinner's done.

NUTRIENTS PER SERVING 29 G PROTEIN 4 G FAT
33 G CARBOHYDRATES 1 G FIBRE 2 MG IRON
29 MG CALCIUM 1999 MG SODIUM 293 CALORIES

Ginger Mojito Pork

PREPARATION TIME 10 MINUTES
GRILLING TIME 25 MINUTES
STANDING TIME 5 MINUTES
MAKES 2 TO 3 SERVINGS

4 limes

2 tbsp (30 mL) honey

4 tsp (20 mL) rum

1 tbsp (15 mL) oil

¼ tsp (1 mL) ground ginger

Generous pinches of salt

**1 large pork tenderloin or small boneless centre-cut pork loin roast,
about 1 ¼ lb (625 g)**

¼ cup (50 mL) shredded fresh mint

BRING IT INDOORS

No grill? No problem. Simply marinate meat as directed. Roast on a foil-lined baking sheet at 375°F (190°C) for 25 to 40 minutes. Let stand 5 minutes before slicing.

1. Oil grill and heat barbecue to medium. Meanwhile, squeeze ⅓ cup (75 mL) juice from limes into a wide shallow bowl or pie plate. Whisk in honey, rum, oil, ginger and salt. Using the tip of a small knife, make shallow slashes all over the pork. Place pork in lime mixture and turn to evenly coat. Leave while the barbecue preheats, at least 10 minutes. Turn occasionally.

2. When grill is hot, add meat. Cook, lid closed, basting often with lime mixture for 10 minutes. Turn occasionally until cooked through and an instant-read thermometer inserted into thickest part of pork reads 160°F (70°C), 15 to 20 more minutes. Remove to a cutting board. Let stand 5 minutes, then slice. Sprinkle with mint.

NUTRIENTS PER SERVING 34 G PROTEIN 8 G FAT
15 G CARBOHYDRATES 1 G FIBRE 3 MG IRON
27 MG CALCIUM 72 MG SODIUM 268 CALORIES

Cumin-Crusted Pork with Citrus Sauce

PREPARATION TIME 10 MINUTES
REFRIGERATION TIME 8 HOURS
ROASTING TIME 1 HOUR,
30 MINUTES
STANDING TIME 5 MINUTES
COOKING TIME 15 MINUTES
MAKES 6 SERVINGS

2 cups (500 mL) orange juice

¼ cup (50 mL) olive oil

1 tbsp (15 mL) ground cumin

1 tsp (5 mL) salt

3 ½ to 4 lb (1.75 to 2 kg) rack of pork, 6 to 8 ribs

1 tsp (5 mL) cumin seeds

¼ cup (50 mL) brandy

2 garlic cloves, minced, or 1 ½ tsp (7 mL) bottled chopped garlic

¼ cup (50 mL) finely chopped fresh parsley or cilantro

DID YOU KNOW?

Cilantro and coriander are often mistaken as the same thing. That's because they practically are. Cilantro is the fresh stem and leaf of a coriander plant. Ground coriander is the crushed dried seeds of the plant.

1. Pour 1 cup (250 mL) orange juice and oil into a large plastic bag, then sprinkle in cumin and salt. If pork is tied with butcher's string, remove and discard. Using the tip of a knife, make shallow slits all over pork. Place pork in bag with marinade. Push meat down into marinade, then squeeze out as much air as you can. Seal tightly with an elastic band as close to meat as possible. Place bag in a bowl. Refrigerate at least 8 hours and preferably overnight.

2. Preheat oven to 375°F (190°C). Line a large, shallow-sided roasting pan or baking dish with foil. Remove pork from bag but do not discard marinade. Place pork, bone-side down, on prepared pan. Sprinkle evenly with cumin seeds. Roast, uncovered, in centre of preheated oven until an instant-read thermometer inserted into thickest part of roast reads 160°F (70°C), about 1 ½ hours. When done, remove roast to a cutting board and let stand 5 minutes before slicing.

3. While meat is roasting, pour marinade into a large, wide frying pan set over high heat. For sauce, stir in remaining 1 cup (250 mL) orange juice, brandy and garlic. Boil, stirring often, until sauce is thickened and reduced by half, about 15 minutes. Just before serving, stir in parsley. Slice pork into chops and serve drizzled with sauce.

NUTRIENTS PER CHOP SERVING ¼ CUP (50 mL) SAUCE
37 G PROTEIN 21 G FAT 14 G CARBOHYDRATES 1 G FIBRE
3 MG IRON 62 MG CALCIUM 473 MG SODIUM 408 CALORIES

Chili-Spiced Chops with Guacamole

PREPARATION TIME 15 MINUTES
GRILLING TIME 10 MINUTES
MAKES 4 SERVINGS

1 tbsp (15 mL) vegetable oil

2 tsp (10 mL) each ground coriander and chili powder

1 tsp (5 mL) garlic salt

½ to 1 tsp (2 to 5 mL) Tabasco sauce

4 pork loin chops, at least 1/2-inch (1 cm) thick

GUACAMOLE

1 ripe avocado

1 lime

1 cup (250 mL) chopped fresh cilantro

½ tsp (2 mL) salt

½ tsp (2 mL) Tabasco sauce

3 plum tomatoes

BRING IT INDOORS

Preheat a grilling machine to medium-high. Place pork on grill. Grill, lid closed, until meat feels firm to the touch, 5 to 7 minutes.

1. Oil grill and heat barbecue to medium-high. For chops, in a small bowl, stir oil with coriander, chili powder, garlic salt and ½ tsp (2 mL) Tabasco sauce. If you like it hot, use 1 tsp (5 mL) Tabasco. Rub over both sides of chops. Let stand at room temperature while preparing sauce.

2. For guacamole, cut avocado in half and discard pit. Scoop flesh from peel into a blender or food processor. Squeeze in about 1 tbsp (15 mL) juice from lime. Add cilantro, ½ cup (125 mL) water, salt and ½ tsp (2 mL) Tabasco sauce. Whirl until smooth. Taste and add more lime juice and Tabasco if you wish. Spoon mixture into a medium bowl. Cut tomatoes in half. Squeeze out and discard seeds. Finely chop tomatoes, then stir into avocado mixture. Guacamole tastes best the same day it's made.

3. Place chops on grill. Barbecue, lid closed, until meat feels firm to the touch, 5 to 7 minutes per side. Place on plates and top with generous dollops of guacamole. Delicious with grilled corn on the cob.

GET AHEAD Cover and refrigerate guacamole for up to 6 hours.

NUTRIENTS PER SERVING 22 G PROTEIN 18 G FAT
7 G CARBOHYDRATES 3 G FIBRE 2 MG IRON
43 MG CALCIUM 659 MG SODIUM 275 CALORIES

179

Fresh Wraps with Saucy Pork

2 tbsp (30 mL) each barbecue sauce and hoisin sauce

1 tbsp (15 mL) hot chili-garlic sauce

1 tsp (5 mL) soy sauce

¼ tsp (1 mL) dark sesame oil

1 pork tenderloin, about ¾ to 1 lb (375 g to 500 g)

2 green onions or 1 carrot

1 avocado or ¼ cucumber

8 medium flour tortillas, about 7 inches (18 cm) in diameter, or small pitas

Handful of fresh parsley (optional)

SERVING SUGGESTION

For a bigger meal, serve this cooked pork over noodles or tossed with a salad.

1. Position oven rack on bottom shelf of oven. Preheat oven to 500°F (260°C). Line a baking sheet with foil, then spray with oil. In a bowl, stir barbecue sauce with hoisin sauce, chili-garlic sauce, soy sauce and sesame oil. Slice pork in half lengthwise. Thinly slice halves. Add to sauce, stirring to coat.

2. Spread pork in a single layer on baking sheet. Roast on bottom shelf of preheated oven until lightly glazed, 7 to 8 minutes. You don't need to turn. Excellent warm, at room temperature or chilled.

3. Just before serving, thickly slice onions. If using carrot, coarsely grate. Slice avocado in half and discard pit. Gently scoop flesh from peel, then slice into thin wedges. If using cucumber, peel if you wish, then thinly slice. Place a few slices of pork in centre of each tortilla and top with slices of onion and avocado, and parsley if you wish. If serving as appetizers, cut each roll in half on the diagonal.

GET AHEAD Cover roasted pork and refrigerate for up to 2 days.

NUTRIENTS PER WRAP 22 G PROTEIN 12 G FAT
35 G CARBOHYDRATES 4 G FIBRE 3 MG IRON
36 MG CALCIUM 517 MG SODIUM 338 CALORIES

Thick Chops Stuffed with Brie

PREPARATION TIME 10 MINUTES
COOKING TIME 19 MINUTES
MAKES 4 SERVINGS

3 oz (90 g) brie or camembert cheese
4 bone-in, centre-cut pork chops, at least 1 inch (2.5 cm) thick
1 large red or green apple, unpeeled
1 tbsp (15 mL) Dijon mustard
½ tsp (2 mL) Italian or poultry seasoning
Fresh rosemary leaves, chopped (optional)

ON THE SIDE

Wonder what we've tucked behind those chops in this photo? Roasted tomatoes on the vine. You can prepare these by drizzling tomatoes (still on the vine) with a bit of olive oil, then roasting on a foil-lined baking sheet in a preheated 400°F (200°C) oven until tender, about 15 minutes.

1. Cut brie into 4 slices (it's okay to leave rind on). Make a slit about 2 inches (5 cm) long in the side of each chop. Stuff each with a slice of brie. Lightly coat a large frying pan with oil and set over medium-high heat. When pan is hot, add chops. Cook until lightly golden, 2 to 3 minutes per side. You may need to do this in 2 batches. Remove chops to a plate as they are done.

2. Meanwhile, slice apple into thin wedges. Once pork is removed from pan, add apple along with a little more oil. Stir occasionally until apple wedges are lightly golden, about 3 minutes. Pour in ¼ cup (50 mL) water. Add Dijon and seasoning. Using a wooden spoon, scrape up and stir in any brown bits from pan bottom. Push apple wedges to side of pan.

3. Return chops to pan. Cover and reduce heat to medium-low. Simmer, stirring occasionally, until pork is springy when pressed, 10 to 12 minutes. Turn chops over halfway through cooking time. Transfer chops and apple to plates. Increase heat to high. Stir constantly until sauce is as thick as you like, about 2 minutes. Sauce will be golden and flecked with flavourful bits. Arrange on platter or individual plates and sprinkle with fresh rosemary if you wish. Wonderful with green beans and baby potatoes.

NUTRIENTS PER SERVING 26 G PROTEIN 21 G FAT
9 G CARBOHYDRATES 1 G FIBRE 1 MG IRON
75 MG CALCIUM 249 MG SODIUM 329 CALORIES

Wilted Spinach Salad with Chipotle Pork

PREPARATION TIME 15 MINUTES
COOKING TIME 15 MINUTES
MAKES 3 TO 4 SERVINGS

1 large pork tenderloin, about ¾ to 1 lb (375 g to 500 g)

2 ripe peaches or nectarines or pears or a mix

¼ red onion

¾ of 10 oz (284 g) pkg baby spinach, about 12 cups (3 L)

1 cup (250 mL) orange juice

1 tbsp (15 mL) chopped fresh rosemary or 1 tsp (5 mL) dried rosemary leaves, crumbled

½ tsp (2 mL) each ground cumin and salt

2 tbsp (30 mL) vegetable or olive oil

1 tbsp (15 mL) honey

1 to 1 ½ tsp (5 to 7 mL) finely minced chipotle chili packed in adobo sauce

SERVING SUGGESTION

This big salad supper makes a great light weeknight meal.

1. Slice pork into thin, round slices. Lightly coat a large frying pan with oil and set over medium-high heat. When pan is hot, add pork and brown on all sides, 2 to 4 minutes. Reduce heat to medium-low. Cover and cook until pork is cooked through.

2. Meanwhile, peel and pit peaches or core pears, then slice into thin wedges. Thinly slice onion. Place all in a very large salad bowl along with spinach. After removing pork from pan, add orange juice, rosemary, cumin and salt. Using a wooden spoon, scrape up and stir in any brown bits from pan bottom. Boil, uncovered, over high heat until liquid is reduced by half, about 5 minutes.

3. Once liquid has reduced, stir in oil, honey and chipotle. Add sliced pork and stir occasionally until warm, about 2 minutes. Turn over spinach and fruit, tossing to coat.

NUTRIENTS PER SERVING 30 G PROTEIN 10 G FAT
20 G CARBOHYDRATES 2 G FIBRE 3 MG IRON
78 MG CALCIUM 399 MG SODIUM 288 CALORIES

Pancetta-Wrapped Pork with Apple Stuffing

PREPARATION TIME 15 MINUTES
ROASTING TIME 50 MINUTES
STANDING TIME 10 MINUTES
MAKES 6 SERVINGS

1 chorizo or cooked spicy sausage

1 small apple, unpeeled

¼ cup (50 mL) dried apricots (optional)

4 green onions

1 tbsp (15 mL) chopped fresh rosemary or ½ tsp (2 mL) dried rosemary leaves, crumbled

½ tsp (2 mL) dried oregano leaves

¼ tsp (1 mL) each salt and freshly ground black pepper

2 to 2 ½ lb (1 to 1.25 kg) boneless pork loin roast

4 thinly sliced pancetta rounds

4 sprigs fresh rosemary

Butcher's string

DINNER TONIGHT

Make it (even on a weeknight) by preparing only the stuffing and placing in an 8-inch (2 L) baking dish. Cover with foil. Lightly oil a pork tenderloin or two, depending on how much you want. Sprinkle with rosemary, salt and pepper. Roast tenderloin on a baking sheet alongside stuffing until tenderloin is cooked through and stuffing is hot, 20 to 25 minutes.

1. Preheat oven to 350°F (180°C). Line a baking sheet with foil. For stuffing, finely chop sausage, apple and apricots (if using). Place all in a medium bowl. Thinly slice onions. Add to sausage along with rosemary, oregano, salt and pepper. Set aside.

2. If pork has netting, discard. Using a long knife, slice meat in half horizontally, but not all the way through, so you can open it up like a book. For a small roast, top one side of the "book" with about two-thirds of stuffing, spreading out evenly but leaving a 1-inch (2.5 cm) uncovered edge. For a large roast, use all the stuffing, also leaving a 1-inch (2.5 cm) uncovered edge. Fold other side of "book" over stuffing. Wrap or cover pork with pancetta, overlapping slightly. Top with rosemary sprigs. Tie with string to hold everything in place. Seal any extra stuffing in a foil package.

3. Place pork on prepared baking sheet and stuffing package beside it. Roast in centre of preheated oven until an instant-read thermometer inserted into thickest part of pork reads 160°F (70°C), 50 to 70 minutes. Remove roast to a carving board. Let stand 10 minutes, loosely covered with foil, then thickly slice and arrange on a platter.

NUTRIENTS PER SERVING 36 G PROTEIN 9 G FAT
4 G CARBOHYDRATES 1 G FIBRE 1 MG IRON
19 MG CALCIUM 302 MG SODIUM 251 CALORIES

Puff Pastry–Wrapped Pork Tenderloin

PREPARATION TIME 20 MINUTES
BAKING TIME 45 MINUTES
STANDING TIME 5 MINUTES
MAKES 6 TO 8 SERVINGS

397 g pkg frozen puff pastry, thawed

8 slices prosciutto

2 pork tenderloins, each about ¾ to 1 lb (375 g to 500 g)

2 tsp (10 mL) Dijon or grainy mustard

Generous pinches of dried rosemary leaves, salt and freshly ground black pepper

1 egg

KITSCHY DECORATION TIP

For a pretty presentation, add decorative leaves to the pastry. Simply roll 1 strip of pastry into a cord and flatten into a long strip. Slice the flat strip diagonally into diamonds or leaf shapes and score them with the knife tip to resemble leaf veins. Brush pastry on meat with egg mixture before gently pressing the decorations on top. Brush decorations with egg mixture.

1. Preheat oven to 350°F (180°C). Have an ungreased baking sheet ready. Cut a ½-inch (1 cm) strip from both ends of pastry. Set aside for decorations. Slice pastry in half. Place half on a lightly floured surface. Using a lightly floured rolling pin, roll dough into a 12-inch (30 cm) square. Edges don't need to be perfect.

2. Vertically lay 4 slices of prosciutto in centre of pastry, overlapping slightly. Place 1 tenderloin horizontally across prosciutto, tucking in thin end of pork so meat is of even thickness. Spread meat with 1 tsp (5 mL) Dijon. Crumble rosemary overtop, then sprinkle with salt and pepper. In a bowl, whisk egg with 1 tbsp (15 mL) water, then lightly brush edges of pastry. Fold bottom part of pastry and prosciutto over pork. Fold in pastry edges. Roll pastry around pork to form a log. Pinch edges to completely seal. Place log, seam-side down, on baking sheet. Repeat with remaining ingredients.

3. With a knife, make 3 small holes in top of each log for steam to escape. Thinly roll out pastry for decorations. Cut half into leaf or petal shapes and roll half into slim strips to use as "stalks" (see sidebar). Brush logs with egg mixture. Press pastry decorations on top of logs and gently press into pastry. Brush decorations with egg mixture. Bake in centre of preheated oven until pastry is deep golden, 45 to 50 minutes. Turn baking sheet halfway through baking time. Let stand 5 minutes before slicing.

NUTRIENTS PER SERVING 25 G PROTEIN 22 G FAT
23 G CARBOHYDRATES 1 G FIBRE 2 MG IRON
14 MG CALCIUM 273 MG SODIUM 395 CALORIES

Pork Tenderloin Parmigiana

PREPARATION TIME 10 MINUTES
ROASTING TIME 30 MINUTES
STANDING TIME 5 MINUTES
MAKES 2 TO 3 SERVINGS

2 tbsp (30 mL) store-bought fine dry bread crumbs or panko (see sidebar)

2 tbsp (30 mL) freshly grated parmesan cheese

1 tbsp (15 mL) chopped fresh rosemary or 1 tsp (5 mL) dried rosemary leaves

2 garlic cloves, minced, or 1 ½ tsp (7 mL) bottled chopped garlic

¼ tsp (1 mL) each salt and freshly ground black pepper

1 pork tenderloin, about ¾ to 1 lb (375 g to 500 g)

2 tsp (10 mL) olive oil

1 pint cherry or grape tomatoes

WHAT IS IT?

Panko are Japanese bread crumbs made from crustless bread. They have a coarser texture than regular bread crumbs and typically result in a crispier texture when cooked. Panko can be found at your local grocery store.

1. Preheat oven to 375°F (190°C). In a pie plate or wide shallow bowl, stir bread crumbs with parmesan, rosemary, garlic, salt and pepper. Rub pork with 1 tsp (5 mL) oil, then place in crumbs and turn to evenly coat, pressing mixture onto meat. Place on a foil-lined, rimmed baking sheet. Press any remaining crumb mixture overtop and onto sides of meat. In a small bowl, toss tomatoes with remaining 1 tsp (5 mL) oil, then scatter around pork.

2. Roast in centre of preheated oven, stirring tomatoes occasionally, until pork is firm when pressed, 30 to 40 minutes. Pork is done when an instant-read thermometer inserted into thickest part of meat reads 160°F (70°C). Let stand 5 minutes before slicing. Excellent with a green salad.

NUTRIENTS PER SERVING 30 G PROTEIN 8 G FAT
9 G CARBOHYDRATES 1 G FIBRE 2 MG IRON
84 MG CALCIUM 373 MG SODIUM 227 CALORIES

Moroccan-Style Lamb Kebabs with Charmoula Mayonnaise

PREPARATION TIME 20 MINUTES
GRILLING TIME 7 MINUTES
MAKES 4 SERVINGS

KEBABS

6 large skewers, preferably metal

2 garlic cloves

2 tbsp (30 mL) olive oil

1 tsp (5 mL) each paprika and ground cumin

½ tsp (2 mL) each ground coriander and salt

¼ tsp (1 mL) cayenne pepper

1 lb (500 g) piece of boneless lamb, such as shoulder or leg

2 small red onions

1 large orange, unpeeled

¼ cup (50 mL) chopped fresh mint or cilantro (optional)

SAUCE (OPTIONAL)

1 lemon

½ cup (125 mL) mayonnaise, preferably light

2 tbsp (30 mL) finely chopped fresh cilantro (optional)

2 garlic cloves, minced

1 tsp (5 mL) ground cumin

1 tsp (5 mL) paprika, preferably smoked

¼ tsp (1 mL) cayenne pepper

WHAT IS IT?

Charmoula is a spice and herb mix that's often used as in marinades in Moroccan and Tunisian cuisine — it's typically a mixture of cilantro, cumin, lemon and garlic.

1. For kebabs, lightly oil grill, then heat barbecue to medium-high. If using wooden skewers, soak in water for 20 minutes (see sidebar). Mince garlic and place in a large bowl. Stir in oil, paprika, cumin, coriander, salt and cayenne. Add more cayenne if you want extra heat. Cut lamb into 1 ½-inch (4 cm) pieces. Add to spice mix and turn to evenly coat. Cut each onion into 6 wedges. Cut orange into 12 wedges. Thread meat and onion and orange wedges, alternating, onto skewers.

2. For sauce, squeeze 2 tbsp (30 mL) juice from lemon into a small bowl. Stir in mayonnaise, cilantro (if using), garlic, cumin, paprika and cayenne.

3. Place kebabs on grill. Barbecue, turning frequently, until meat is lightly charred around edges, 7 to 10 minutes. Remove kebabs to a platter. Sprinkle with chopped mint if you wish. Serve sauce alongside kebabs.

NUTRIENTS PER SERVING WITHOUT SAUCE 21 G PROTEIN
15 G FAT 16 G CARBOHYDRATES 3 G FIBRE 2 MG IRON
62 MG CALCIUM 351 MG SODIUM 278 CALORIES

Lamb Chops with Chèvre Crust

PREPARATION TIME 5 MINUTES
BROILING TIME 12 MINUTES
MAKES 4 SERVINGS

8 lamb loin chops, about 1 ½ inches (4 cm) thick

5 oz (140 g) log goat cheese

¼ cup (50 mL) chopped roasted red pepper, store-bought or homemade (see sidebar, page 107)

¼ cup (50 mL) snipped fresh chives, or chopped fresh parsley or cilantro

Handful of Italian-style bread crumbs, preferably with pecorino cheese, for sprinkling

WHAT IS IT?

Chèvre is the French word for goat and the name given to goat's milk cheese. The cheese's tangy flavour and creamy texture stands up well to roasting.

1. Place oven rack about 3 inches (8 cm) from broiler. Preheat broiler. Line a baking sheet with shallow sides with foil. Place a rack on baking sheet and arrange chops on top. Broil 4 minutes. Turn and broil 4 more minutes.

2. Meanwhile, in a small bowl, stir cheese with a spoon or mash with a fork to soften a little. Stir in pepper and chives just until evenly distributed. After chops are broiled, remove baking sheet from oven to a heatproof surface. Spread about 2 tbsp (30 mL) cheese mixture over each chop. Generously sprinkle bread crumbs overtop. Return to oven and broil until bread crumbs turn golden, 4 to 6 more minutes.

NUTRIENTS PER SERVING 21 G PROTEIN 13 G FAT
1 G CARBOHYDRATES 0 G FIBRE 1 MG IRON
45 MG CALCIUM 213 MG SODIUM 206 CALORIES

Trio of Lamb

PREPARATION TIME 10 MINUTES
ROASTING TIME 25 MINUTES
STANDING TIME 5 MINUTES
MAKES 4 SERVINGS

3 racks of lamb, each about 8 ribs

PESTO AND MINT CRUST

2 slices toasted white bread, crusts trimmed

½ cup (125 mL) coarsely chopped fresh mint

½ cup (125 mL) freshly grated parmesan or asiago cheese

1 tsp (5 mL) olive oil

3 tbsp (45 mL) pesto, store-bought or homemade (see sidebar, page 76)

CURRY-CHUTNEY GLAZE

⅓ cup (75 mL) sweet mango chutney

¼ tsp (1 mL) each curry powder and ground cumin

¼ cup (50 mL) chopped fresh cilantro (optional)

SESAME-GARLIC GLAZE

1 tbsp (15 mL) each hot chili-garlic sauce and honey

2 tsp (10 mL) Dijon mustard

1 tsp (5 mL) dark sesame oil

CARVING TIP

Serving lamb racks is much easier than carving a leg; just slice right in between the bones.

1. Preheat oven to 375°F (190°C). For pesto and mint crust, tear toast into large pieces and place in a food processor. Add mint, cheese and oil. Pulse until coarse crumbs form. Smear fat-side of 1 lamb rack with pesto. Generously mound with bread crumb mixture, gently pressing so it sticks. Place lamb, coated-side up, on a rack set on a baking sheet or in a baking dish.

2. For curry-chutney glaze, place chutney in a small bowl. Remove any chunks and finely chop, then return to bowl. Stir in curry powder, cumin and cilantro (if using). Smear over fat-side of 1 lamb rack. Place lamb, coated-side up, beside other rack on baking sheet.

3. For sesame-garlic glaze, in a small bowl, combine chili-garlic sauce, honey, Dijon and sesame oil. Smear over fat-side of remaining lamb rack. Place lamb, coated-side up, beside other racks, arranging at least 1 inch (2.5 cm) apart.

4. Roast in centre of preheated oven until an instant-read thermometer inserted into centre of meat reads 140°F (60°C) for medium-rare, about 25 minutes, depending on size of rack.

5. Let stand 5 minutes. Slice into chops. Excellent served with Coconut Milk–Infused Rice (page 303) and a green salad.

NUTRIENTS PER PESTO AND MINT CHOP
7 G PROTEIN 6 G FAT 4 G CARBOHYDRATES
1 G FIBRE 1 MG IRON 94 MG CALCIUM
204 MG SODIUM 100 CALORIES

NUTRIENTS PER CURRY-CHUTNEY CHOP
4 G PROTEIN 2 G FAT 6 G CARBOHYDRATES
0 G FIBRE 0 MG IRON 4 MG CALCIUM
145 MG SODIUM 53 CALORIES

NUTRIENTS PER SESAME-GARLIC CHOP
4 G PROTEIN 2 G FAT 2 G CARBOHYDRATES
0 G FIBRE 0 MG IRON 4 MG CALCIUM
32 MG SODIUM 44 CALORIES

seafood

Seafood is so healthy that we're always looking for quick and easy ways to get more of it into the weekly lineup. Seared scallops, halibut tacos and salmon with a pistachio crust do the trick nicely.

Seared Scallops on Tender Greens

PREPARATION TIME 10 MINUTES
COOKING TIME 8 MINUTES
MAKES 2 SERVINGS

6 fresh large sea scallops

1 tsp (5 mL) ground cumin

½ tsp (2 mL) paprika

Pinch of salt

2 tbsp (30 mL) butter

⅓ cup (75 mL) dry white wine

2 cups (500 mL) arugula, baby spinach or mixed greens

1 plum tomato

SCALLOP SCOOP

Scallops come in all sizes, with the large ones being the most prized. Before cooking, gently tear off any tough muscle from their sides.

1. Pat scallops dry with paper towels and place in a small bowl. Sprinkle with cumin, paprika and salt. Using your hands, gently toss to evenly coat.

2. Melt butter in a large non-stick frying pan over medium-high heat. Add scallops and cook until golden, about 2 minutes per side. Pour in wine and reduce heat to medium-low. Using a wooden spoon, scrape up and stir in brown bits from pan bottom. Cover and continue cooking until scallops give some resistance when pressed, 2 to 3 more minutes.

3. Meanwhile, arrange arugula on 2 plates. Chop tomato, then scatter over arugula. Top with scallops. Increase heat and boil liquid in pan until reduced by half, about 2 more minutes. Drizzle over scallops and greens.

NUTRIENTS PER SERVING 20 G PROTEIN 13 G FAT
7 G CARBOHYDRATES 2 G FIBRE 3 MG IRON
154 MG CALCIUM 595 MG SODIUM 239 CALORIES

Great Grilled Side of Salmon

PREPARATION TIME 10 MINUTES
GRILLING TIME 15 MINUTES
MAKES 4 TO 6 SERVINGS

3 to 4 lb (1.5 to 2 kg) side of salmon

2 tbsp (30 mL) olive oil

2 tsp (10 mL) each ground cumin and ground coriander (optional)

1 tbsp (15 mL) fresh thyme or 1 tsp (5 mL) dried thyme leaves

½ tsp (2 mL) cayenne pepper (optional)

Generous pinches of salt and freshly ground black pepper

CITRUS BUTTER

Make a terrific topper for salmon by mixing softened butter with finely grated lemon or lime peel. Form into a log and wrap. Refrigerate until firm. Slice into rounds and place on fish.

1. Oil grill, then heat barbecue to medium. Using a ruler, measure thickness of salmon to figure out how long to cook it. The general rule is 10 to 12 minutes for every 1 inch (2.5 cm) of thickness, so a fish that's 1 ½ inches (4 cm) thick will take 15 to 18 minutes, and one that's 2 inches (5 cm) thick will take 20 to 24 minutes.

2. Run your fingers along the middle portion of salmon to check for bones. If you find any, use tweezers to gently pluck them out and discard. In a small bowl, stir oil with seasonings. Rub or brush over fish to evenly coat.

3. Place salmon, skin-side down, on grill. Barbecue, lid closed, until skin is lightly charred and a knife tip inserted into thickest part of fish and held for 10 seconds comes out warm, 15 to 24 minutes. Don't turn.

4. Use 2 long, wide metal spatulas to remove fish. To serve without skin, slip spatulas between skin and flesh, then carefully lift salmon, leaving the skin on the grill. Slide onto a large platter or cutting board. Garnish with sliced lemon.

NUTRIENTS PER SERVING 35 G PROTEIN 24 G FAT
0 G CARBOHYDRATES 0 G FIBRE 1 MG IRON
25 MG CALCIUM 96 MG SODIUM 362 CALORIES

Curried Catfish with Coriander Cream

PREPARATION TIME 10 MINUTES
COOKING TIME 14 MINUTES
MAKES 2 SERVINGS

1 tbsp (15 mL) curry powder

1 tbsp (15 mL) vegetable oil

1 garlic clove, minced

1 tsp (5 mL) grated fresh ginger

¼ tsp (1 mL) cinnamon

Pinch each of ground cloves and salt

2 large catfish or tilapia fillets

1 tbsp (15 mL) butter or vegetable oil

1 onion, chopped

⅓ cup (75 mL) plain yogourt or regular sour cream

⅓ cup (75 mL) chopped fresh cilantro

DINNER TONIGHT

This is a terrific high-protein main course for any night of the week.

1. In a small bowl, stir curry powder with oil, garlic, ginger, cinnamon, cloves and salt. Rub mixture all over fish. Melt half of butter in a large non-stick frying pan over medium heat. If using oil, pour half into frying pan. When pan is hot, add onion. Stir often until soft and light golden, about 5 minutes, then push to side of pan.

2. Melt remaining butter in pan or add oil, then add fish. Cover and cook for 4 minutes. Using a wide spatula, turn fish over and continue cooking until a knife tip inserted into thickest part of fish and held for 10 seconds comes out warm, about 4 more minutes. It's okay if onion becomes dark golden. Using a wide spatula, remove only the fish to dinner plates. Reduce heat to low. Add yogourt and cilantro to onion. Stir until heated through, about 30 seconds. Spoon over fish.

NUTRIENTS PER SERVING 63 G PROTEIN 22 G FAT
10 G CARBOHYDRATES 2 G FIBRE 2 MG IRON
123 MG CALCIUM 377 MG SODIUM 502 CALORIES

Oven "Fried" Fish

PREPARATION TIME 15 MINUTES
BAKING TIME 12 MINUTES
MAKES 4 SERVINGS

4 fish fillets such as tilapia, catfish or halibut, each about 6 oz (170 g)

1 egg white

½ cup (125 mL) buttermilk

½ cup (125 mL) each all-purpose flour and store-bought bread crumbs

2 tsp (10 mL) paprika

1 tsp (5 mL) salt

½ tsp (2 mL) cayenne pepper

1 tbsp (15 mL) vegetable oil

TARTAR SAUCE

Stir ⅓ cup (75 mL) each light mayonnaise and sour cream or yogourt with ¼ cup (50 mL) chopped dill pickles, 1 tbsp (15 mL) green pickle relish, 1 tsp (5 mL) finely chopped capers, 1 thinly sliced green onion and a pinch of cayenne pepper.

Makes about ⅔ cup (150 mL)

1. Position rack on top shelf in oven. Preheat oven to 500°F (260°C). Line a rimmed baking sheet with foil and set a wire rack on top. Lightly spray or brush rack with vegetable oil.

2. Pat fish dry with paper towels. Slice fillets in half lengthwise to form long pieces. In a pie plate or wide shallow dish, whisk egg white with buttermilk. In another dish, stir flour with bread crumbs, paprika, salt and cayenne.

3. Working with 1 piece of fish at a time, lightly coat with flour mixture. Shake off excess flour, then dip into buttermilk mixture. Turn to evenly coat. Shake off excess liquid. Coat fish in flour mixture again. Shake off excess coating, then place on rack. Repeat with remaining fish, 1 piece at a time. Discard any remaining buttermilk and flour mixtures.

4. Using a brush, lightly dab oil as evenly as possible over coating (or lightly spray fish with vegetable oil). Do not skip this step — it is essential for crispy fish. Bake on top rack of preheated oven until coating is crisp and golden, 12 to 15 minutes. Do not turn. Serve with Tartar Sauce (see sidebar). Terrific with Light and Creamy Coleslaw (page 75) and sliced dill pickles.

NUTRIENTS PER SERVING 34 G PROTEIN 9 G FAT
18 G CARBOHYDRATES 1 G FIBRE 2 MG IRON
66 MG CALCIUM 698 MG SODIUM 292 CALORIES

Warm Cucumber and Shrimp Sauté

PREPARATION TIME 10 MINUTES
COOKING TIME 8 MINUTES
MAKES 4 SERVINGS

340 g pkg frozen uncooked medium or large shrimp, peeled

2 field cucumbers or 1 English cucumber

1 yellow pepper

½ red onion

2 garlic cloves

2 tbsp (30 mL) butter

2 tsp (10 mL) curry paste, such as Indian or Thai red curry

½ cup (125 mL) shredded fresh basil or chopped fresh cilantro or 3 green onions, sliced

¼ tsp (1 mL) salt (optional)

SERVING SUGGESTION

Delicious over cinnamon-scented basmati rice. Cook rice according to package directions, throwing in a stick of cinnamon. Remove cinnamon stick and discard just before serving.

1. Thaw shrimp according to package directions (or see sidebar, page 246). Peel cucumbers only if skin is thick. Slice in half lengthwise. Using a spoon, scrape out seeds and discard. Thickly slice diagonally. Slice pepper and red onion into thin bite-sized strips. Mince garlic.

2. Melt butter in a large frying pan over medium heat. Add onion and stir frequently until it starts to soften, about 2 minutes. Add garlic and curry paste, stirring until fragrant, about 30 seconds. Increase heat to medium-high. Scatter in shrimp and stir-fry until they start to turn bright pink, 1 to 3 minutes. Add cucumber and pepper. Continue stir-frying until pepper is done as you like, about 4 more minutes. Stir in basil. Taste and add salt if you wish.

NUTRIENTS PER SERVING 19 G PROTEIN 9 G FAT
12 G CARBOHYDRATES 2 G FIBRE 3 MG IRON
87 MG CALCIUM 395 MG SODIUM 201 CALORIES

Mussels with Fennel

PREPARATION TIME 15 MINUTES
COOKING TIME 11 MINUTES
MAKES 2 SERVINGS

2 lb (1 kg) bag mussels

½ small fennel bulb

1 onion or 2 large leeks

4 plum tomatoes

1 tbsp (15 mL) olive oil

½ cup (125 mL) white wine or dry vermouth

2 tsp (10 mL) hot chili-garlic sauce or ½ tsp (2 mL) hot chili flakes

¼ tsp (1 mL) salt

¼ cup (50 mL) snipped fresh chives

MUSSELS 101

When it comes to seafood, mussels are a cinch. Just a quick simmer in a delicate but flavourful broth is the trick. The rules: Before cooking, discard any that are open. Once cooked, discard any that remained closed.

1. Scrub mussels and pull off beards. Discard any that are open. Core fennel, then chop. If using onion, finely chop. If using leeks, cut off and discard root ends and dark green tops of leeks. Cut leeks in half lengthwise. Fan out under cold running water to remove grit. Thinly slice. Chop tomatoes.

2. Heat oil in a large saucepan over medium heat. Add fennel and onion. Sauté, stirring often, until softened slightly, 5 minutes. Stir in wine, chili-garlic sauce and salt. Increase heat to medium-high. When boiling, stir in tomatoes, then mussels. Cover and cook, stirring once, until mussels have opened, about 6 minutes. Discard any mussels that haven't opened. Spoon mussels into bowls, and sprinkle with chives.

NUTRIENTS PER SERVING 19 G PROTEIN 10 G FAT
20 G CARBOHYDRATES 4 G FIBRE 6 MG IRON
81 MG CALCIUM 596 MG SODIUM 263 CALORIES

Fast-Fix Paella

PREPARATION TIME 10 MINUTES
COOKING TIME 9 MINUTES
STANDING TIME 5 MINUTES
MAKES 2 TO 3 SERVINGS

½ lb (250 g) fresh or frozen cooked medium shrimp, peeled

2 hot Italian sausages

2 tomatoes

1 large onion

2 tsp (10 mL) each paprika and garlic powder

10 oz (284 mL) can undiluted chicken broth

2 cups (500 mL) frozen peas

2 cups (500 mL) couscous

WHAT IS IT?
Couscous is a precooked granular pasta that needs only a hot liquid and 5 minutes of standing time before it's ready to serve.

1. If using frozen shrimp, do not thaw. Place in a sieve and rinse under cold running water until ice crystals melt. Then drain well and pat dry with paper towels.

2. Lightly coat a large saucepan with olive oil and set over medium heat. Cut sausages in half. Squeeze meat from casings and crumble into oil. Discard casings. Using a fork, stir frequently to keep meat crumbly. Cook until meat is no longer pink, 3 to 4 minutes. Meanwhile, coarsely chop tomatoes and onion.

3. Once sausages are cooked, add onion. Stir frequently until onion starts to soften, about 3 minutes. Add tomatoes along with any juice and seeds. Sprinkle with paprika and garlic powder. Stir occasionally, uncovered, until tomatoes start to break down, about 3 minutes. Pour in broth and 1 ¼ cups (300 mL) water. Bring to a boil. Using a wooden spoon, scrape up and stir in any brown bits from pan bottom.

4. Stir in shrimp, peas and couscous. Cover and remove from heat. Let stand until liquid is absorbed, about 5 minutes. Fluff paella with a fork, then spoon onto dinner plates. Red wine is the perfect accompaniment.

NUTRIENTS PER SERVING 31 G PROTEIN 19 G FAT
50 G CARBOHYDRATES 4 G FIBRE 2 MG IRON
93 MG CALCIUM 1460 MG SODIUM 495 CALORIES

Prosciutto-Wrapped Fish with Sautéed Olives and Tomatoes

Sprinkle 2 halibut fillets with a pinch of salt and pinches of smoked paprika, along with pinches of dried oregano leaves or Italian seasoning if you wish. Wrap each fillet in a slice of prosciutto. Lightly oil a large frying pan set over medium heat. When pan is hot, add prosciutto-wrapped fish. Scatter 1 lb (500 g) grape or cherry tomatoes and a handful of pitted kalamata olives (see sidebar, page 162) around fish. Cook, stirring tomatoes and olives occasionally, until a knife inserted into thickest part of fish and held for 10 seconds comes out warm, 3 to 5 minutes per side. Remove fish to individual plates. Continue to cook tomatoes and olives, stirring occasionally, until tomatoes soften slightly, 2 to 3 minutes. Serve fish topped with tomato and olive mixture.

MAKES 2 SERVINGS

COOKING TIP

We used halibut for this recipe, but feel free to use any fish you like. Cooking time may vary depending on the thickness of the fish.

SMOKED PAPRIKA

This spice hails from Spain. The peppers used to make paprika are wood-smoked before they are ground into a fine powder, which gives the spice its robust smoky flavour. There are three varieties of smoked paprika: dulce (sweet), agridulce (semi-sweet) and picante (hot). All work well for this recipe.

Roasted Halibut with Minted Pea Coulis

PREPARATION TIME 12 MINUTES
COOKING TIME 16 MINUTES
ROASTING TIME 5 MINUTES
MAKES 6 SERVINGS AND 1 CUP
(250 mL) COULIS

COULIS

2 large shallots or ½ small onion

½ tsp (2 mL) salt

½ cup (125 mL) dry white wine

2 cups (500 mL) frozen peas

2 to 4 tbsp (30 to 60 mL) chopped fresh mint

½ cup (125 mL) whipping cream

FISH

6 halibut or salmon fillets, each about 6 oz (170 g)

1 tsp (5 mL) salt

Pinches of freshly ground black pepper

1 tbsp (15 mL) butter

1 tsp (5 mL) vegetable oil

1 lime, cut in half

COULIS

Coulis is a purée that's been strained. It often is made with fruit, but we love to make it with vegetables too. The key to the smooth texture? Using the bottom of a ladle to push the purée through a sieve.

1. For coulis, finely chop shallots. Place in a small saucepan. Sprinkle with salt. Pour in wine. Bring to a boil, then reduce heat to medium-low. Simmer, stirring often, until shallots are soft, about 5 minutes. Add peas, 2 tbsp (30 mL) mint and whipping cream. Cook until peas are soft, about 5 minutes. Remove from heat.

2. Purée coulis mixture in a food processor, scraping down sides of bowl as necessary. Taste and add remaining mint if you wish, then purée. Press mixture through a sieve into a clean saucepan or small bowl. Mash as much pea pulp as possible through sieve. Discard any pulp that doesn't pass through. If not serving right away, refrigerate, uncovered, until cool. This will help keep the colour vibrant for up to 4 hours.

3. Preheat oven to 400°F (200°C). For fish, line a baking sheet with foil. Don't oil. Sprinkle fish with salt and pepper. Heat butter and oil in a large frying pan over medium-high heat. Add 3 of the fillets, skin-side up. Cook until golden-tinged, about 3 minutes. Place skin-side down on prepared baking sheet. Repeat with remaining fillets, adding more butter and oil to pan if needed. Roast in centre of preheated oven until a knife tip inserted into thickest part of fish and held for 10 seconds comes out warm, 5 to 7 minutes.

4. To serve, reheat pea coulis. Spoon a little in centre of each plate. Place fish on top, leaving skin in pan. Squeeze a little lime juice overtop.

NUTRIENTS PER SERVING 39 G PROTEIN 14 G FAT
6 G CARBOHYDRATES 0 G FIBRE 2 MG IRON
110 MG CALCIUM 735 MG SODIUM 319 CALORIES

Halibut and Zucchini Soft Tacos

PREPARATION TIME 10 MINUTES
GRILLING TIME 10 MINUTES
MAKES 3 SERVINGS

3 to 6 small skewers

2 tbsp (30 mL) vegetable oil

1 tbsp (15 mL) honey

1 tsp (5 mL) five-spice powder or ground cumin

Pinches of salt and freshly ground black pepper

1 lb (500 g) skinless halibut or salmon fillets

1 small zucchini

3 medium flour tortillas, about 7 inches (18 cm) in diameter, or small pitas

Shredded lettuce (optional)

ZESTY HOT SAUCE

Try these tacos with a zesty hot sauce: Finely grate peel from ½ lime into a small bowl. Squeeze in juice from lime. Stir in 1 tsp (5 mL) hot chili-garlic sauce, 1 tsp (5 mL) dark sesame oil and pinches of granulated sugar and salt. Taste and stir in more chili-garlic sauce if you want it spicier. Drizzle over taco filling.

1. Oil grill and heat barbecue to medium. If using wooden skewers, soak in water for 20 minutes (see sidebar, page 124). In a large bowl, stir oil with honey, five-spice powder, salt and pepper. Slice fish into approximately 1-inch (2.5 cm) pieces. Slice zucchini in half lengthwise, then into ½-inch (1 cm) pieces. Add fish and zucchini to spice mixture, gently stirring to coat.

2. Thread skewers, alternating fish with zucchini. (For easy turning, use 2 skewers through each kebab.) Barbecue kebabs, lid closed, turning halfway through cooking time, until a knife inserted into thickest piece of fish comes out warm, about 10 minutes. Remove skewers. Scatter fish and zucchini over tortillas, along with lettuce if you wish. Serve immediately.

NUTRIENTS PER SKEWER (WITH NO SAUCE)
36 G PROTEIN 15.5 G FAT 25 G CARBOHYDRATES 2 G FIBRE
3 MG IRON 83 MG CALCIUM 283 MG SODIUM 374 CALORIES

Cedar-Planked Salmon

PREPARATION TIME 10 MINUTES
SOAKING TIME 1 HOUR
GRILLING TIME 20 MINUTES
MAKES 4 SERVINGS

PLANKS 101

When barbecuing, be sure to buy an untreated plank, sold in most supermarkets, then follow these quick steps:

Check the plank frequently during cooking. If the plank catches fire, spray it with water. (You may need to reduce the heat under the plank to medium-low.) Note: The plank is easier to remove from a barbecue after it cools down.

1 **untreated cedar plank**
1 **tbsp (15 mL) each soy sauce and maple syrup**
¼ **tsp (1 mL) cayenne pepper**
4 **salmon fillets, each about 6 oz (170 g) and 1 inch (2.5 cm) thick**

1. Place cedar plank in the kitchen sink or a large bucket or dish. Cover with water. Weigh plank down with a couple of heavy cans so it stays submerged. Soak at least 1 hour, and preferably overnight (see sidebar, page 124).

2. When ready to grill, heat both sides of the barbecue to high, then turn one side down to medium. In a bowl, stir soy sauce with maple syrup and cayenne. Place salmon, skin-side down, on the presoaked unoiled plank. Brush tops and sides of the salmon with the maple mixture.

3. Place plank on side of grill that is set to medium. Barbecue, lid closed, until a knife tip inserted into thickest part of fish and held there for 10 seconds comes out warm, 20 to 30 minutes. Transfer salmon to dinner plates or a platter. Delicious served with Grilled Sweet Peppers with Basil Drizzle (page 293).

NUTRIENTS PER SERVING 28 G PROTEIN 15 G FAT
4 G CARBOHYDRATES 0 G FIBRE 1 MG IRON
23 MG CALCIUM 334 MG SODIUM 271 CALORIES

Crab and Artichoke Crêpes with Béchamel Sauce

PREPARATION TIME 20 MINUTES
COOKING TIME 26 MINUTES
MAKES 12 CRÊPES

DRESS IT UP

For special occasions, use real crab meat. Before using, squeeze the crab meat with paper towels to remove excess moisture.

CRÊPES

2 eggs

¾ cup (175 mL) milk

½ cup (125 mL) all-purpose flour

4 tsp (20 mL) melted butter

¼ tsp (1 mL) salt

2 tbsp (30 mL) snipped fresh chives

FILLING

3 tbsp (45 mL) butter

2 garlic cloves

¼ cup (50 mL) all-purpose flour

1 ½ cups (375 mL) milk

½ tsp (2 mL) Tabasco sauce

½ tsp (2 mL) salt

1 lemon

2 227-g pkgs imitation crab, sliced

170-mL jar marinated artichoke halves, chopped

¼ cup (50 mL) chopped fresh dill

1. Whirl crêpe ingredients in a blender until smooth. For filling, melt butter in a saucepan over medium heat. Add garlic. Stir for 30 seconds. Whisk in flour until it bubbles. Gradually add milk, whisking constantly to prevent lumps. Whisk in Tabasco sauce and salt. Whisking constantly, bring mixture to a boil over high heat. Reduce heat to medium-low. Stir often until mixture thickens, about 2 minutes. Remove from heat. Finely grate 2 tsp (10 mL) peel and squeeze 2 tsp (10 mL) juice from lemon. Stir into sauce along with crab, artichokes and dill.

2. Spray a medium non-stick frying pan with oil and set over medium heat. When pan is hot, pour 2 tbsp (30 mL) batter into pan. Lift pan from burner and tilt to form a very thin pancake. Return to burner and cook until top is set, about 1 minute, then turn over. Cook until golden, 1 minute. Remove to a plate. Repeat with remaining batter. Roll up about ⅓ cup (75 mL) filling in each crêpe. Serve topped with more chopped dill if you wish.

GET AHEAD Prepare and fill crêpes. Arrange in an oiled 9- × 13-inch (3 L) casserole dish. Cover with foil. Refrigerate overnight. Bake directly from fridge, covered, in preheated 300°F (150°C) oven until hot, about 40 minutes.

NUTRIENTS PER CRÊPE 17 G PROTEIN 15 G FAT
27 G CARBOHYDRATES 2 G FIBRE 2 MG IRON
142 MG CALCIUM 1060 MG SODIUM 310 CALORIES

Pistachio-Crusted Salmon

PREPARATION TIME 5 MINUTES
BAKING TIME 14 MINUTES
MAKES 6 SERVINGS

6 skinless salmon fillets, at least 1 inch (2.5 cm) thick
Pinches of salt and freshly ground black pepper
¼ cup (50 mL) maple syrup
1 tsp (5 mL) each curry powder and Dijon mustard
½ cup (125 mL) shelled pistachios

TEST KITCHEN TIP
Try the maple and
pistachio crust on
Cedar-Planked Salmon
(page 214).

1. Preheat oven to 400°F (200°C). Line a baking sheet with foil and spray with oil. Place fillets on foil and sprinkle with salt and pepper. In a bowl, stir maple syrup with curry powder and Dijon. Coarsely chop pistachios. Brush half of maple mixture on fillets, then sprinkle with pistachios. Spoon remaining maple mixture over nuts.

2. Bake in centre of preheated oven until a knife tip inserted into thickest part of fish and held there for 10 seconds comes out warm, 14 to 16 minutes.

NUTRIENTS PER SERVING 32 G PROTEIN 21 G FAT
12 G CARBOHYDRATES 1 G FIBRE 1 MG IRON
43 MG CALCIUM 93 MG SODIUM 369 CALORIES

Classic Risotto with Shrimp and Sweet Peas

PREPARATION TIME 10 MINUTES
COOKING TIME 26 MINUTES
MAKES 2 TO 3 SERVINGS

VARIATIONS

Classic risotto
Prepare recipe as directed but omit shrimp and peas.

Roasted squash
Prepare recipe as directed but omit shrimp and peas. Roast 1 lb (500 g) oiled butternut-squash cubes at 400°F (200°C) until tender. Stir into cooked hot risotto.

Double mushroom
Prepare recipe as directed but omit shrimp and peas. Add ½ oz (14 g) dried mushrooms to broth. Cook 8 oz (250 g) sliced mushrooms with onion. Continue with recipe as directed.

900 mL carton chicken broth

¾ cup (175 mL) dry white wine

1 large onion or 2 small onions or 2 leeks

2 tbsp (30 mL) butter

1 tbsp (15 mL) olive oil

1 cup (250 mL) arborio rice

½ lb (250 g) fresh or frozen uncooked peeled shrimp, preferably medium or large

1 cup (250 mL) frozen peas

1 cup (250 mL) freshly grated parmesan or asiago cheese

½ cup (125 mL) snipped fresh chives, about 1 bunch

1. Pour broth and ½ cup (125 mL) wine into a medium saucepan. Bring to a boil. Reduce heat to low. Finely chop onion, or slice off and discard root ends and dark green tops of leeks. Cut leeks in half lengthwise. Fan out under cold running water to remove grit. Finely chop by slicing lengthwise, then crosswise.

2. Heat 1 tbsp (15 mL) butter with oil in a large pot set over medium heat. Add onion and stir often until soft, 3 to 5 minutes. Add rice and stir until glossy and coated, about 1 minute.

3. While stirring constantly, add remaining ¼ cup (50 mL) wine to rice. Stir until rice has absorbed wine. Ladle in about ½ cup (125 mL) hot broth mixture. Gently stir until most of the liquid is absorbed. Repeat this process with remaining broth, about ½ cup (125 mL) at a time. Adjust heat as needed so mixture is just simmering.

4. Stir gently and constantly until rice is tender and almost all broth is absorbed, 22 to 25 minutes. Mixture should be slightly saucy but not soupy. Meanwhile, if using frozen shrimp, thaw according to package directions (or see sidebar, page 246). Five minutes before rice is cooked, stir in shrimp and peas. When risotto is tender and slightly saucy (but not soupy) remove from heat. Stir in remaining 1 tbsp (15 mL) butter, parmesan and chives. Taste and add salt, pepper and more cheese if needed.

NUTRIENTS PER SERVING 38 G PROTEIN 24 G FAT
67 G CARBOHYDRATES 4 G FIBRE 4 MG IRON
463 MG CALCIUM 1878 MG SODIUM 666 CALORIES

Big-Batch Bouillabaisse

PREPARATION TIME 25 MINUTES
COOKING TIME 15 MINUTES
MAKES 14 CUPS (3.5 L) FOR
6 TO 8 SERVINGS

900 mL carton chicken broth

2 cups (500 mL) dry white wine

236 mL bottle clam juice

1 tbsp (15 mL) butter

½ cup (125 mL) coarsely chopped shallots, about 3 large

1 Spanish or red onion

3 jalapeño peppers

1 small orange

1 tsp (5 mL) fennel seeds (optional)

½ tsp (2 mL) each dried thyme leaves and salt

½ tsp (2 mL) saffron threads

1 pint cherry or grape tomatoes

1 lb (500 g) mussels

1 lb (500 g) sea or bay scallops

1 lb (500 g) fresh or frozen uncooked large shrimp

1 cooked lobster (optional)

TIMING TIP

Make the broth a day ahead so that you need only reheat and add the seafood.

SHOPPING TIP

Purchasing a cooked lobster will save you a lot of time. Many supermarkets and fish shops offer this option.

1. Pour chicken broth, wine and clam juice into a large pot and bring to a boil over medium heat. Add butter and shallots. Meanwhile, cut onion in half and thinly slice. Add to the simmering broth. Slice jalapeños in half lengthwise and seed, then finely chop. Stir into broth. Finely grate peel from half of orange. Add to broth along with fennel seeds (if using), thyme and salt. Crumble in saffron threads. Slice tomatoes in half and stir in. Reduce heat to low. Cover pot and simmer to develop flavour, at least 10 minutes.

2. Meanwhile, scrub mussels and pull off beards. Discard any that are open. If sea scallops are large, slice in half crosswise to form 2 rounds. Leave small bay scallops whole. If using frozen shrimp, thaw according to package directions (or see sidebar, page 246). Peel and devein shrimp, if necessary. Crack the lobster shell and remove the meat (if using). Discard shell or set aside a claw or two for garnish. Slice lobster into large bite-sized pieces.

3. Just before serving, bring broth mixture to a boil. Stir in mussels. Cover and simmer, without stirring, until mussels partially open, about 2 minutes. Stir in scallops and shrimp so they are submerged in broth. Cover and cook just until shrimp turn pink, 3 to 4 minutes. Remove from heat. Discard any mussels that have not opened. Stir in lobster (if using). Ladle bouillabaisse into large wide soup bowls.

NUTRIENTS PER SERVING 26 G PROTEIN 4 G FAT
12 G CARBOHYDRATES 2 G FIBRE 3 MG IRON
92 MG CALCIUM 1043 MG SODIUM 198 CALORIES

pasta

From an indulgent penne with brie to a healthier take on mac and cheese, pasta's versatility makes it the ideal weeknight meal. Then again, a dish of creamy carbonara is posh enough for Saturday night guests.

Classic Arrabbiata Sauce

PREPARATION TIME 25 MINUTES
COOKING TIME 1 HOUR,
15 MINUTES
MAKES 5 CUPS (1.25 L)

12 regular or 20 plum tomatoes, about 5 lb (2.5 kg)

8 garlic cloves

2 large onions

¼ cup (50 mL) olive oil

5 ½ oz (156 mL) can tomato paste

1 tbsp (15 mL) each dried basil and oregano leaves

2 tsp (10 mL) hot chili flakes

1 tsp (5 mL) salt

1 tbsp (15 mL) granulated sugar (optional)

½ cup (125 mL) chopped fresh basil (optional)

SAUCY MAKEOVERS

Puttanesca-style:
Add capers, chopped
black olives and finely
chopped anchovies.

Vodka cream sauce:
Add a splash of vodka
near the end of cooking.
Finish with a little
whipping cream.

Too hot to handle: For a
mellower, classic tomato
sauce, simply skip the
chili flakes.

1. Easily remove tomato skins by slicing an X in the bottom of each tomato. Add several at a time to a pot filled with boiling water. Boil tomatoes for about 30 seconds. Use a slotted spoon to remove tomatoes to a large bowl of ice water. Let stand about 2 minutes. Drain, then slip off skins and discard.

2. Coarsely chop tomatoes. Mince garlic and chop onions. Heat oil in a large pot over medium-low heat. Add garlic and onions and cook, stirring often, until onions are very soft, about 15 minutes.

3. Stir in tomatoes, including juice and seeds, tomato paste, dried basil, oregano, chili flakes and salt. Increase heat to high and bring mixture to a boil, then reduce to medium-low. Simmer, partially covered and stirring often, to thicken and develop flavour, about 1 hour. Taste and add sugar if needed. Stir fresh basil into sauce if you wish. Serve over hot cooked pasta.

GET AHEAD Cover sauce and refrigerate for up to 1 week, or freeze for up to 3 months. Freeze in 1- or 2-cup (125 or 250 mL) portions and you'll have sauce on hand for single- or double-serving dinners.

NUTRIENTS PER 1 CUP (250 mL) 3 G PROTEIN 6 G FAT
18 G CARBOHYDRATES 4 G FIBRE 2 MG IRON
38 MG CALCIUM 376 MG SODIUM 124 CALORIES

Herbed Chicken Meatballs with Spaghetti

PREPARATION TIME 15 MINUTES
COOKING TIME 25 MINUTES
MAKES 4 SERVINGS

1 slice white bread

2 tbsp (30 mL) milk

1 egg

1 tsp (5 mL) each Dijon mustard and Worcestershire sauce

1 tsp (5 mL) dried oregano leaves

¾ tsp (4 mL) salt

1 lb (500 g) ground chicken

½ cup (125 mL) snipped fresh chives or 1 bunch green onions, thinly sliced

½ cup (125 mL) finely chopped fresh mint (optional)

½ of 450 g pkg spaghetti, fusilli or rotini

4 garlic cloves

4 plum tomatoes

¼ tsp (1 mL) freshly ground black pepper

¼ cup (50 mL) dry red or white wine

1 cup (250 mL) freshly grated parmesan cheese

COOKING TIP

Overmixing makes meatballs tough.

1. If crust on bread is hard, cut off and discard. Tear bread into small pieces and place in a small bowl. Add milk and mash with a fork until pasty.

2. In a large bowl, whisk egg with Dijon, Worcestershire sauce, oregano and ½ tsp (2 mL) salt until blended. Stir in the bread mixture. Crumble in chicken. Sprinkle with 2 tbsp (30 mL) each chives and mint (if using). Using your hands or a fork, work just until evenly mixed.

3. Bring a large pot of water to a boil over high heat. Meanwhile, lightly coat a large frying pan with oil and set over medium heat. Slightly dampen your hands and roll meat mixture into 1-inch (2.5 cm) balls, adding to the oil as each is formed. Don't crowd pan. The meatballs will need to be cooked in at least 2 batches. Turn often until lightly browned, 5 to 7 minutes. Remove each to a large plate when done. Repeat with remaining meatballs, adding more oil to pan if needed.

4. While meatballs are browning, add pasta to boiling water and cook according to package directions until al dente, 7 to 9 minutes. Mince garlic and chop tomatoes. When all meatballs are removed from pan, add garlic, tomatoes and ¼ tsp (1 mL) each salt and pepper. Stir frequently until tomatoes start to break down, 2 to 3 minutes. Pour in wine. Scrape up and stir in any brown bits from

pan bottom. Cook, uncovered and stirring occasionally, until tomatoes become saucy, about 4 minutes. Add meatballs. Cover and stir often until they are cooked through, 2 to 4 more minutes.

5. Drain cooked pasta, then stir, along with parmesan, into tomato-meatball mixture. Serve in individual bowls sprinkled with remaining herbs.

NUTRIENTS PER SERVING 41 G PROTEIN 22 G FAT
52 G CARBOHYDRATES 4 G FIBRE 4 MG IRON
341 MG CALCIUM 382 MG SODIUM 582 CALORIES

Homemade Mushroom Meat Lasagna

PREPARATION TIME 50 MINUTES
COOKING TIME 25 MINUTES
BAKING TIME 1 HOUR, 15 MINUTES
STANDING TIME 5 MINUTES
MAKES 8 SERVINGS

300 g pkg frozen chopped spinach or 8 cups (2 L) baby spinach

½ cup (125 mL) dry white wine

½ oz (14 g) pkg dried mushrooms of your choice

2 skinless, boneless chicken breasts (optional)

5 or 6 hot Italian sausages

½ cup (125 mL) Marsala or sherry

700 mL bottle flavourful tomato pasta sauce

1 tsp (5 mL) each dried basil and oregano leaves

6 tbsp (90 mL) butter

1 onion, chopped

2 8-oz (227 g) pkgs sliced mushrooms

1 ½ tsp (7 mL) salt

⅓ cup (75 mL) all-purpose flour

2 ½ cups (625 mL) homogenized milk

½ tsp (2 mL) ground nutmeg

2 cups (500 mL) grated mozzarella cheese

1 cup (250 mL) freshly grated parmesan cheese

9 to 15 oven-ready lasagna noodles

FLAVOUR TIP

Don't hesitate to make ahead or even freeze — this lasagna gets better as it sits.

1. Thaw spinach at room temperature. Don't thaw in microwave. If using baby spinach, leave as is. In a measuring cup, microwave wine on high until hot, 1 minute. Chop dried mushrooms, then add to wine. Cover with plastic wrap. Let stand at room temperature.

2. For meat sauce, slice chicken (if using) into bite-sized pieces. Coat a large frying pan with oil and set over medium heat. Slice sausages in half, then crumble meat into pan. Using a fork to keep meat crumbly, cook until no pink remains, 3 to 4 minutes. Add Marsala and chicken. Increase heat to high. Stir often until most of Marsala has evaporated, about 5 minutes. Add pasta sauce, basil and oregano. Stir often until hot, about 2 minutes. Remove from heat.

3. For mushroom sauce, melt 1 tbsp (15 mL) butter in a large frying pan over medium-high heat. Add onion. Sauté until softened, about 3 minutes. Add 1 tbsp (15 mL) butter and sliced mushrooms. Sprinkle with 1 tsp (5 mL) salt. Stir often until mushrooms start to soften, about 4 minutes. Add soaked dried mushrooms and wine. Increase heat to high and stir often until most of liquid is absorbed, about 5 minutes. Remove from heat.

4. For white sauce, melt remaining 4 tbsp (60 mL) butter in a large saucepan over medium heat. Gradually whisk in flour. Whisk constantly until mixture bubbles. Gradually whisk in milk. Whisk until mixture comes to a boil. Reduce heat to medium-low. Whisk often until thickened, 3 to 5 minutes. Stir in nutmeg and remaining ½ tsp (2 mL) salt. Stir half of sauce into mushroom mixture. Set remaining sauce aside.

5. Preheat oven to 350°F (180°C). In a bowl, mix cheeses. Spread enough meat sauce to barely cover bottom of a 9- × 13-inch (3 L) baking dish. Top with 3 to 5 noodles. Don't overlap. Spread with half of mushroom sauce, then half of meat sauce. Sprinkle with 1 cup (250 mL) cheese. Top with 3 to 5 noodles, then remaining mushroom mixture. Do not squeeze water from partially frozen spinach. Scatter spinach overtop. Sprinkle with 1 cup (250 mL) cheese. Finish with remaining noodles, then remaining meat sauce. Dollop white sauce overtop. It won't cover, but it will spread during baking. Sprinkle with remaining 1 cup (250 mL) cheese. Cover pan with foil. Place on a rimmed baking sheet. Bake in centre of preheated oven for 1 hour. Remove foil. Continue to bake until sauce is bubbly and top is light golden, 15 to 20 more minutes. Let stand 5 minutes before serving.

NUTRIENTS PER SERVING 30 G PROTEIN 40 G FAT
44 G CARBOHYDRATES 5 G FIBRE 4 MG IRON
510 MG CALCIUM 1729 MG SODIUM 660 CALORIES

Spicy Saffron Tomato-Pepper Sauce

PREPARATION TIME 35 MINUTES
COOKING TIME 45 MINUTES
MAKES 10 CUPS (2.5 L)

6 large tomatoes

4 peppers, preferably 2 red and 2 green

3 large onions

12 garlic cloves

¼ cup (50 mL) olive oil

1 tbsp (15 mL) paprika

1 tsp (5 mL) each hot chili flakes, saffron threads and salt

¼ tsp (1 mL) cayenne pepper

1 ⅔ cup (400 mL) homemade tomato sauce or 14 oz (398 mL) can tomato sauce

1 cup (250 mL) chopped fresh cilantro

COOKING TIP

If you want to use a homemade tomato sauce in this recipe, try Classic Arrabbiata Sauce (page 226).

SAFFRON

This fragrant spice comes from the stigmas of the crocus. Although its price tag is high, a little goes a long way. Some of the most popular recipes that call for this delicate flavour include paella, bouillabaisse and risotto. It's also commonly used in Middle Eastern cooking. When purchasing, look for Persian or Spanish saffron — "safflower" or "saffron flower," which is often mistaken for saffron, costs less but is far inferior.

1. Coarsely chop tomatoes, peppers and onions. Mince garlic. Heat oil in a large pot over medium heat. When pot is hot, add onions and garlic. Stir often until onions are softened, about 10 minutes. Reduce heat if onions begin to brown.

2. Add peppers and tomatoes, including seeds and juice, to softened onions, along with paprika, chili flakes, saffron, salt and cayenne. Stir in tomato sauce. Increase heat and bring to a boil. Reduce heat to medium-low and simmer, uncovered and stirring occasionally, until liquid is slightly reduced, 35 to 40 minutes. Stir in cilantro.

GET AHEAD Prepare as directed but do not add cilantro. Cover sauce and refrigerate for up to 3 days, or freeze for up to 1 month. Reheat, adding cilantro just before serving.

NUTRIENTS PER 1 CUP (250 mL) 3 G PROTEIN 6 G FAT
16 G CARBOHYDRATES 4 G FIBRE 1 MG IRON
36 MG CALCIUM 490 MG SODIUM 119 CALORIES

Singapore Noodles

PREPARATION TIME 20 MINUTES
COOKING TIME 8 MINUTES
MAKES 2 SERVINGS

½ of 250 g pkg rice vermicelli

½ of 454 g pkg frozen uncooked peeled large shrimp

1 skinless, boneless chicken breast

2 green onions

1 carrot

½ red pepper

2 tbsp (30 mL) freshly squeezed lime juice

1 tbsp (15 mL) soy sauce

2 tbsp (30 mL) vegetable oil

1 garlic clove, minced, or 1 tsp (5 mL) bottled chopped garlic

1 tsp (5 mL) finely grated fresh ginger or bottled minced ginger

2 tsp (10 mL) curry powder

½ tsp (2 mL) salt

⅓ cup (75 mL) chopped fresh cilantro (optional)

SUBSTITUTION

Threadlike vermicelli made from rice is sold in many supermarkets and Asian food markets. If you can't find it, use the same amount of spaghettini or cappellini and instead of soaking noodles, cook them according to package directions before adding to sauce.

1. Separate noodles as best you can, then soak according to package directions or in very hot water for 20 minutes. If noodles soften before you need them, drain and toss with a little vegetable oil to help prevent sticking.

2. Meanwhile, rinse shrimp under cold running water to remove any ice crystals. Pat dry with paper towels. Cut chicken in half lengthwise, then slice into thin strips. Slice onions into 1-inch (2.5 cm) pieces. Slice carrot into thin julienne strips. Thinly slice pepper. In a small bowl, stir lime juice with soy sauce, 1 tbsp (15 mL) water and 1 tbsp (15 mL) oil.

3. Heat remaining 1 tbsp (15 mL) oil in a large non-stick frying pan or wok over medium-high heat. Add chicken. Stir-fry until light golden, about 3 minutes. Add shrimp, carrot, pepper, garlic and ginger. Sprinkle with curry powder and salt. Stir often until shrimp turn bright pink, about 3 minutes. Add drained noodles, then pour in lime mixture. Stir often, separating noodles, until hot and noodles turn yellow, about 2 minutes. Remove from heat and stir in onions, and cilantro if you wish.

NUTRIENTS PER SERVING 42 G PROTEIN 18 G FAT
64 G CARBOHYDRATES 4 G FIBRE 5 MG IRON
112 MG CALCIUM 1367 MG SODIUM 590 CALORIES

Whole-Wheat Mac and Cheese

PREPARATION TIME 30 MINUTES
COOKING TIME 10 MINUTES
BROILING TIME 4 MINUTES
STANDING TIME 5 MINUTES
MAKES 8 SERVINGS

3 slices whole-wheat bread

1 tbsp (15 mL) melted butter

¼ cup (50 mL) snipped fresh chives (optional)

3 cups (750 mL) grated old cheddar cheese, about 10 oz (300 g)

1 butternut squash or small sugar pumpkin, about 2 lb (1 kg)

10 oz (284 mL) can undiluted chicken broth

½ tsp (2 mL) ground nutmeg

450 g pkg whole-wheat elbow macaroni or fusilli

8 oz (250 g) block cream cheese, cubed

1 cup (250 mL) whipping cream

1 tbsp (15 mL) Dijon mustard

¼ tsp (1 mL) salt

CHATELAINE KITCHEN TIP

This is no ordinary mac and cheese — its über-creamy sauce is thanks to blended, cooked squash, rather than the standard cheese-and-cream mixture.

1. For topping, trim crusts from bread and lightly toast bread. Tear into large pieces and pulse in a food processor until coarse crumbs form. Add butter and pulse to mix. Or crumble toast with your fingers and stir in butter. Add chives (if using) and ½ cup (125 mL) cheddar. Pulse once or stir to mix.

2. Peel squash (see sidebar, page 97). Cut in half, scoop out and discard pulp and seeds, then cut into small chunks. You should have about 4 cups (1 L). Place in a large pot. Add broth, 1 can water and nutmeg. Cover and bring to a boil over high heat. Reduce heat and simmer, covered and stirring occasionally, until pumpkin is very tender, 10 to 15 minutes.

3. Meanwhile, bring a large pot of water to a boil over high heat. Add pasta and cook according to package directions until al dente, 8 to 10 minutes. Place rack in top third of oven and preheat broiler. Using a slotted spoon, remove half of the pumpkin to a bowl. Using a potato masher, mash remaining pumpkin with broth until fairly smooth. Add cream cheese. Continue mashing until almost melted. Stir in cream, Dijon and salt. Remove from heat. Stir in remaining 2 ½ cups (625 mL) cheddar until melted. Stir in pumpkin pieces.

4. Drain cooked pasta and place in a bowl. Stir in pumpkin mixture. Spread evenly in a 9- × 13-inch (3 L) baking dish. Sprinkle evenly with crumb mixture. Broil until crust is golden, 4 to 5 minutes. Let stand 5 minutes before serving. Lovely served with a tomato salad.

NUTRIENTS PER SERVING 25 G PROTEIN 38 G FAT
59 G CARBOHYDRATES 8 G FIBRE 3 MG IRON
411 MG CALCIUM 1033 MG SODIUM 650 CALORIES

Broccoli and Boursin Lasagna Rolls

PREPARATION TIME 30 MINUTES
COOKING TIME 23 MINUTES
BAKING TIME 40 MINUTES
STANDING TIME 10 MINUTES
MAKES 6 TO 8 SERVINGS

6 garlic cloves

1 onion

1 tbsp (15 mL) butter

1 head broccoli

5 oz (140 g) pkg baby spinach, about 8 cups (2 L)

2 cups (500 mL) grated asiago cheese

1 tsp (5 mL) ground nutmeg

16 to 20 lasagna noodles (not oven-ready)

Olive oil

3 cups (750 mL) tomato pasta sauce

150 g pkg Boursin cheese

STALK TALK

There's no reason to toss out broccoli stalks — you can use them in lots of dishes. We suggest that you peel their tough skin, then chop or slice. Use in stir-fry and pasta recipes that call for florets. They may take a few more minutes to cook than florets, so add them ahead of time.

1. Mince garlic and chop onion. Melt butter in a large frying pan set over medium heat. Add garlic and onion. Stir frequently until onion starts to soften, 3 to 4 minutes. Meanwhile, slice broccoli stalks from florets. Using a vegetable peeler, peel stalks, then chop. Add to onion mixture along with ¾ cup (175 mL) water. Cover and boil, stirring occasionally, to partially cook, 5 minutes. Meanwhile, coarsely chop florets. Add to stalks after 5 minutes of cooking. Cover and boil, stirring occasionally, until broccoli is very tender, 5 to 7 more minutes.

2. Meanwhile, bring a large pot of water to a boil over high heat. Place cooked broccoli mixture, including liquid, in a food processor. Pulse to chop. Whirl in spinach, in 2 batches, until almost puréed. Scrape down side of bowl as needed. Turn mixture into a large bowl. Stir in asiago and nutmeg. Refrigerate until cool, 10 to 15 minutes. Add pasta to boiling water and cook according to package directions until al dente, 10 to 12 minutes. Drain and rinse under cold water. Place in a large bowl, drizzle with oil and toss to evenly coat.

3. Preheat oven to 350°F (180°C). Spread about ¼ cup (50 mL) pasta sauce over bottom of a 9- × 13-inch (3 L) baking dish. Lay a few lasagna noodles flat on the counter. Spread about ¼ cup (50 mL) broccoli mixture over each noodle. Roll up noodles. Place rolls, seam-side down, in a single layer in dish. Repeat with remaining noodles (you may not need them all). Evenly crumble Boursin overtop, then cover with remaining sauce. Lay a piece of foil overtop. Bake in centre of preheated oven until a knife tip inserted into centre of a roll comes out warm, 40 to 45 minutes. Let stand 10 minutes before serving. If you prefer the lasagna saucy, heat extra pasta sauce and spoon overtop.

GET AHEAD Completely prepare dish but don't bake. Cover and refrigerate overnight. When ready to cook, remove from refrigerator. Lay a piece of foil overtop. Bake in centre of preheated oven until a knife tip inserted into centre of a roll comes out warm, about 1 hour and 50 minutes.

NUTRIENTS PER SERVING 15 G PROTEIN 16 G FAT
49 G CARBOHYDRATES 5 G FIBRE 2 MG IRON
285 MG CALCIUM 541 MG SODIUM 397 CALORIES

Herbed Pasta with Spinach

PREPARATION TIME 5 MINUTES
COOKING TIME 10 MINUTES
MAKES 2 TO 3 SERVINGS

½ of 450 g pkg chunky pasta, such as rigatoni, about 2 cups (500 mL)

19 oz (540 mL) can stewed tomatoes

1 tsp (5 mL) Italian seasoning or ½ tsp (2 mL) each dried basil and oregano leaves

Pinch of hot chili flakes

1 cup (250 mL) crumbled goat cheese

3 cups (750 mL) baby spinach

COOKING TIP

Stewed tomatoes have added herbs and spices, making them a great ingredient for shortcut pasta sauce.

1. If you like your pasta saucy, use only 1 ½ cups (375 mL) pasta; otherwise, use the whole 2 cups (500 mL). Bring a large pot of water to a boil over high heat. Add pasta and cook according to package directions until al dente, 10 to 12 minutes.

2. Meanwhile, pour tomatoes with their juices into a large, wide frying pan and set over medium-high heat. Add seasonings. Boil, uncovered and stirring often, to develop flavours, about 3 minutes. Reduce heat to low. Simmer, uncovered, stirring occasionally, while pasta cooks.

3. When pasta is cooked, ladle out and reserve about ¼ cup (50 mL) pasta water, then drain pasta. Stir pasta into tomato mixture along with half of cheese. If sauce is thicker than you like, add pasta water, a little at a time, to desired consistency. Stir in spinach. Serve with remaining cheese sprinkled overtop.

NUTRIENTS PER SERVING 21 G PROTEIN 12 G FAT
70 G CARBOHYDRATES 6 G FIBRE 8 MG IRON
194 MG CALCIUM 861 MG SODIUM 470 CALORIES

Prosciutto and Sugar Snap Peas Penne

PREPARATION TIME 10 MINUTES
COOKING TIME 7 MINUTES
MAKES 3 TO 4 SERVINGS

½ of 450 g pkg penne or rotini
2 handfuls of sugar snap peas, about 7 oz (200 g)
1 small, thin zucchini
3 garlic cloves
2 tbsp (30 mL) olive oil, preferably extra-virgin
1 tbsp (15 mL) drained capers
4 slices prosciutto or ham
1 tsp (5 mL) Dijon mustard
½ cup (125 mL) freshly grated parmesan cheese
Pinch of salt (optional)

WHAT IS IT?

In the olive-oil making process, the first pressing of olives yields what is known as extra-virgin oil. The fruitiest and least acidic of the olive oils, extra-virgin is considered to be the finest grade. A dark-coloured oil usually indicates deeper flavour, but the region where the olives are from also has a bearing on the taste of their oil.

1. Bring a large pot of water to a boil over high heat. Cook pasta according to package directions until al dente, 7 to 9 minutes. Trim peas and add to pasta water for the last 1 minute of cooking. Drain.

2. Meanwhile, slice zucchini in half lengthwise, then into semicircles. Mince garlic. Heat oil in a large frying pan over medium heat. Add zucchini, garlic and capers. Stir often until zucchini starts to soften and capers begin to pop, 3 to 4 minutes.

3. Slice prosciutto into thin strips. Add pasta to zucchini mixture. Dot with Dijon and toss to evenly coat. Sprinkle with parmesan. Stir in prosciutto slices. Taste and add a pinch of salt or more capers if needed. Serve in wide bowls.

NUTRIENTS PER SERVING 16 G PROTEIN 13 G FAT
48 G CARBOHYDRATES 4 G FIBRE 3 MG IRON
178 MG CALCIUM 615 MG SODIUM 373 CALORIES

Rustic Mediterranean Pasta with Tomatoes

PREPARATION TIME 20 MINUTES
COOKING TIME 8 MINUTES
MAKES 8 CUPS (2 L)

1 pint each red and yellow cherry or grape tomatoes
¼ red onion
½ cup (125 mL) pitted kalamata or green olives (see sidebar, page 162)
¼ cup (50 mL) each red wine vinegar and olive oil
½ cup (125 mL) crumbled feta
⅓ cup (75 mL) chopped fresh dill
1 tsp (5 mL) each dried oregano leaves and salt
½ tsp (2 mL) each garlic powder and freshly ground black pepper
½ of 450 g pkg fusilli
¼ cup (50 mL) raisins
¼ cup (50 mL) toasted pine nuts (optional)

COOKING TIP

Hydrating raisins gives the sweet morsels a plump, juicy texture. In this recipe we just add them to the pasta water, but you can also plump them for other recipes, such as salads and butter tarts. Simply microwave in a bit of liquid until warm, then remove from liquid once they're cool.

1. Cut tomatoes in half. Place in a very large bowl. Thinly slice onion. Coarsely chop olives. Add onion and olives to tomatoes. Drizzle with vinegar and oil. Sprinkle with feta, dill, oregano, salt, garlic powder and pepper. Stir to blend. Let stand at room temperature.

2. Meanwhile, bring a large pot of water to a boil over high heat. Add pasta and cook according to package directions until al dente, 8 to 10 minutes. Add raisins to boiling pasta water for last minute of cooking.

3. When pasta is cooked, ladle out and reserve about ¼ cup (50 mL) pasta water. Drain pasta and raisins, then stir into tomato mixture. If pasta is too dry, add pasta water, a little at a time. Taste and add more dill or cheese if you wish. Spoon into bowls, and sprinkle with pine nuts if you wish.

NUTRIENTS PER 1 CUP (250 mL) 6 G PROTEIN 12 G FAT
33 G CARBOHYDRATES 3 G FIBRE 2 MG IRON
63 MG CALCIUM 756 MG SODIUM 258 CALORIES

Lemon Chicken Spaghettini

PREPARATION TIME 10 MINUTES
COOKING TIME 6 MINUTES
MAKES 2 TO 3 SERVINGS

½ of 450 g pkg cappellini or spaghettini

1 lemon

1 tbsp (15 mL) Dijon mustard

¼ tsp (1 mL) each granulated sugar and salt

2 skinless, boneless chicken breasts

Pinches of salt and freshly ground black pepper

3 tbsp (45 mL) butter

3 garlic cloves, minced

8 oz (250 g) snow peas or green beans, trimmed

1 cup (250 mL) coarsely chopped fresh cilantro or snipped fresh chives

CHATELAINE KITCHEN TIP

Prepare snow peas by snapping off the ends, then pulling away the tough string that runs from one end of the pea to the other.

1. Bring a large pot of water to a boil over high heat. Add pasta and cook according to package directions until al dente, about 6 to 8 minutes. Meanwhile, finely grate 2 tsp (10 mL) lemon peel into a small bowl, then squeeze in about 2 tbsp (30 mL) juice. Whisk in Dijon, sugar and salt. Slice chicken into thin strips. Sprinkle with pinches of salt and pepper. Melt 2 tbsp (30 mL) butter in a large non-stick frying pan over medium-high heat. Add garlic and stir constantly for 1 minute. Add chicken and stir-fry until golden, 3 to 4 minutes. Remove from heat.

2. Add peas to pasta water for last 1 minute of cooking. If using beans, add for last 3 minutes. Drain pasta and peas. Return to pasta pot. Drizzle with lemon mixture. Stir in chicken and garlic, cilantro and remaining 1 tbsp (15 mL) butter. Taste and add more salt and pepper if you wish.

NUTRIENTS PER SERVING 34 G PROTEIN 15 G FAT
70 G CARBOHYDRATES 6 G FIBRE 5 MG IRON
71 MG CALCIUM 790 MG SODIUM 556 CALORIES

Spicy Sausage with Dilled Orzo

4 large sausages, preferably hot Italian

4 ripe but firm tomatoes

2 peppers, preferably different colours

3 tbsp (45 mL) olive oil

2 cups (500 mL) orzo or other small pasta

1 head broccoli, cut into small florets

1 lemon

½ tsp (2 mL) each salt and freshly ground black pepper

3 green onions

½ cup (125 mL) each chopped fresh basil and dill or 2 tsp (10 mL)
dried basil leaves and 1 ½ tsp (7 mL) dried dillweed

BRING IT INSIDE

If you prefer, roast sausage, peppers and tomatoes on baking sheets in a preheated 400°F (200°C) oven. Continue with preparation instructions.

1. Oil grill. Heat barbecue to medium-high. Prick sausages in several places. Thickly slice tomatoes and halve peppers, then core and seed. Brush with about 1 tbsp (15 mL) oil. Place all on grill. If they won't fit, add only half the tomatoes. Cook, lid closed, turning often. Remove tomatoes to a large baking sheet when grill marks form, 2 to 4 minutes. Add any remaining tomatoes to grill. When peppers are charred and sausages cooked, 12 to 16 minutes, remove to the baking sheet.

2. Meanwhile, bring a large pot of salted water to a boil over high heat. Add orzo. Stir to separate. Boil, uncovered and stirring occasionally, until al dente, about 7 minutes. Add broccoli for the last 2 minutes of cooking. Drain and turn into a large bowl. Squeeze 2 tbsp (30 mL) juice from lemon into a small bowl. Whisk in remaining 2 tbsp (30 mL) oil, salt and pepper. Stir into orzo mixture. Chop grilled tomatoes and peppers. Thickly slice sausages, diagonally. Thinly slice onions. Stir all into orzo along with basil and dill. Taste, adding more lemon juice and salt, if you wish. Delicious warm or at room temperature.

GET AHEAD Cover salad and refrigerate overnight.

NUTRIENTS PER SERVING 16 G PROTEIN 12 G FAT
42 G CARBOHYDRATES 5 G FIBRE 3 MG IRON
60 MG CALCIUM 669 MG SODIUM 337 CALORIES

Linguine with Spicy Gremolata Shrimp

PREPARATION TIME 10 MINUTES
COOKING TIME 10 MINUTES
MAKES 2 TO 3 SERVINGS

340 g pkg frozen uncooked large shrimp, peeled

1 large lemon

1 small bunch asparagus

1 large jalapeño pepper

2 garlic cloves

½ of 450 g pkg linguine or fettuccine

3 tbsp (45 mL) butter

¼ tsp (1 mL) salt

½ cup (125 mL) chopped fresh parsley

DEFROSTING SHRIMP

The best way to thaw shrimp: Place in a sieve and rinse with cold running water until ice crystals melt. This way they don't sit for long and will keep their fresh flavour. Make sure to pat dry with paper towels.

1. Thaw shrimp according to package directions (or see sidebar). Bring a large pot of water to a boil over high heat. Meanwhile, finely grate about 1 tbsp (15 mL) peel and squeeze 3 tbsp (45 mL) juice from lemon. Snap tough ends from asparagus and discard. Cut spears into bite-sized pieces. Finely chop jalapeño and mince garlic.

2. Add pasta to boiling water and cook according to package directions until al dente, 7 to 9 minutes. Add asparagus to pasta for last 2 minutes of cooking. Ladle out and reserve about ¼ cup (50 mL) pasta water before draining pasta and asparagus.

3. Meanwhile, melt 2 tbsp (30 mL) butter in a large frying pan over medium heat. Add shrimp, jalapeño, garlic and salt. Stir-fry until shrimp are pink, 3 to 4 minutes. Toss pasta and asparagus with shrimp mixture, remaining 1 tbsp (15 mL) butter, lemon peel and juice, parsley and 2 tbsp (30 mL) pasta water. If dry, stir in more pasta water, a little at a time. Taste and add salt, if you wish. Serve in large bowls.

NUTRIENTS PER SERVING 29 G PROTEIN 15 G FAT
63 G CARBOHYDRATES 6 G FIBRE 6 MG IRON
102 MG CALCIUM 816 MG SODIUM 500 CALORIES

Penne with Creamy Brie and Tomatoes

PREPARATION TIME 10 MINUTES
COOKING TIME 8 MINUTES
MAKES 4 SERVINGS

½ of 450 g pkg farfalle or penne

4 tomatoes, preferably a mix of red and yellow

4 slices prosciutto

3 garlic cloves, minced

1 cup (250 mL) shredded fresh basil

2 tbsp (30 mL) olive oil

Generous pinches of salt

5 oz (140 g) brie or camembert cheese

BRIE TIP

It's okay to eat and cook the rind of brie and other semi-ripened cheeses — the rind helps the cheese keep its shape when cooked.

1. Bring a large pot of water to a boil over high heat. Add pasta and cook according to package directions until al dente, about 8 to 10 minutes. Meanwhile, coarsely chop tomatoes. Slice prosciutto into thin strips. Place in a large bowl with the garlic and basil. Add oil and salt, stirring to mix. Cut brie into small pieces. It should measure about 1 cup (250 mL).

2. When pasta is cooked, ladle out and reserve about ¼ cup (50 mL) pasta water. Drain pasta, then return to pasta pot. Add tomato mixture and brie. Toss to mix. If needed, stir in pasta water, a little at a time, just until moist. Serve immediately.

NUTRIENTS PER SERVING 19 G PROTEIN 19 G FAT
53 G CARBOHYDRATES 5 G FIBRE 4 MG IRON
107 MG CALCIUM 577 MG SODIUM 457 CALORIES

Orecchiette with Herbed Garlic Tomatoes

PREPARATION TIME 10 MINUTES
COOKING TIME 8 MINUTES
MAKES 4 SERVINGS

½ of 450 g pkg orecchiette, about 2 cups (500 mL)

1 small orange

2 garlic cloves

1 pint teardrop, cherry or grape tomatoes, preferably orange or yellow

Pinches of salt and freshly ground black pepper

4 cups (1 L) arugula

½ cup (125 mL) chopped fresh basil or snipped fresh chives

1 ½ cups (375 mL) crumbled feta or 5 oz (140 g) log goat cheese

TURN A NEW LEAF

Arugula has a nutty, almost peppery flavour. If you can't find it, substitute baby spinach.

1. Bring a large pot of water to a boil over high heat. Cook pasta according to package directions until al dente, 8 to 11 minutes. Meanwhile, finely grate peel from half of the orange. Mince garlic. Lightly coat a large frying pan with olive oil and set over medium heat. Add tomatoes, garlic, salt and pepper. Stir frequently, uncovered, until tomatoes start to break down, 3 to 5 minutes. If arugula leaves are large, tear into smaller pieces.

2. When pasta is cooked, ladle out and reserve about ¼ cup (50 mL) pasta water. Drain pasta and add to tomato-garlic mixture along with pasta water, orange peel and basil. Toss well, then gradually stir in the arugula and about 1 cup (250 mL) feta. Taste and add salt if needed. Serve in large wide bowls and sprinkle remaining feta overtop.

NUTRIENTS PER SERVING 19 G PROTEIN 15 G FAT
56 G CARBOHYDRATES 5 G FIBRE 4 MG IRON
400 MG CALCIUM 835 MG SODIUM 425 CALORIES

Not-So-Classic Creamy Carbonara

PREPARATION TIME 10 MINUTES
COOKING TIME 8 MINUTES
MAKES 4 TO 6 SERVINGS

450 g pkg linguine or fettuccine

6 thin slices pancetta or bacon strips

½ red onion

8 oz (227 g) pkg sliced mushrooms

1 cup (250 mL) whipping cream

1 ½ cups (375 mL) freshly grated parmesan cheese

2 tbsp (30 mL) cold butter, cubed

6 cups (1.5 L) baby spinach

SWITCH IT UP

This recipe is flexible, so feel free to swap a bit. For example, green onions, oyster and cremini mushrooms and asiago cheese all work well in this dish.

1. Bring a large pot of water to a boil over high heat. Add pasta and cook according to package directions until al dente, 8 to 10 minutes, then drain. Meanwhile, slice pancetta into long, thin strips. If using bacon, thinly slice. Thinly slice onion. Set a large frying pan (preferably non-stick) over medium heat. Add pancetta. Stir often until it begins to crisp, 2 to 3 minutes. Bacon will take about 6 minutes. Add onion and mushrooms. Pan will be very full. Stir often until onion begins to soften and mushrooms begin to brown, about 6 minutes. Remove to a large bowl.

2. Pour cream into frying pan. Increase heat to medium-high. Stir frequently until cream comes to a boil, 1 to 2 minutes. Reduce heat to low. Gradually stir in cheese, then butter, stirring constantly until melted, about 1 minute. Remove from heat. Add spinach and drained pasta to pancetta mixture in large bowl. Pour cream sauce overtop and stir to evenly mix. Serve immediately, sprinkled with a little more parmesan if you wish.

NUTRIENTS PER SERVING 40 G PROTEIN 56 G FAT
105 G CARBOHYDRATES 9 G FIBRE 9 MG IRON
700 MG CALCIUM 1377 MG SODIUM 1077 CALORIES

vegetarian mains

No meat one night a week? Why not, when there's easy eggplant parmesan, spicy peanut tofu and a luxurious vegetable curry.

Roasted Vegetable and Kale Salad with Maple Dressing

PREPARATION TIME 10 MINUTES
ROASTING TIME 20 MINUTES
MAKES 4 SERVINGS

4 carrots or 2 carrots and 2 parsnips

2 peppers, preferably a mix of colours

1 small red onion

⅓ cup (75 mL) plus 1 tbsp (15 mL) olive oil

Pinches of salt

3 tbsp (45 mL) white or cider vinegar

1 tbsp (15 mL) maple syrup

1 tbsp (15 mL) Dijon mustard

1 tsp (5 mL) dried thyme leaves

Generous pinches of dried sage leaves

Pinches of freshly ground black pepper

½ bunch kale leaves or 5 oz (140 g) pkg baby spinach, about 8 cups (2 L)

19 oz (540 mL) can chickpeas or 6-bean medley

GOOD FOR YOU

Kale, a vegetable underdog, is loaded with flavour and nutrients, including vitamins A and C and folate, a B vitamin. Choose leaves that are dark green and pert. Not sure how to use it? Kale is usually a great substitute for spinach.

1. Preheat oven to 450°F (230°C). Peel carrots and parsnips. Cut in half lengthwise. Halve peppers, then core and seed. Slice onion into thick wedges. Place all on a large baking sheet. Drizzle 1 tbsp (15 mL) oil and sprinkle with pinches of salt. Toss to coat. Roast in centre of preheated oven until tender, 20 to 25 minutes. You don't need to turn. Remove from oven and coarsely chop.

2. Meanwhile, in a small bowl, whisk vinegar with maple syrup (if using), Dijon, thyme, sage, and pinches of salt and pepper. Slowly whisk in remaining ⅓ cup (75 mL) oil. Cut kale into bite-sized pieces. It should measure about 8 cups (2 L). Rinse and drain chickpeas. Place warm vegetables, kale and chickpeas in a large bowl. Drizzle with as much dressing as you like, tossing to coat.

NUTRIENTS PER SERVING 12 G PROTEIN 16 G FAT
56 G CARBOHYDRATES 12 G FIBRE 5 MG IRON
253 MG CALCIUM 422 MG SODIUM 395 CALORIES

Faux Pho

PREPARATION TIME 10 MINUTES
COOKING TIME 13 MINUTES
MAKES 2 SERVINGS

900 mL carton vegetable or chicken broth

1 cinnamon stick

1 thin slice ginger

1 star anise (optional)

½ tsp (2 mL) each hot chili-garlic sauce and granulated sugar

½ of 350 g pkg extra-firm tofu

2 cups (500 mL) sliced shiitake or button mushrooms, about 8 oz (250 g)

2 green onions

Small bundle of thick rice vermicelli

1 lime

¼ cup (50 mL) fresh mint or basil leaves

Handful of bean sprouts (optional)

WHAT IS IT?

Star anise is a star-shaped dark brown pod that has a strong licorice flavour. It plays a major role in traditional pho's unique flavour and it's available in the spice section of grocery stores and at Asian food markets.

1. Pour broth into a large pot and set over high heat. Add cinnamon, ginger, star anise (if using), chili-garlic sauce and sugar. Bring to a boil. Reduce heat to medium-low and simmer until flavourful, about 5 minutes. Remove and discard cinnamon, ginger and star anise.

2. Meanwhile, cut tofu into slices. If using shiitake mushrooms, remove and discard stems. Slice mushrooms and onions. Coat a large frying pan with oil and set over medium-high heat. Add tofu and mushrooms. Stir often until tofu is golden, about 5 minutes. Add to broth. Bring to a boil, then stir in noodles, separating as you add. Boil gently, stirring often, until noodles are tender, 3 to 5 minutes. Cut lime into wedges. Serve soup with onions, mint, bean sprouts if using, and lime wedges on the side.

NUTRIENTS PER SERVING 16 G PROTEIN 6 G FAT
41 G CARBOHYDRATES 4 G FIBRE 3 MG IRON
156 MG CALCIUM 1484 MG SODIUM 245 CALORIES

Grilled Vegetable Pizza

PREPARATION TIME 5 MINUTES
GRILLING TIME 5 MINUTES
MAKES 2 SERVINGS

2 ripe but firm plum tomatoes

1 small zucchini

2 green onions

Olive oil

Generous pinches of dried basil leaves, salt and freshly ground black pepper

1 large or 2 small naan or Greek-style flat pitas

½ cup (125 mL) goat cheese or crumbled feta cheese

FETA TIP

If you've purchased block feta, taste before using. If it's really salty, quickly rinse under cold running water in its block form, then pat dry with paper towels.

1. Lightly oil grill and heat barbecue to medium-high. Thickly slice tomatoes. Cut zucchini diagonally into long ovals. Place in a large bowl along with whole onions. Drizzle with just enough olive oil to coat. Sprinkle with basil, salt and pepper, tossing to coat. Brush bread with olive oil.

2. Place vegetables on grill and barbecue until tender and lightly charred, 2 to 5 minutes per side, removing them as they are done.

3. When vegetables are cooked, place bread on grill and barbecue, lid closed, just until grill marks form, about 1 to 2 minutes per side. Remove from grill and sprinkle with goat cheese, then arrange tomatoes and zucchini on top. Slice onions and scatter overtop.

NUTRIENTS PER SERVING 20 G PROTEIN 21 G FAT
71 G CARBOHYDRATES 4 G FIBRE 5 MG IRON
131 MG CALCIUM 1355 MG SODIUM 552 CALORIES

Harvest Vegetable Curry

PREPARATION TIME 20 MINUTES
COOKING TIME 31 MINUTES
MAKES 6 TO 8 SERVINGS

1 large onion
1 tbsp (15 mL) vegetable oil
4 large tomatoes
2 tbsp (30 mL) Indian curry paste
2 tbsp (30 mL) grated fresh ginger
1 tbsp (15 mL) ground coriander
1 small eggplant
2 zucchini
1 cup (250 mL) vegetable broth
¼ cup (50 mL) mango chutney
1 small cauliflower
19 oz (540 mL) can chickpeas (optional)

OMNIVORE OPTION

If you like your meat, add chunks of cooked chicken or beef.

1. Finely chop onion. Heat oil in a very large, wide pot over medium heat. Add onion and sauté to soften a little, 2 to 3 minutes. Coarsely chop tomatoes and add to onion along with seeds and juice. Stir in curry paste, ginger and coriander. Stir frequently until saucy, 4 to 6 minutes.

2. Meanwhile, slice eggplant into bite-sized strips. Cut zucchini in half lengthwise, then slice into semicircles. Add to tomato mixture. Stir often until softened slightly, about 5 minutes. Add broth and chutney. Bring to a boil. Cut cauliflower into florets and mix in. Cover and simmer, stirring often, until saucy and cauliflower is tender, 20 to 30 minutes. Rinse and drain chickpeas (if using) and add for the last 1 minute of cooking. Good over basmati rice.

GET AHEAD Cover curry and refrigerate for up to 3 days, or freeze for up to 2 months.

NUTRIENTS PER SERVING 3 G PROTEIN 4 G FAT
19 G CARBOHYDRATES 5 G FIBRE 1 MG IRON
36 MG CALCIUM 318 MG SODIUM 116 CALORIES

Spiced Squash and Corn Chili

PREPARATION TIME 20 MINUTES
COOKING TIME 55 MINUTES
MAKES 15 CUPS (3.75 L) FOR
8 TO 12 SERVINGS

6 garlic cloves or 1 tbsp (15 mL) bottled chopped garlic

3 onions

1 small butternut squash or about 4 cups (1 L) squash pieces

2 28-oz (796 mL) cans diced tomatoes

14 oz (398 mL) can tomato sauce

¼ cup (50 mL) chili powder

1 tbsp (15 mL) each ground coriander and cumin

1 to 2 tsp (5 to 10 mL) hot chili flakes (optional)

1 tsp (5 mL) each cinnamon ground, allspice and salt

3 peppers, preferably a mix of colours

12 oz (341 mL) can corn niblets or 2 cups (500 mL) frozen corn

19 oz (540 mL) can black beans

WAYS WITH CHILI

This chili can be served over rice or wrapped up in tortillas.

1. Coarsely chop garlic and onions. Lightly coat a large pot with oil and set over medium heat. Add garlic and onions. Stir occasionally until onions start to soften, about 10 minutes. Meanwhile, peel squash (see sidebar, page 97). Cut in half, scoop out and discard pulp and seeds, then cut into 1-inch (2.5 cm) pieces.

2. Add squash, tomatoes and tomato sauce to softened onions. Sprinkle with chili powder, coriander, cumin, chili flakes, cinnamon, allspice and salt. Stir and bring to a boil. Meanwhile, cut peppers into 1-inch (2.5 cm) pieces. Stir into chili. Reduce heat to medium-low.

3. Cover and simmer, stirring often, until squash is fork-tender, 40 to 50 minutes. Meanwhile, drain corn and beans, then rinse and drain again. Once squash is tender, stir corn and beans into chili. Simmer until warmed through, about 5 minutes.

NUTRIENTS PER 1 CUP (250 mL) 5 G PROTEIN 1 G FAT
25 G CARBOHYDRATES 6 G FIBRE 3 MG IRON
85 MG CALCIUM 669 MG SODIUM 112 CALORIES

Sweet and Spicy Pepper Tortilla Casserole

PREPARATION TIME 20 MINUTES
BAKING TIME 35 MINUTES
STANDING TIME 10 MINUTES
MAKES 6 SERVINGS

2 19-oz (540 mL) cans red kidney beans or 6-bean medley

2 cups (500 mL) sour cream

340 g jar roasted red peppers, drained well, thickly sliced

5 green onions, thinly sliced

3 garlic cloves, minced

1 small chipotle chili packed in adobo sauce, finely chopped, or 2 tbsp (30 mL) finely chopped pickled jalapeño peppers

½ tsp (2 mL) each paprika, ground cumin and salt

3 cups (750 mL) chopped fresh cilantro

2 cups (500 mL) grated cheddar cheese

8 to 10 medium tortillas, about 7 inches (18 cm) in diameter

2 cups (500 mL) salsa

SERVING SUGGESTION

Guacamole is a natural accompaniment to this meal. You'll find the recipe for a homemade version on page 179.

1. Preheat oven to 350°F (180°C). Rinse and drain beans. In a large bowl, stir beans with sour cream, peppers, onions, garlic, chipotle, paprika, cumin and salt. Stir in 1 cup (250 mL) each cilantro and cheddar until evenly mixed. Lightly coat a 9- × 13-inch (3 L) baking dish with oil. Completely cover bottom with a single layer of tortillas, trying not to overlap too much. If necessary, use scissors to cut to fit.

2. Spread one-third of bean mixture over tortillas. Spoon ⅔ cup (150 mL) salsa overtop. Sprinkle with ½ cup (125 mL) cilantro. Repeat layering two more times. Finish with 1 cup (250 mL) cheese.

3. Bake, uncovered, in centre of preheated oven until casserole is bubbly and cheese is melted, 35 to 40 minutes. Let stand 10 minutes before serving. Sprinkle with remaining ½ cup (125 mL) cilantro.

GET AHEAD Cover unbaked casserole and refrigerate for up to 1 day. Bake cold casserole, tightly covered with foil, in centre of preheated 350°F (180°C) oven for 45 minutes. Uncover and bake until bubbly and cheese is melted, 30 more minutes. Best eaten the day it's made, but baked, cooled casserole will keep, covered and refrigerated, for up to 1 day. Reheat leftovers in microwave on medium.

NUTRIENTS PER SERVING 26 G PROTEIN 28 G FAT
61 G CARBOHYDRATES 14 G FIBRE 5 MG IRON
455 MG CALCIUM 1601 MG SODIUM 589 CALORIES

Savoury Sesame-Tofu Cakes

PREPARATION TIME 25 MINUTES
STANDING TIME 30 MINUTES
COOKING TIME 16 MINUTES
MAKES 32 TO 36 CAKES

TOFU CAKES

350 g pkg extra-firm tofu

1 egg

1 carrot

3 tbsp (45 mL) finely chopped fresh cilantro

2 tbsp (30 mL) hoisin sauce

2 tsp (10 mL) each dark sesame oil and hot chili-garlic sauce

¼ tsp (1 mL) salt

½ cup (125 mL) all-purpose flour

SAUCE

¼ cup (50 mL) rice vinegar

2 tbsp (30 mL) each hoisin sauce and hot chili-garlic sauce

TOFU

Made from soybean milk, tofu is high in both protein and iron. It comes in a range of textures, from soft to extra-firm. Soft is more commonly used for dessert dishes, and extra-firm is well suited to frying.

1. For tofu cakes, remove tofu from packaging, wrap in a clean kitchen towel and place on a large plate. Cover with another plate. Weigh down with a heavy can. Let stand 30 minutes. This removes excess liquid from tofu.

2. Meanwhile, in a large bowl, whisk egg. Finely grate carrot. It should measure about ½ cup (125 mL). Squeeze carrot with a kitchen towel to remove excess liquid. Stir into egg along with cilantro, hoisin, sesame oil, chili-garlic sauce and salt.

3. Unwrap tofu and finely crumble into egg mixture. Using a fork or your hands, mash together to evenly mix. Sprinkle in 3 tbsp (45 mL) flour and stir to evenly mix. Scoop out about 1 tbsp (15 mL) tofu mixture and shape into a ball, then flatten into a cake about 1 ½ inches (4 cm) thick. Place on waxed paper or a baking sheet. Repeat with remaining tofu mixture.

4. Coat a large, wide frying pan (preferably non-stick) with oil and set over medium heat. Place remaining flour on a plate. Lightly dip one-quarter of the cakes into remaining flour, coating both sides. Shake off any excess flour. Place in pan, being careful not to crowd. Cook until golden, about 2 minutes per side. Remove to a large platter lined with paper towels. Repeat with remaining cakes in 3 more batches, adding more oil if needed. Serve warm or at room temperature. Meanwhile, for sauce, stir vinegar with hoisin and chili-garlic sauce in a bowl. When cakes are ready, serve with sauce for dipping.

GET AHEAD Refrigerate cooked cakes in a covered container between layers of waxed paper for up to 1 day. Reheat on baking sheet at 350°F (180°C), 3 to 5 minutes.

NUTRIENTS PER CAKE 1 G PROTEIN 1 G FAT
2 G CARBOHYDRATES 0 G FIBRE 0 MG IRON
17 MG CALCIUM 54 MG SODIUM 26 CALORIES

Grilled Eggplant Parmesan

PREPARATION TIME 10 MINUTES
GRILLING TIME 10 MINUTES
MAKES 2 SERVINGS

1 large eggplant

2 tbsp (30 mL) vegetable or olive oil

1 tsp (5 mL) Italian seasoning

¼ tsp (1 mL) salt and freshly ground black pepper

4 ripe but firm tomatoes

1 ½ cups (375 mL) coarsely grated parmesan or asiago cheese

½ cup (125 mL) shredded fresh basil

BASIL TRICK

The easiest way to shred basil is to stack the large leaves, roll, then shred. Basil is delicate and bruises easily, so use a sharp knife to prevent the leaves from browning quickly.

1. Oil grill and heat barbecue to medium. Thickly slice eggplant lengthwise. Brush both sides with some of the oil, then sprinkle with seasonings. Place on grill. Cover and barbecue until grill marks form on one side, about 5 minutes.

2. Meanwhile, cut tomatoes into thick slices and brush with remaining oil. Place on grill with eggplant after it has cooked 5 minutes. Turn eggplant. Continue barbecuing until tomatoes are warm and eggplant is tender, 5 to 8 more minutes. Turn occasionally, keeping an eye on tomatoes, as they cook quickly. Remove each to a baking sheet as soon as it's done.

3. To layer, place a piece of eggplant on each dinner plate. Top with a couple slices of tomato. Sprinkle with one-quarter of the cheese and basil. Repeat layering, finishing with basil.

NUTRIENTS PER SERVING 30 G PROTEIN 39 G FAT
35 G CARBOHYDRATES 10 G FIBRE 2 MG IRON
813 MG CALCIUM 1253 MG SODIUM 582 CALORIES

Portobello Burgers

PREPARATION TIME 10 MINUTES
ROASTING TIME 12 MINUTES
MAKES 2 SANDWICHES

PORTOBELLO TIP

Removing the dark-coloured gills from portobellos by gently scraping them out with a spoon makes for a nicer presentation.

TAKE IT OUTDOORS

If you're cooking on the barbecue, prepare recipe as above, but lightly oil grill and heat barbecue to medium-high. Grill mushrooms until tender and marks form on both sides, 3 to 4 minutes per side. Just before mushrooms are done, lightly grill bread.

2 large or 4 small portobello mushrooms
1 tbsp (15 mL) dark sesame or olive oil
Pinches of salt and freshly ground black pepper
1 large plum tomato
½ avocado, peeled and pitted
4 pieces thickly sliced bread or 2 crusty buns, split in half
1 cup (250 mL) baby spinach or arugula
2 thick slices Cambozola or cheddar cheese
Thin slices red onion (optional)

1. Preheat oven to 500°F (260°C). Discard stems from mushrooms. Using a spoon, gently scrape out dark gills from underside of mushrooms and discard. Brush mushrooms all over with oil. Place gill-side up on a foil-lined baking sheet. Generously sprinkle with salt and pepper. Roast in preheated oven for 8 minutes. Turn mushrooms (it's all right if liquid from centre of caps spills out) and continue to roast until dark brown and tender, about 4 more minutes. Remove from oven.

2. Meanwhile, thickly slice tomato. Thinly slice avocado. Lay 2 pieces of bread on counter. Cover with spinach, tomato and warm mushrooms, gill-side up. Place cheese in centre of mushrooms, then top with avocado and onion (if using). Cover with remaining bread or bun tops. Serve warm or at room temperature. Great with Light and Creamy Coleslaw (page 75) and crisp dill pickles.

NUTRIENTS PER SANDWICH 17 G PROTEIN 26 G FAT
45 G CARBOHYDRATES 7 G FIBRE 4 MG IRON
247 MG CALCIUM 737 MG SODIUM 465 CALORIES

Tarragon Tofu Scramble

Coat a large frying pan with oil and set over medium-high heat. Add 8 oz (250 g) sliced mushrooms, preferably a mix. Sauté until mushrooms are lightly browned around edges, about 5 minutes. When mushrooms are done, crumble in a 350 or 450 g pkg medium-firm tofu and sprinkle with generous pinches of salt and freshly ground black pepper. Stir often until tofu is warmed through, about 5 minutes. Stir in a handful of chopped fresh herbs, such as tarragon, basil or chives. Serve immediately.

MAKES 3 TO 4 SERVINGS

TARRAGON

This fragrant fresh herb is commonly used in French cooking. Its strong anise taste really brightens the flavour of a dish — try adding it to tofu, egg, chicken and even lemonade recipes.

Vegetable Phyllo Pockets

PREPARATION TIME 15 MINUTES
BAKING TIME 12 MINUTES
MAKES 8 POCKETS, FOR ABOUT
4 SERVINGS

4 cups (1 L) finely chopped fresh vegetables such as cauliflower, carrots, onions, snow peas, celery and broccoli

1 tbsp (15 mL) melted butter

1 tbsp (15 mL) vegetable oil

8 sheets frozen phyllo pastry, thawed

1 cup (250 mL) cooked rice

1 cup (250 mL) creamy goat cheese

⅓ cup (75 mL) chopped fresh basil

Pinches of salt and freshly ground black pepper

VARIATIONS

Use these phyllo instructions to make pockets with different fillings, such as chopped antipasto ingredients, including sun-dried tomatoes, artichokes, olives and feta-stuffed peppers. Just make sure that the filling is not too wet or it will make the pastry soggy.

1. Preheat oven to 375°F (190°C). Steam, boil or microwave vegetables just until bright in colour. Rinse with cold water and drain well. Stir butter with oil. Lightly brush some over a sheet of phyllo pastry. (Cover remaining phyllo with a damp kitchen towel to prevent drying out.) Fold in half lengthwise and brush top surface with oil-butter mixture.

2. Mound ½ cup (125 mL) vegetables at one end, slightly off centre. Top with 2 tbsp (30 mL) rice, 2 tbsp (30 mL) goat cheese, 2 tsp (10 mL) basil and pinches of salt and pepper. Fold as if folding a flag to form a triangle. Brush with oil-butter mixture. Place on an ungreased baking sheet. Repeat with remaining ingredients to make 8 triangles. Bake in preheated oven until browned, 12 to 15 minutes.

NUTRIENTS PER 2 POCKETS
8 G PROTEIN 11 G FAT 25 G CARBOHYDRATES
1 MG IRON 59 MG CALCIUM 230 CALORIES

Spicy Peanut Tofu and Spinach Stir-Fry

PREPARATION TIME 10 MINUTES
COOKING TIME 3 MINUTES
MAKES 3 SERVINGS

GOOD FOR YOU

This dish is high in protein and iron and an excellent source of vitamins A and C.

½ cup (125 mL) orange juice

⅓ cup (75 mL) smooth all-natural peanut butter

⅓ cup (75 mL) vegetable broth or teriyaki sauce, preferably low-sodium

2 tbsp (30 mL) hot chili-garlic sauce

350 or 454 g pkg extra-firm tofu

1 red pepper

5 oz (140 g) pkg baby spinach, about 8 cups (2 L)

1. In a small bowl, whisk juice with peanut butter, broth and chili-garlic sauce. Slice tofu into thin french fry–shaped sticks. Slice pepper into thick strips.

2. Lightly coat a large frying pan with oil and set over medium-high heat. When pan is hot, add tofu and pepper. Gently stir-fry until tofu is hot and pepper is tender, 3 to 5 minutes. Don't worry if tofu breaks a bit. Stir in sauce and spinach. Remove from heat and stir until spinach is just wilted. Good served over quinoa, couscous or steamed rice.

NUTRIENTS PER SERVING 25 G PROTEIN 25 G FAT
20 G CARBOHYDRATES 5 G FIBRE 5 MG IRON
319 MG CALCIUM 188 MG SODIUM 374 CALORIES

Thai Basil Noodles with Tofu

PREPARATION TIME 20 MINUTES
SOAKING TIME 5 MINUTES
COOKING TIME 12 MINUTES
MAKES 4 TO 6 SERVINGS

2 eggs

¼ cup (50 mL) each fish sauce and ketchup

¼ cup (50 mL) granulated sugar

2 tbsp (30 mL) each Worcestershire sauce and hot chili-garlic sauce

3 garlic cloves

3 green onions

3 red or green peppers

3 carrots

350 g pkg extra-firm tofu

¾ of 400 g pkg rice-stick noodles, about ¼ inch (5 mm) wide

3 tbsp (45 mL) vegetable oil

2 cups (500 mL) vegetable broth

1 cup (250 mL) chopped fresh basil

Lime wedges (optional)

SECRET INGREDIENT

You'd be surprised at how many Thai restaurants rely on the table condiment ketchup for flavour. But take it from us, this recipe wouldn't taste the same without it.

1. Put a full kettle of water on to boil. Meanwhile, in a bowl, whisk eggs with fish sauce, ketchup, sugar, and Worcestershire and chili-garlic sauces. Mince garlic. Slice onions. Cut peppers and carrots into thin bite-sized strips. Cut tofu into 1-inch (2.5 cm) cubes.

2. Place noodles in a large bowl and cover with very hot water. Soak until almost tender, 5 to 15 minutes, stirring often to separate. (Or cook noodles according to package directions.) Drain and set aside.

3. Meanwhile, heat oil in a wide saucepan over medium-high heat. Add tofu. Cook, turning occasionally, until light golden, 5 to 8 minutes. (Tofu may stick a little.) Remove when done to a bowl. Add more oil to pan if needed, then add garlic, peppers and carrots. Stir-fry for 3 minutes.

4. Add broth. Using a wooden spoon, scrape up and stir in brown bits from pan bottom. Bring broth to a boil. Stir egg mixture, then pour and stir into broth. Add tofu. Stir constantly until sauce thickens slightly, about 2 minutes. Add noodles. Pan will be very full. Gently toss until noodles are coated and hot, about 2 minutes. Sprinkle with onions and basil. Serve with lime wedges if you wish.

NUTRIENTS PER SERVING 17 G PROTEIN 19 G FAT
77 G CARBOHYDRATES 6 G FIBRE 4 MG IRON
232 MG CALCIUM 2065 MG SODIUM 535 CALORIES

Hearty Middle Eastern Supper Salad

PREPARATION TIME 10 MINUTES
BAKING TIME 2 MINUTES
MAKES 2 TO 3 SERVINGS

SALAD

1 pita, preferably whole wheat, split in half

Vegetable oil

1 tsp (5 mL) ground cumin

1 red pepper

1 cup (250 mL) marinated artichoke hearts, drained

3 ripe plum tomatoes or 2 cups (500 mL) small multi-coloured cherry tomatoes

¼ cup (50 mL) pitted kalamata olives (see sidebar, page 162)

¼ cup (50 mL) chopped fresh mint or basil

¾ cup (175 mL) crumbled feta

DRESSING

½ lemon

2 tbsp (30 mL) olive oil

1 garlic clove, minced

SWITCH IT UP

Try replacing artichokes or olives with slivers of oil-packed sun-dried tomatoes.

1. For salad, lightly brush both sides of pita with vegetable oil and sprinkle with ½ tsp (2 mL) cumin. Crisp in a toaster oven or preheated 450°F (230°C) oven, 2 to 4 minutes. Meanwhile, slice pepper into bite-sized pieces. If artichokes are large, slice into halves or quarters. Coarsely chop plum tomatoes. Place all in a large bowl. Slice olives in half. Add to bowl along with mint and feta. Tear pita into bite-sized pieces and add to bowl.

2. For dressing, squeeze about 1 tbsp (15 mL) lemon juice into a small bowl. Whisk in oil and garlic until evenly mixed. Drizzle over salad, tossing to coat. Taste and add more cumin or lemon juice, if needed.

GET AHEAD Prepare salad up to 2 hours before serving (it gets better as it stands).

NUTRIENTS PER SERVING 11 G PROTEIN 28 G FAT
26 G CARBOHYDRATES 7 G FIBRE 4 MG IRON
255 MG CALCIUM 955 MG SODIUM 379 CALORIES

Baked Tomato Risotto

PREPARATION TIME 10 MINUTES
COOKING TIME 9 MINUTES
BAKING TIME 30 MINUTES
MAKES 4 CUPS (1 L)

1 onion

2 tbsp (30 mL) butter

1 cup (250 mL) arborio rice

19 oz (540 mL) can stewed tomatoes

2 cups (500 mL) vegetable broth

1 tbsp (15 mL) dried oregano leaves

1 tsp (5 mL) each garlic powder, salt and granulated sugar

5 oz (140 g) log goat cheese, crumbled

5 oz (140 g) pkg baby spinach, about 8 cups (2 L)

SUBSTITUTION

Risotto is traditionally made with Italian-grown (arborio) rice, but this cheater version works with long-grain rice too.

1. Preheat oven to 400°F (200°C). Finely chop onion. Melt butter in a large, ovenproof pot over medium heat. Add onion and stir often until soft, about 5 minutes. Add rice, stirring to coat. Add tomatoes, stir often until liquid is almost absorbed, 4 to 5 minutes. Stir in broth, oregano, garlic powder, salt and sugar.

2. Bring mixture to a boil, stirring often. Tightly cover pot and bake in centre of preheated oven until all liquid is absorbed, 30 to 40 minutes. Remove from oven, then stir in cheese and half of the spinach. Spoon into bowls and top with remaining spinach.

NUTRIENTS PER 1 CUP (250 mL) 12 G PROTEIN 14 G FAT
54 G CARBOHYDRATES 3 G FIBRE 4 MG IRON
159 MG CALCIUM 1494 MG SODIUM 388 CALORIES

sides

Spicy green beans, gingery carrots, homemade sweet potato fries . . . it's the trimmings that show off a great main. These fast and flavourful dishes keep things delicious and interesting.

Warm Beets with Horseradish Vinaigrette

PREPARATION TIME 15 MINUTES
COOKING TIME 30 MINUTES
MAKES 4 SERVINGS

1 large bunch beets, 4 to 5 beets, unpeeled

2 tbsp (30 mL) each red wine vinegar and prepared horseradish

1 tbsp (15 mL) granulated sugar

1 tbsp (15 mL) olive oil

1 tsp (5 mL) salt

1 green onion, thinly sliced

CHATELAINE KITCHEN TIP

Don't throw the beets' leafy tops away — they're a tasty addition to a stir-fry or sautéed side dish. Chop and add for the last few minutes of cooking.

1. Trim green tops from beets. Wash beets well. Place in a large pot, cover with water and bring to a boil over high heat. Reduce heat to medium and simmer, partially covered, until fork-tender, 30 to 35 minutes. In a large bowl, stir vinegar with horseradish, sugar, oil and salt.

2. When beets are tender, drain and rinse under cold water until cool enough to handle. Trim root ends. Remove and discard skins. Slice beets into wedges, thick strips or rounds.

3. Add warm beets to vinaigrette and toss to evenly coat. Sprinkle with onion. Serve warm or at room temperature.

GET AHEAD Cover salad and refrigerate for up to 3 days.

NUTRIENTS PER SERVING 1 G PROTEIN 2 G FAT
5 G CARBOHYDRATES 1 G FIBRE 0 MG IRON
9 MG CALCIUM 314 MG SODIUM 37 CALORIES

Asparagus with Pine-Nut Butter

PREPARATION TIME 5 MINUTES
COOKING TIME 4 MINUTES
MAKES 4 SERVINGS

ASPARAGUS TRICK

Hold each spear by its point and cut ends. Place pressure on the thick cut end so the spear snaps. It will naturally break off right where the asparagus becomes tough.

1 bunch asparagus
4 tsp (20 mL) butter
¼ cup (50 mL) pine nuts
Pinches of salt and freshly ground black pepper

1. Partially fill a large frying pan with water and bring to a boil over high heat. Meanwhile, snap tough ends from asparagus and discard. Boil asparagus until tender-crisp, about 2 minutes. Drain. Pat dry with a kitchen towel and place on a platter.

2. Wipe pan dry and place over medium heat. Add butter. When melted, add pine nuts and stir continuously until they begin to turn golden, about 2 minutes. Pour butter mixture over asparagus. Taste and add pinches of salt and pepper. Serve immediately.

NUTRIENTS PER SERVING 3 G PROTEIN 10 G FAT
4 G CARBOHYDRATES 2 G FIBRE 1 MG IRON
21 MG CALCIUM 38 MG SODIUM 108 CALORIES

Baby Zucchini with Blue Cheese

PREPARATION TIME 5 MINUTES
ROASTING TIME 18 MINUTES
MAKES 2 SERVINGS

SERVING SUGGESTION

This zucchini is a great sidekick for grilled steak or roasted chicken.

If you can't find baby zucchini, the regular ones will do — just give them a few more minutes of roasting time.

6 baby zucchini

½ cup (125 mL) crumbled stilton or roquefort cheese, about 2 oz (60 g)

1. Preheat oven to 450°F (230°C). Slice zucchini in half lengthwise and lightly rub with oil. Place cut-side down on a foil-lined baking sheet. Roast zucchini, uncovered, in centre of preheated oven until cut sides are lightly golden, 15 to 20 minutes.

2. Remove from oven and turn cut-side up. Sprinkle cheese overtop. Return to oven and continue roasting just until cheese starts to melt, 3 to 5 minutes.

NUTRIENTS PER SERVING 5 G PROTEIN 6 G FAT
5 G CARBOHYDRATES 2 G FIBRE 1 MG IRON
71 MG CALCIUM 447 MG SODIUM 89 CALORIES

Colourful Squash Ratatouille

PREPARATION TIME 30 MINUTES
ROASTING TIME 35 MINUTES
MAKES 12 CUPS (3 L)

2 zucchini

1 large eggplant

1 each red, green and yellow pepper

2 to 3 leeks

1 small butternut squash

1 pint cherry or grape tomatoes

¼ cup (50 mL) plus 3 tbsp (45 mL) olive oil

2 tsp (10 mL) dried basil leaves

1 tsp (5 mL) salt

1 tsp (5 mL) each dried thyme and rosemary leaves, crumbled

1 lemon

2 garlic cloves

1 tsp (5 mL) granulated sugar

EGGPLANT TIP

It's usually best to leave the skins on, otherwise the eggplants can lose their shape and turn to mush..

1. Arrange oven racks in top and bottom thirds of oven. Preheat oven to 400°F (200°C). Slice zucchini in half lengthwise, then into large chunks. Chop eggplant into similar-sized chunks. Coarsely chop peppers. Slice off and discard root ends and dark green tops of leeks. Slice leeks in half lengthwise. Fan out under cold running water to remove grit. Thinly slice. Peel squash (see sidebar, page 97). Cut in half, scoop out and discard pulp and seeds, then cut into pieces same size as zucchini. Place vegetables and tomatoes in a very large bowl. Add ¼ cup (50 mL) oil, basil, salt, thyme and rosemary. Toss to coat. Spread on 2 large baking sheets.

2. Roast in top and bottom thirds of preheated oven until squash is tender but not mushy, 35 to 45 minutes. Rotate baking sheets and stir vegetables halfway through cooking time. For dressing, squeeze juice from lemon into a small bowl. Mince garlic and add to bowl. Stir in sugar. Whisk in remaining 3 tbsp (45 mL) oil. Turn cooked vegetables into a large bowl. Drizzle with half of dressing, tossing to coat. Taste and add more dressing if you wish. Delicious served warm or at room temperature.

GET AHEAD Cover ratatouille and refrigerate for up to 2 days.

NUTRIENTS PER 1 CUP (250 mL) 2 G PROTEIN 7 G FAT
14 G CARBOHYDRATES 3 G FIBRE 1 MG IRON
40 MG CALCIUM 198 MG SODIUM 112 CALORIES

Spicy Szechuan Eggplant

PREPARATION TIME 7 MINUTES
COOKING TIME 8 MINUTES
MAKES 6 TO 8 SERVINGS

SERVING SUGGESTION

Serve in bowls over rice, toss with pasta or serve with chicken.

EGGPLANTS 101

Often thought of as a vegetable, eggplant is actually a relative of the tomato and a member of the fruit family. There are several varieties, including the long, skinny and mild Japanese eggplant; Italian eggplants, which are small and pear-shaped; and the larger variety that's most commonly available at your local market. If you find the flavour of eggplant to be too bitter, before preparing recipe, slice eggplant into long pieces, then sprinkle with salt. Let stand until the moisture comes to the surface, about 15 minutes. Rinse salt and moisture off. Pat eggplant dry with a kitchen towel. This removes some of the bitter juices and gives the eggplant a milder flavour.

2 medium eggplants, about 2 lb (1 kg) total

1 tbsp (15 mL) vegetable oil

5 garlic cloves, minced, or 2 tsp (10 mL) bottled chopped garlic

2 tsp (10 mL) minced fresh ginger or 1 tbsp (15 mL) bottled minced ginger

½ cup (125 mL) chicken or vegetable broth

2 tbsp (30 mL) each soy sauce and rice vinegar

1 tbsp (15 mL) granulated sugar

1 tsp (5 mL) each dark sesame oil and hot chili-garlic sauce

4 green onions, thinly sliced

1 to 2 tomatoes, coarsely chopped

Pinch of salt (optional)

Sesame seeds (optional)

1. Peel eggplants and cut into 1-inch (2.5 cm) pieces. Heat oil in a large non-stick frying pan or wok set over medium-high heat. Stir-fry eggplants until slightly darkened, 2 to 3 minutes. Reduce heat to medium. Add garlic and ginger and stir-fry for 1 minute.

2. Add broth, soy sauce, vinegar, sugar, sesame oil and chili-garlic sauce and bring to a boil. Cook, uncovered and stirring often, until eggplants are very tender and sauce has thickened, about 5 minutes. Stir in onions and tomatoes. Taste and add salt if needed. Sprinkle with sesame seeds if you wish.

NUTRIENTS PER SERVING 2 G PROTEIN 3 G FAT
10 G CARBOHYDRATES 3 G FIBRE 1 MG IRON
16 MG CALCIUM 321 MG SODIUM 65 CALORIES

Grilled Sweet Peppers with Basil Drizzle

PREPARATION TIME 15 MINUTES
GRILLING TIME 6 MINUTES
MAKES 6 TO 8 SERVINGS

TIMING TIP

This dish can be served at room temperature, so don't hesitate to make it ahead of time. Simply prepare the peppers, then loosely cover and leave at room temperature for up to 4 hours. This is a great way to ease time pressures

TEST KITCHEN TIP

Whip up the basil drizzle in this recipe, then save it for serving over any of your favourite vegetables. It works well over barbecued zucchini, stirred into mashed potatoes or tossed with roasted squash.

1 garlic clove, minced
½ lemon
½ tsp (2 mL) salt
¼ tsp (1 mL) freshly ground black pepper
¼ cup (50 mL) plus 1 tbsp (15 mL) olive oil
1 cup (250 mL) coarsely chopped fresh basil
6 colourful peppers
½ cup (125 mL) crumbled feta

1. Place garlic in a blender. Squeeze in 1 tbsp (15 mL) juice from lemon. Add salt, pepper and ¼ cup (50 mL) oil. Blend. Add basil. Purée until smooth.

2. Oil grill and heat barbecue to medium-high. Halve peppers, then core and seed. Slice into quarters and place in a large bowl. Drizzle with remaining 1 tbsp (15 mL) oil, tossing to coat. Place on grill. Depending on size of grill, you may need to barbecue in 2 batches. Barbecue, lid closed, until peppers are lightly charred, turning often, 6 to 8 minutes. Remove peppers to bowl when done.

3. Evenly drizzle basil sauce overtop peppers, then toss. Place on a platter and scatter feta overtop.

GET AHEAD Cover basil drizzle and refrigerate for up to 2 days. Bring to room temperature before using. For peppers, see sidebar.

NUTRIENTS PER SERVING 2 G PROTEIN 10 G FAT
7 G CARBOHYDRATES 1 G FIBRE 1 MG IRON
56 MG CALCIUM 232 MG SODIUM 122 CALORIES

Husk-On Barbecued Corn with Herbed Butter

PREPARATION TIME 10 MINUTES
GRILLING TIME 8 MINUTES
MAKES 8 COBS

½ **bunch cilantro**

1 **green onion**

⅓ **cup (75 mL) cold butter**

8 **cobs of corn with husks**

BRING IT INSIDE

If you prefer, bring a large pot of salted water to a boil. Remove and discard husk and silk from cobs. Place in large pot. If all cobs won't fit, break some in half. Boil, partially covered, until you can smell the corn and the kernels feel tender, 6 to 8 minutes. Drain well and serve.

1. Remove cilantro leaves from stems and coarsely chop. Roughly chop onion. Place both in a food processor fitted with a metal blade. Whirl until finely chopped. Cut butter into cubes, then add to cilantro mixture. Whirl until cilantro and onion are evenly distributed throughout butter. Remove from food processor. Form butter into 2 small logs.

2. To grill corn, peel back husks without entirely removing from cobs. Peel off and discard silk. Recover corn with husks and tie with butcher's string or a piece of husk. Soak cobs in water at least 5 minutes before grilling. Oil grill, then heat barbecue to medium-high. Place cobs on grill, turning frequently until charred, at least 8 minutes. Watch closely for flare-ups. When cool enough to handle, remove and peel back husk. Serve with herbed butter.

GET AHEAD Wrap butter in plastic wrap or place in an airtight container and refrigerate for up to 5 days, or freeze for up to 1 month.

NUTRIENTS PER COB WITH 2 TSP (10 mL) BUTTER
4 G PROTEIN 5 G FAT 30 G CARBOHYDRATES 5 G FIBRE
1 MG IRON 7 MG CALCIUM 56 MG SODIUM 161 CALORIES

Indian-Spiced Cauliflower

PREPARATION TIME 5 MINUTES
MICROWAVING TIME 6 MINUTES
COOKING TIME 4 MINUTES
MAKES 4 TO 6 SERVINGS

1 small head cauliflower

⅓ cup (75 mL) store-bought fine dry bread crumbs

1 tsp (5 mL) curry powder

½ tsp (2 mL) each ground cumin, garlic powder and ground ginger

¼ tsp (1 mL) salt

3 tbsp (45 mL) butter

2 tbsp (30 mL) chopped fresh cilantro or parsley (optional)

CHATELAINE KITCHEN TIP

To mellow curry powder's harsh flavour, cook in oil or butter, stirring constantly, over medium heat for at least 1 minute.

1. Cut out and discard core from cauliflower. Place whole cauliflower on a plate. Microwave on medium until tender, 6 to 8 minutes. Meanwhile, place bread crumbs in a small bowl. Stir in curry powder, cumin, garlic powder, ginger and salt. Cut cooked cauliflower into small florets.

2. Melt butter in a large frying pan set over medium heat. When bubbly, stir in crumb mixture until evenly moist, about 30 seconds. Add cauliflower. Stir often, spooning crumbs over cauliflower, until cauliflower is well coated and crumbs are golden, 3 minutes. Sprinkle with cilantro if you wish.

NUTRIENTS PER SERVING 2 G PROTEIN 7 G FAT
8 G CARBOHYDRATES 2 G FIBRE 1 MG IRON
30 MG CALCIUM 216 MG SODIUM 93 CALORIES

Country Vegetable Bake

PREPARATION TIME 25 MINUTES
COOKING TIME 3 MINUTES
BAKING TIME 56 MINUTES
STANDING TIME 10 MINUTES
MAKES 8 TO 10 SERVINGS

4 slices white bread

1 cup (250 mL) freshly grated parmesan or asiago cheese

¼ cup (50 mL) snipped fresh chives

2 tbsp (30 mL) butter, at room temperature

½ tsp (2 mL) each salt and freshly ground black pepper, plus generous pinches of both

2 leeks

2 garlic cloves, minced

1 head cauliflower

1 each green and yellow pepper

1 zucchini

300 g pkg frozen chopped spinach, thawed

¼ cup (50 mL) all-purpose flour

1 tsp (5 mL) dried sage leaves, crumbled

¼ tsp (1 mL) ground nutmeg

3 tbsp (45 mL) Dijon mustard

1 ½ cups (375 mL) whipping cream

1. Preheat oven to 400°F (200°C). For topping, trim crusts from bread. Place slices on a baking sheet. Toast in centre of preheated oven until lightly golden, 3 to 4 minutes per side. Tear toasted bread into large pieces and place in a food processor. Add ½ cup (125 mL) cheese, chives, 1 tbsp (15 mL) butter, and generous pinches of salt and pepper. Pulse until coarse crumbs form.

2. Reduce oven temperature to 375°F (190°C). Slice off and discard root ends and dark green tops of leeks. Cut leeks in half lengthwise. Fan out under cold running water to remove grit. Thinly slice. Melt remaining 1 tbsp (15 mL) butter in a large frying pan over medium heat. Add leeks and garlic. Stir often until leeks begin to soften, 3 to 5 minutes. Transfer to a large bowl.

3. Meanwhile, cut cauliflower into small bite-sized florets, and peppers into similar-sized pieces. Slice zucchini in half lengthwise, then slice into semicircles.

SERVING SUGGESTION
Pair with a roast chicken
or beef dinner.

Add to leeks. Squeeze excess water from spinach. Add spinach to vegetables. Sprinkle with remaining ½ cup (125 mL) cheese, flour, sage, ½ tsp (2 mL) each salt and pepper, and nutmeg. Toss to evenly mix.

4. Turn into a lightly buttered 9- × 13-inch (3 L) baking dish and evenly spread out. Gently press down to lightly pack. Using a fork, beat Dijon into cream until blended. Pour over vegetables. Sprinkle bread crumbs overtop. Cover pan tightly with foil.

5. Bake in centre of preheated oven for 35 to 40 minutes. Uncover and continue to bake until vegetables are fork-tender and topping is golden, 15 to 20 more minutes. Let stand 10 to 15 minutes before serving.

GET AHEAD Prepare casserole, but don't sprinkle with bread crumb mixture. Store topping in resealable plastic bag. Cover casserole and refrigerate both overnight. When ready to bake, remove casserole from refrigerator and leave at room temperature for 1 hour. Preheat oven to 375°F (190°C). Evenly sprinkle bread crumb mixture overtop vegetables. Cover pan tightly with foil and bake for 45 to 50 minutes, then remove foil. Continue baking until vegetables are fork-tender and topping is golden, 15 to 20 more minutes.

NUTRIENTS PER SERVING 9 G PROTEIN 19 G FAT
16 G CARBOHYDRATES 4 G FIBRE 2 MG IRON
231 MG CALCIUM 472 MG SODIUM 258 CALORIES

Jewelled Rice

PREPARATION TIME 15 MINUTES
COOKING TIME 20 MINUTES
MAKES 7 CUPS (1.75 L) FOR 8 TO
12 SERVINGS

LEFTOVERS?

Refrigerate leftover rice in a sealed plastic bag for up to 2 days. Just before reheating, break up any clumps with your hands while the rice is still in the bag. Turn into a microwavable dish. Microwave on medium-high, stirring halfway through cooking time, until warm, 8 to 10 minutes.

3 cups (750 mL) water or chicken broth

1 tsp (5 mL) salt

1 ½ cups (375 mL) rice, preferably basmati

1 large orange

½ cup (125 mL) each dried apricots and dried cranberries

½ tsp (2 mL) saffron threads

¾ cup (175 mL) pistachios in shells

¾ cup (175 mL) finely chopped parsley or fresh cilantro

1. In a large pot, bring water and salt to a boil over high heat. If using chicken broth, omit salt. Add rice to boiling water. Stir, then cover and reduce heat to medium-low. Cook for 10 minutes.

2. Meanwhile, finely grate peel from orange. Chop apricots. After rice has cooked 10 minutes, stir in peel, apricots, cranberries and saffron threads. Cover and continue to cook until water is completely absorbed, 10 to 15 more minutes. Meanwhile, shell nuts and coarsely chop. Taste rice and add more salt if needed. Stir in pistachios and parsley.

NUTRIENTS PER SERVING 3 G PROTEIN 2 G FAT
28 G CARBOHYDRATES 2 G FIBRE 1 MG IRON
24 MG CALCIUM 195 MG SODIUM 141 CALORIES

Orzo Salad with Vibrant Greens

PREPARATION TIME 5 MINUTES
COOKING TIME 7 MINUTES
MAKES 12 CUPS (3 L)

450 g pkg uncooked orzo, about 3 cups (750 mL)

¼ cup (50 mL) white wine vinegar

2 tbsp (30 mL) regular or grainy Dijon mustard

1 tbsp (15 mL) honey

1 tsp (5 mL) salt

⅓ cup (75 mL) olive oil

2 cups (500 mL) frozen peas

2 Belgian endives

½ cup (125 mL) chopped fresh dill

4 green onions

6 oz (170 g) pkg baby spinach

1 cup (250 mL) freshly grated parmesan cheese (optional)

SERVING SUGGESTIONS

Terrific served alongside roast chicken or packed up for a fresh take on a picnic salad.

1. Bring a large pot of salted water to a boil over high heat. Add orzo. Stir to separate. Boil, uncovered and stirring occasionally, until al dente, about 7 minutes. Meanwhile, in a small bowl, whisk vinegar with mustard, honey and salt. Slowly whisk in oil. When orzo is cooked, drain well and place in a large bowl. Add dressing and stir to coat. Refrigerate, stirring occasionally, until cool.

2. Meanwhile, cook peas in boiling water for 3 minutes. Drain, then rinse under cold water to cool. Cut out and discard endive cores. Thickly slice crosswise. Chop dill and slice onions. When orzo is cool, stir in peas, onions, endive, dill and spinach. Sprinkle with parmesan if you wish. Taste and add more dill, salt and a drizzle of vinegar if needed.

GET AHEAD Prepare salad according to recipe but don't add the spinach or cheese (if using). Cover and refrigerate for up to 2 days. Just before serving, stir in spinach and cheese. Taste and add more dill, salt and vinegar if needed.

NUTRIENTS PER CUP (250 mL) 4 G PROTEIN 4 G FAT
19 G CARBOHYDRATES 2 G FIBRE 1 MG IRON
18 MG CALCIUM 180 MG SODIUM 121 CALORIES

Coconut Milk–Infused Rice

PREPARATION TIME 5 MINUTES
COOKING TIME 20 MINUTES
MAKES 4 SERVINGS

400 mL can unsweetened coconut milk

1 cup (250 mL) basmati rice

1 tsp (5 mL) ground cardamom

1 large cinnamon stick, broken in half

1 bay leaf

½ tsp (2 mL) salt

2 green onions, thinly sliced

BASMATI

This long-grained rice is aged, which gives it a fragrant nutty flavour.

Simmering it in coconut milk with a hint of cinnamon, cardamom and a bay leaf turns rice into a rich, creamy base for an Indian or Thai vegetable curry.

1. Pour coconut milk into a large measuring cup and add enough water to make 2 cups (500 mL). Pour into a large saucepan and set over high heat. Add rice, cardamom, cinnamon stick, bay leaf and salt. Cover and bring to a boil. Stir and reduce heat to low. Simmer, covered, until all water is absorbed, about 20 minutes.

2. When rice is cooked, remove and discard cinnamon stick and bay leaf. Stir in onions. Turn onto a platter or individual plates.

NUTRIENTS PER SERVING 6 G PROTEIN 21 G FAT
40 G CARBOHYDRATES 1 G FIBRE 4 MG IRON
33 MG CALCIUM 301 MG SODIUM 359 CALORIES

Chunky Sweet Potato Fries with Herbed Yogourt Dip

PREPARATION TIME 10 MINUTES
ROASTING TIME 25 MINUTES
MAKES 4 SERVINGS

3 sweet potatoes

1 tbsp (15 mL) olive oil

1 tbsp (15 mL) brown sugar

1 tsp (5 mL) ground cumin

½ tsp (2 mL) garlic salt

¼ tsp (1 mL) cayenne pepper (optional)

½ cup (125 mL) Balkan-style plain yogourt (5.9% MF)

1 tsp (5 mL) dried rosemary leaves, crumbled, or dill weed

1 tsp (5 mL) finely grated lemon, orange or lime peel

SERVING SUGGESTION

Pair these healthy fries with nutritious mains such as Fiery Asian Burgers (page 143) or BBQ Chicken with Piri Piri Sauce (page 120).

1. Preheat oven to 450°F (230°C). Lightly oil a large rimmed baking sheet and place in oven to heat. Peel potatoes. Slice in half lengthwise, then in half crosswise. Place each piece cut-side down, then slice lengthwise into thin wedges. In a large bowl, toss potatoes with olive oil. Sprinkle with sugar, cumin, garlic salt and cayenne (if using). Stir to coat. Tumble onto hot baking sheet.

2. Roast potatoes in preheated oven, turning every 10 minutes, until tender and lightly browned, about 25 minutes. Meanwhile, in a small bowl, stir yogourt with rosemary and lemon peel. Serve alongside warm roasted potatoes for dunking, or drizzle over potatoes.

NUTRIENTS PER SERVING WITH 2 TBSP (30 mL) DIP
4 G PROTEIN 6 G FAT 30 G CARBOHYDRATES 4 G FIBRE
1 MG IRON 105 MG CALCIUM 208 MG SODIUM 183 CALORIES

Shortcut Scalloped Potatoes

PREPARATION TIME 20 MINUTES
COOKING TIME 10 MINUTES
BAKING TIME 30 MINUTES
STANDING TIME 15 MINUTES
MAKES 10 TO 12 SERVINGS

VARIATIONS

• Use crumbled stilton or gorgonzola, or freshly grated parmesan or asiago cheese, in place of gruyère.

• Try red-skinned potatoes (unpeeled, of course) or a mix of white and sweet potatoes.

• Stir crumbled cooked pancetta into potatoes just before turning into baking dish.

CHATELAINE KITCHEN TIP

If you usually keep peeled potatoes in water so they don't brown too quickly, don't do it for this recipe. The water will remove some of the starch and the water will absorb into the potatoes, preventing the creamy sauce from thickening.

1 tbsp (15 mL) butter

3 lb (1.5 kg) potatoes, such as russet or Yukon gold, about 6 medium

1 ½ cups (375 mL) whipping cream

10 oz (284 mL) can undiluted chicken broth

1 garlic clove, minced

1 bay leaf

½ tsp (2 mL) each ground nutmeg and salt

1 small onion, preferably red

1 tbsp (15 mL) fresh thyme leaves

1 ½ cups (375 mL) grated gruyère cheese, about 3 oz (90 g)

1. Preheat oven to 375°F (190°C). Rub butter over bottom and sides of a 9- × 13-inch (3 L) baking dish or broiler pan. Peel potatoes. Using a very sharp knife, and working quickly so potatoes don't brown too much, thinly slice potatoes into pieces no thicker than ½ inch (1 cm). Or for easier slicing, use a mandoline (see sidebar, page 59) or food processor to thinly slice potatoes.

2. Pour whipping cream and chicken broth into a large pot. Stir in garlic, bay leaf, nutmeg and salt, then add potatoes, separating as you add. Cover and bring to a boil over medium-high heat. Once at a boil, uncover and simmer gently, stirring occasionally, until potatoes are almost fork-tender, 10 to 13 minutes. Meanwhile, thinly slice onion into rings. Discard bay leaf from potato mixture.

3. Turn potatoes and cream mixture into baking dish. Scatter with onion and thyme, then sprinkle cheese overtop. Cover tightly with foil.

4. Bake in centre of preheated oven for 15 minutes. Uncover and continue to bake until bubbly and cheese is golden, about 15 minutes. Let stand 15 minutes before serving.

NUTRIENTS PER SERVING 7 G PROTEIN 16 G FAT 19 G CARBOHYDRATES 1 G FIBRE 1 MG IRON 179 MG CALCIUM 353 MG SODIUM 244 CALORIES

Greek Herb-Roasted Potatoes

PREPARATION TIME 15 MINUTES
ROASTING TIME 1 HOUR,
30 MINUTES
MAKES 6 SERVINGS

CHATELAINE KITCHEN TIP

You can roast this side dish at the same time as the main course. Position oven racks in top and bottom thirds of oven. Roast potatoes on bottom rack, below the main course.

1 large lemon

1 tbsp (15 mL) olive oil

1 tsp (5 mL) each dried oregano leaves and salt

6 medium potatoes, preferably Yukon gold

2 bay leaves (optional)

1. Preheat oven to 350°F (180°C). Squeeze 3 tbsp (45 mL) juice from lemon into a 9- × 13-inch (3 L) baking dish. Whisk ¼ cup (50 mL) water with oil, oregano and salt. Peel potatoes, then cut into large chunks. Place in dish, toss to coat and tuck in bay leaves (if using).

2. Roast, uncovered, in centre of preheated oven, stirring occasionally, until potatoes are tender, about 1 ½ hours. If water evaporates before potatoes are done, pour in about 3 tbsp (45 mL) water. Remove bay leaves before serving. Great with Stuffed Greek Chicken (page 124).

NUTRIENTS PER SERVING 4 G PROTEIN 3 G FAT
32 G CARBOHYDRATES 3 G FIBRE 1 MG IRON
15 MG CALCIUM 395 MG SODIUM 161 CALORIES

Sautéed Spinach with Pancetta and Shallots

PREPARATION TIME 5 MINUTES
COOKING TIME 7 MINUTES
MAKES 3 TO 4 SERVINGS

6 thick slices pancetta, cut into strips

1 tbsp (15 mL) olive oil or butter

1 shallot, thinly sliced, or 2 garlic cloves, minced

8 oz (227 g) pkg spinach or 2 large bunches

½ lemon

SHALLOTS

Shallots are a member of the onion family, so it's no surprise that they're used in cooking in a similar fashion. The distinct differences between a shallot and a regular cooking onion (or "dry onion") are the shallot's almost pinkish-brown papery skin that surrounds its garlic clove-shaped bulbs, and its much milder, delicate flavour.

1. Place pancetta in a large frying pan and set over medium-high heat. Cook, stirring occasionally, until crisp, about 3 minutes. Add oil, then shallot. Stir until shallot has softened, 1 to 2 minutes. Add spinach and stir until wilted, about 3 minutes. Pan will be very full, so you may need to add spinach gradually. Squeeze 1 tbsp (15 mL) juice from lemon overtop. Stir to mix. Serve immediately.

NUTRIENTS PER SERVING 5 G PROTEIN 19 G FAT
3 G CARBOHYDRATES 1 G FIBRE 2 MG IRON
76 MG CALCIUM 251 MG SODIUM 198 CALORIES

Lacy Double Potato Latkes

PREPARATION TIME 15 MINUTES
COOKING TIME 6 MINUTES
PER BATCH
MAKES 16 TO 18 LATKES

3 eggs

¼ cup (50 mL) all-purpose flour

2 tsp (10 mL) baking powder

¼ cup (50 mL) chopped fresh parsley (optional)

1 tsp (5 mL) each celery salt and salt

¼ tsp (1 mL) freshly ground black pepper

3 medium potatoes, preferably Yukon gold, peeled

1 large sweet potato, peeled

1 small onion

2 cups (500 mL) vegetable oil

INDULGE

Make these potato delights even better by serving with sour cream or apple sauce.

1. In a large bowl, whisk eggs with flour, baking powder, parsley (if using), celery salt, salt and pepper. Using the large holes on a box grater or food processor, grate potatoes and sweet potato. Squeeze as much liquid as you can from potatoes. Place on a kitchen towel–lined baking sheet. Cover with another towel and press down to absorb any excess liquid. Thinly slice onion. Add onion and potatoes to egg mixture. Stir to evenly mix.

2. Pour enough oil into a large deep frying pan (do not use non-stick) to come ½ inch (1 cm) up the side and set over medium-high heat. When pan is hot, pack potato mixture into ¼ cup (50 mL) dry measure. Carefully turn into pan and flatten slightly using a fork or spatula. Repeat, fitting 2 more latkes in pan. Do not crowd pan. Fry until golden, 3 to 4 minutes per side. Remove to a paper towel–lined plate. Repeat with remaining mixture.

NUTRIENTS PER LATKE 2 G PROTEIN 7 G FAT
11 G CARBOHYDRATES 1 G FIBRE 1 MG IRON
29 MG CALCIUM 244 MG SODIUM 113 CALORIES

Brussels Sprouts in Parmesan Cream

PREPARATION TIME 10 MINUTES
COOKING TIME 16 MINUTES
MAKES 8 SERVINGS

¼ cup (50 mL) butter

¼ cup (50 mL) all-purpose flour

10 oz (284 mL) can undiluted chicken broth

1 cup (250 mL) whipping cream

1 tsp (5 mL) dried tarragon or dried thyme leaves

½ tsp (2 mL) salt

2 lb (1 kg) brussels sprouts

½ cup (125 mL) freshly grated parmesan cheese

2 slices prosciutto, cut in thin strips (optional)

½ cup (125 mL) toasted pine nuts, chopped walnuts or
    slivered almonds (optional)

BRUSSELS SPROUTS TRICK

To clean well, remove stems. Add a generous squeeze of lemon juice or splash of white vinegar to water, to draw out anything undesirable, such as dirt or bugs, that may be lingering. Soak brussels sprouts in water for 15 minutes. Then rinse and drain.

1. Melt butter in a large saucepan over medium heat. Add flour and stir constantly until bubbly, about 2 minutes. Whisking constantly, gradually add broth, cream, tarragon and salt. Reduce heat and simmer, whisking often, until sauce has thickened enough to coat the back of a spoon, 8 to 10 minutes.

2. Meanwhile, bring a large pot of water to a boil over high heat. Remove tough outer leaves and trim stems from sprouts. Cut sprouts in half. Cook in boiling water until almost fork-tender, 3 to 5 minutes. Drain well. Stir sprouts into cream sauce in pan. Cook over medium heat, stirring often, until hot, about 3 minutes. Stir in parmesan. Turn sprouts into a serving bowl and scatter with prosciutto and pine nuts if you wish. Taste and add more salt if needed.

NUTRIENTS PER SERVING 7 G PROTEIN 19 G FAT
14 G CARBOHYDRATES 4 G FIBRE 2 MG IRON
133 MG CALCIUM 594 MG SODIUM 236 CALORIES

Chili-Garlic Beans

PREPARATION TIME 10 MINUTES
COOKING TIME 7 MINUTES
MAKES 4 TO 6 SERVINGS

1 lb (500 g) green beans
1 tbsp (15 mL) vegetable oil
2 tsp (10 mL) bottled minced ginger or freshly grated ginger
2 tbsp (30 mL) oyster sauce
1 to 2 tsp (5 to 10 mL) hot chili-garlic sauce
Generous pinch of salt (optional)

MAKE MORE

If you're cooking for a crowd, this recipe is easily doubled, tripled or even quadrupled.

1. Trim ends from beans. Heat oil in a large frying pan or wok over medium-high heat. Add beans. Stir-fry for 2 minutes. Carefully pour in ⅓ cup (75 mL) water (it may splatter). Stir often until beans are tender-crisp and most of water has evaporated, 4 to 5 minutes.

2. Stir in ginger, oyster sauce and 1 tsp (5 mL) chili-garlic sauce. Stir to evenly coat, about 1 minute. Add salt and remaining chili-garlic sauce if you wish. Serve immediately.

NUTRIENTS PER SERVING 1 G PROTEIN 3 G FAT
6 G CARBOHYDRATES 2 G FIBRE 1 MG IRON
32 MG CALCIUM 152 MG SODIUM 47 CALORIES

Lemony Snow Peas and Mixed Mushrooms

PREPARATION TIME 30 MINUTES
COOKING TIME 6 MINUTES
MAKES 8 TO 10 SERVINGS

2 lb (1 kg) snow peas or sugar snap peas
1 lb (500 g) mixed mushrooms, such as button, cremini and shiitake
2 tbsp (30 mL) butter
1 garlic clove, minced
1 tsp (5 mL) salt
1 lemon
Pinch of freshly ground black pepper

MUSHROOMS 101

Clean mushrooms with a damp kitchen towel or mushroom brush. Don't rinse under water or they may absorb the water and some of the dirt you are attempting to rinse, and won't brown in the pan.

1. Pull tough strings from peas and cut off stems. Slice mushrooms. If using shiitake, discard stems. Thinly slice caps.

2. Melt butter in a large wide frying pan or saucepan over medium-high heat. When bubbly, add garlic and mushrooms. Sprinkle with salt. Stir often until mushrooms begin to soften and turn brown around edges, 4 to 6 minutes.

3. Meanwhile, finely grate 1 tbsp (15 mL) peel and squeeze 2 tbsp (30 mL) juice from lemon. When mushrooms are brown, stir in peas, lemon peel, lemon juice and pepper. Stir often until snow peas are tender-crisp, 2 to 3 minutes.

NUTRIENTS PER SERVING 4 G PROTEIN 3 G FAT
8 G CARBOHYDRATES 3 G FIBRE 2 MG IRON
41 MG CALCIUM 261 MG SODIUM 66 CALORIES

Rapini Sauté

PREPARATION TIME 5 MINUTES
COOKING TIME 9 MINUTES
MAKES 4 SERVINGS

GOOD FOR YOU

Rapini is a rich source of iron, calcium, potassium, magnesium and vitamins K, C and E, as well as the B vitamins. The darker the colour, the more phytonutrients the rapini contains.

1 bunch rapini

3 large sun-dried tomatoes (packed in oil) plus 1 tbsp (15 mL) marinating oil from sun-dried tomatoes

1 tbsp (15 mL) olive oil

2 garlic cloves, minced

¼ tsp (1 mL) hot chili flakes

Pinch of salt

⅓ cup (75 mL) crumbled feta cheese

1. Trim about 2 inches (5 cm) from rapini stems and discard. Place rapini in a large frying pan along with 1 cup (250 mL) water. Cover and bring to a boil over medium-high heat, turning rapini occasionally. Reduce heat. Simmer, covered, for 8 minutes. Drain well, gently pressing rapini to remove any extra moisture. Remove rapini to a platter. Meanwhile, chop sun-dried tomatoes and set aside marinating oil.

2. Wipe pan dry. Heat olive and marinating oils in pan over medium heat. Stir in garlic and chili flakes. Sauté until garlic is tender and fragrant, about 1 minute. Return rapini to pan and toss with oil mixture and salt. Remove to same platter, then sprinkle with feta and sun-dried tomatoes.

NUTRIENTS PER SERVING 6 G PROTEIN 11 G FAT
6 G CARBOHYDRATES 3 G FIBRE 3 MG IRON
180 MG CALCIUM 190 MG SODIUM 131 CALORIES

Roasted Tomato–Pepper Salsa

PREPARATION TIME 15 MINUTES
ROASTING TIME 15 MINUTES
MAKES 2 CUPS (500 mL)

3 plum tomatoes

1 sweet pepper, preferably yellow, orange or green

2 jalapeño peppers

2 large garlic cloves, unpeeled

2 tbsp (30 mL) olive oil

Generous pinches of salt and freshly ground black pepper

1 lime

¼ cup (50 mL) chopped fresh cilantro, basil or parsley

1. Preheat oven to 400°F (200°C). Slice tomatoes in half and place on a large baking sheet. Core and seed all peppers, then cut sweet pepper into chunks. Leave jalapeños whole. Add peppers to baking sheet along with garlic. Drizzle with 1 tbsp (15 mL) oil, then sprinkle with salt and pepper. Roast in centre of preheated oven until tomatoes and peppers are tender and garlic is soft, about 15 minutes. Stir halfway through roasting time.

2. Meanwhile, squeeze 1 tsp (5 mL) juice from lime into a medium bowl. Stir in remaining 1 tbsp (15 mL) oil along with cilantro. When vegetables are roasted, coarsely chop tomatoes and sweet pepper and mince jalapeños. Remove and discard skins from garlic and finely chop. Stir all into lime mixture, then taste and add salt and pepper if needed.

GET AHEAD Cover salsa and refrigerate for up to 3 days.

NUTRIENTS PER ¼ CUP (50 mL) 1 G PROTEIN 4 G FAT
2 G CARBOHYDRATES 1 G FIBRE 0 MG IRON
6 MG CALCIUM 2 MG SODIUM 40 CALORIES

COOKING TIP

This salsa also works well as a sauce for cooked meats or fish, or in place of regular tomato sauce on pizza.

Multi-Coloured Carrots with Ginger Brown Butter

Partially fill a large pot with water. Bring to a boil over high heat. Meanwhile, peel a couple of big bunches of carrots and thoroughly clean the green tops, leaving them intact. The carrots should all be the same thickness, so you may need to slice some in half lengthwise. When water is boiling, add carrots, cover, then reduce heat to medium. Boil gently until fork-tender, 10 to 15 minutes. Drain well.

Meanwhile, melt ¼ cup (50 mL) butter in a small pan over medium heat. Cook, stirring continuously, until butter is amber coloured, 2 to 4 minutes. Immediately pour into a small bowl. Stir in 2 tsp (10 mL) freshly grated ginger. Transfer carrots to individual plates or a platter. Drizzle with ginger brown butter.

MAKES 3 TO 4 SERVINGS

MULTI-COLOURED CARROTS

You don't need to peel heirloom varieties, especially not the purple ones — the purple pigment in the skin is high in antioxidants. Eat these colourful root vegetables raw or prepare them as you would regular carrots.

desserts

Time to indulge your sweet tooth . . . but how to choose? The best chocolate chip cookies, sweet strawberry shortcake or rich, smooth cheesecake — break the rules and eat dessert first.

Pastry

Place 1 ¾ cups (425 mL) flour, 1 tbsp (15 mL) granulated sugar and ½ tsp (2 mL) salt in a large bowl. Stir to mix. Cut ¾ cup (175 mL) cold unsalted butter into cubes. Using your fingers or a pastry blender, cut butter into flour mixture until coarse crumbs form. Using a fork, work in water, 1 tbsp (15 mL) at a time, until dough can be shaped into a ball. Flatten into a disc and wrap in plastic wrap. Refrigerate until cold enough to easily roll out, about 20 minutes.

PIE SHELL

Using a floured rolling pin, roll out disc on a floured surface into a circle about 12 inches (30 cm) in diameter. Roll from centre to (but not over) the edge. Keep edges even as best you can. Loosely roll pastry around rolling pin. Then unroll over a 9- or 10-inch (23 or 25 cm) deep-dish pie plate. Gently press over bottom and up sides of plate, leaving a ½ inch (1 cm) overhang. Continue with your recipe as instructed.

TART SHELLS

Roll dough so it's ¼ inch (5 mm) thick. Using a 4-inch (10 cm) round cookie cutter, cut out circles. Reroll dough if necessary. Ease pastry circles into muffin cups. Continue with your recipe as instructed.

BLIND BAKING INSTRUCTIONS

Blind baking is a method in which you bake an empty pastry shell. This helps the pastry maintain its flaky texture after being baked with a filling. Prepare your pastry and pie or tart shell(s) as directed above. To prevent shell from shrinking while baking, line the shell with a piece of parchment paper. It should overhang slightly. Fill the parchment with dried beans. Bake on a baking sheet at 400°F (200°C) for 10 minutes. Prepare your recipe as instructed.

PASTRY SHORTCUT

Whirl dry ingredients in a food processor. Add butter and pulse until coarse crumbs form. Add 1 tbsp (15 mL) water at a time, pulsing just until dough comes together.

Carrot Cake with Fluffy White-Chocolate Icing

PREPARATION TIME 30 MINUTES
BAKING TIME 25 MINUTES
STANDING TIME 10 MINUTES
REFRIGERATION TIME
15 MINUTES
MAKES 16 SERVINGS

CAKE

2 cups (500 mL) all-purpose flour

1 ½ tsp (7 mL) baking powder

1 tsp (5 mL) baking soda

**1 tsp (5 mL) each cinnamon and ground allspice or
    2 tsp (10 mL) cinnamon**

½ tsp (2 mL) salt

5 to 6 medium carrots, peeled

4 eggs

1 ¼ cups (300 mL) lightly packed brown sugar

1 cup (250 mL) vegetable oil

1 tsp (5 mL) vanilla extract

1 cup (250 mL) coarsely chopped pecans or walnuts

ICING

6 oz (170 g) white chocolate, coarsely chopped

2 8-oz (250 g) blocks cream cheese, cubed, at room temperature

¾ cup (175 mL) unsalted butter, at room temperature

3 cups (750 mL) sifted icing sugar

1 tsp (5 mL) vanilla extract

TIME-SAVING TIP

If you're pressed for time, skip cutting the cakes in half and make it a two-layered dessert instead. Freeze any leftover icing for up to 1 month.

1. Preheat oven to 350°F (180°C). Oil two 8- or 9-inch (20 or 23 cm) round cake pans. Line pan bottoms with parchment paper. For cake, in a large bowl, stir flour with baking powder, baking soda, cinnamon, allspice and salt until evenly mixed. Grate carrots, using a box grater or the grating disc of a food processor. Measure out 3 ½ cups (875 mL) grated carrots.

2. In another bowl, whisk eggs with brown sugar, oil and vanilla. Stir in grated carrots. Make a well in the centre of dry ingredients. Add carrot mixture and nuts. Stir just until mixed. Pour batter into pans, dividing equally. Smooth tops.

3. Bake in centre of preheated oven until a cake tester inserted into centre of a cake comes out clean, 25 to 30 minutes. Run a knife around edges of cakes. Cool in pan, on a rack, 10 minutes, then turn out cakes onto rack and cool.

4. For icing, place chocolate in a bowl. Microwave on medium until almost melted, 1 to 2 minutes. Stir until smooth. Set aside to cool. In a large bowl, using an electric mixer on medium, beat cream cheese and butter until creamy.

Beat in icing sugar, then cooled chocolate and vanilla. Refrigerate icing to firm up a little, 15 to 30 minutes.

5. To assemble a 4-layer cake, carefully slice each cake in half horizontally. Place 1 layer on a cake plate. Spread with 1 scant cup (225 mL) icing. Top with another layer and repeat icing. Continue with remaining layers and icing. Spread leftover icing over sides.

GET AHEAD Wrap unfrosted, cooled cakes in plastic wrap and leave at room temperature for up to 3 days, or overwrap with foil and freeze for up to 1 month. Icing will keep well, covered and refrigerated, for up to 1 week. When ready to use, let icing stand at room temperature until soft enough to spread easily. Frosted cake will keep well, covered and refrigerated, for 3 days.

NUTRIENTS PER SERVING 10 G PROTEIN 57 G FAT
77 G CARBOHYDRATES 2 G FIBRE 3 MG IRON
135 MG CALCIUM 423 MG SODIUM 844 CALORIES

Free-Form Berry Pie

PREPARATION TIME 12 MINUTES
BAKING TIME 40 MINUTES
STANDING TIME 10 MINUTES
MAKES 8 SERVINGS

All-purpose flour for rolling

½ of 397 g pkg frozen puff-pastry, thawed

5 cups (1.25 L) strawberries, about 1 1/2 lb (750 g)

½ cup (125 mL) granulated sugar, plus more as needed

¼ cup (50 mL) cornstarch

1 egg

Pinches of granulated sugar

1 tbsp (15 mL) apricot or seedless raspberry jam, or apple jelly, for glaze (optional)

TASTY TWEAKS

• Perk up the filling by stirring 1 tsp (5 mL) grated orange or lemon peel into berry mixture.

• Add a nutty topping: 5 minutes before end of baking, remove foil. Scatter berries with sliced almonds and continue baking.

• Try it with a summer garnish. Just before serving, sprinkle finely chopped fresh mint overtop.

1. Position rack on bottom shelf of oven. Preheat oven to 475°F (240°C). Line baking sheet with parchment paper or foil. Lightly sprinkle counter with flour and place pastry on top. Dust rolling pin with flour. Roll pastry into a thin circle, about 14 to 16 inches (35 to 40 cm) in diameter. Don't worry if it's not a perfect circle. Loosely roll pastry around rolling pin, then unroll over baking sheet. It may overhang.

2. Hull, then halve or quarter berries. Lay on paper towels and pat very dry. In a large bowl, stir ½ cup (125 mL) sugar with cornstarch. If berries are not sweet, add another 2 tbsp (30 mL) sugar. Stir in berries to coat. Mound berries in centre of pastry, leaving a 3-inch (8 cm) edge uncovered. Fold pastry over fruit, overlapping as needed. Centre of pie should not be covered.

3. In a bowl, whisk egg with 1 tbsp (15 mL) cold water. Brush over pastry edges. Don't let it pool, or it may form streaks when baked. Sprinkle pastry with pinches of sugar. Place on bottom rack of preheated oven. Immediately reduce temperature to 375°F (190°C). Bake until pastry is golden, 40 to 45 minutes. If berries begin to dry out, loosely cover with circle of foil for the last 15 minutes of baking.

4. Remove pie from oven. Let stand 10 minutes before slicing. Meanwhile, to make glaze (if using), discard any chunks of fruit from jam, then microwave in a small bowl on medium-high until melted, about 30 seconds. Brush over warm berries. Serve pie topped with whipped cream, vanilla ice cream or frozen yogourt. Pie is best warm.

GET AHEAD Cover pie and store at room temperature for up to 1 day.

NUTRIENTS PER SERVING 3 G PROTEIN 10 G FAT
34 G CARBOHYDRATES 2 G FIBRE 1 MG IRON
20 MG CALCIUM 71 MG SODIUM 238 CALORIES

Hazelnut Meringue Cake

PREPARATION TIME 10 MINUTES
BAKING TIME 1 HOUR,
30 MINUTES
STANDING TIME 30 MINUTES
MAKES 12 SLICES

1 ½ cups (375 mL) granulated sugar

2 tbsp (30 mL) cornstarch

6 large egg whites, at room temperature

¼ tsp (1 mL) salt

2 tsp (10 mL) white vinegar

1 tsp (5 mL) vanilla extract

100 g pkg sliced hazelnuts

2 cups (500 mL) whipping cream

Fresh berries, such as raspberries, blackberries and blueberries

White or red currants

Cherries (optional)

COOKING TIP

Bring the eggs to room temperature before using to get the best results. Separate eggs carefully. Even a small amount of yolk in the whites can prevent stiff peaks from forming.

1. Arrange racks in top and bottom thirds of oven. Preheat oven to 275°F (140°C). Cut three 8-inch (20 cm) circles from parchment paper and place on 2 baking sheets. In a small bowl, stir ½ cup (125 mL) sugar with cornstarch. Set aside.

2. Place egg whites in a large bowl. Using an electric mixer on high, beat until soft peaks form when beaters are lifted. Gradually beat in remaining 1 cup (250 mL) sugar. Continue beating until stiff, glossy peaks form when beaters are lifted. Gradually beat in cornstarch mixture, salt, vinegar and vanilla. Using a spatula, gently fold in nuts.

3. Divide meringue mixture evenly among parchment circles. Using a spatula, spread to edges of circles. Smooth tops. Reduce oven temperature to 225°F (110°C). Bake meringues in top and bottom thirds of preheated oven until crisp and dry, 1 ½ to 2 hours, rotating baking sheets halfway through cooking time. Turn off oven and let meringues dry in oven for 30 more minutes. Remove from oven and leave on baking sheets until completely cool.

4. Using an electric mixer on medium-high, whip cream until definite peaks form when beaters are lifted. Place 1 meringue round on cake plate. Spread one-third of cream over meringue just to edge. Scatter with one-third of berries. Top with another meringue round. Spread with half of remaining cream, then scatter with half of remaining berries. Place another meringue round on top. Add the remaining cream. Decorate with remaining berries and top with currants. Serve right away, or refrigerate until ready to serve.

GET AHEAD Store meringues in an airtight container at room temperature for up to 2 days. Assembled cake will keep, refrigerated, for up to 2 hours.

NUTRIENTS PER SLICE 4 G PROTEIN 19 G FAT
29 G CARBOHYDRATES 1 G FIBRE 0 MG IRON
38 MG CALCIUM 88 MG SODIUM 292 CALORIES

Lemon Meringue Pie

PREPARATION TIME 20 MINUTES
BAKING TIME 22 MINUTES
COOKING TIME 7 MINUTES
MAKES 8 TO 10 SERVINGS

9-inch (23 cm) deep-dish pie shell, store-bought frozen or homemade (page 323)

FILLING

3 lemons

6 eggs

1 ¼ cups (300 mL) granulated sugar

½ cup (125 mL) cornstarch

¼ tsp (1 mL) salt

2 tbsp (30 mL) unsalted butter, at room temperature

MERINGUE

¼ tsp (1 mL) cream of tartar

⅓ cup (75 mL) granulated sugar

½ tsp (2 mL) vanilla extract

MERINGUE 101

Lift the beaters to see if meringue is ready — peaks should form and hold their shape without deflating.

To stop the meringue from shrinking during baking, spread it over the filling until it touches the pastry's edge.

CHATELAINE KITCHEN TIP

Be sure the pie is completely cooled before cutting so that it holds its beautiful shape.

1. Bake empty store-bought pie shell according to package directions, at least 12 minutes. If making homemade pastry, follow blind baking instructions (page 323). Set aside. Reduce oven temperature to 350°F (180°C). Meanwhile, for filling, finely grate 1 tbsp (15 mL) peel and squeeze ½ cup (125 mL) juice from lemons. Add 1 tsp (5 mL) extra peel if you like a tangy filling. Separate eggs, placing 4 whites in a large bowl and 6 yolks in another bowl. Set both aside. Save the 2 whites for future use.

2. In a small saucepan, mix sugar with cornstarch and salt. Stir in 1 ½ cups (375 mL) water. Set over medium heat and stir occasionally until mixture begins to thicken, 5 to 10 minutes. Stir frequently toward the end. Remove from heat. Whisk in peel, juice and butter. Gradually add yolks, whisking constantly so they don't scramble. Cook over medium-low, stirring often, until thick, 2 to 3 minutes. Pour into a bowl. Press plastic wrap onto surface of filling.

3. For meringue, using an electric mixer on medium, beat egg whites until foamy, about 1 minute. Add cream of tartar, then beat in sugar, 1 tbsp (15 mL) at a time. Scrape down sides of bowl as needed. Add vanilla. Beat until stiff peaks form when beaters are lifted, 2 to 3 minutes.

4. Pour warm lemon filling into pie shell. Smooth top. Spoon meringue overtop. Spread with a spoon or spatula until it touches the edge of the pie shell. Using the back of a spoon, create small peaks and swirls in meringue, using a dabbing and pulling outward motion.

5. Bake in centre of preheated oven until peaks are light golden, about 10 to 12 minutes. Let pie cool completely. If pie is not completely cool when cut, it will run.

GET AHEAD Tent foil over pie and refrigerate for up to 2 days. Slice just before serving.

NUTRIENTS PER SERVING 5 G PROTEIN 10 G FAT
46 G CARBOHYDRATES 0 G FIBRE 1 MG IRON
22 MG CALCIUM 193 MG SODIUM 292 CALORIES

Coconut-Lemon Cake

PREPARATION TIME 25 MINUTES
BAKING TIME 30 MINUTES
STANDING TIME 10 MINUTES
REFRIGERATION TIME 1 HOUR
MAKES 12 SLICES

CAKE

2 ¼ cups (550 mL) all-purpose flour

¾ cup (175 mL) sweetened shredded coconut

1 tbsp (15 mL) baking powder

½ tsp (2 mL) salt

¾ cup (175 mL) unsalted butter, at room temperature

1 ½ cups (375 mL) granulated sugar

3 eggs

2 tsp (10 mL) vanilla extract

400 mL can unsweetened coconut milk

ICING

½ cup (125 mL) unsalted butter, at room temperature

3 ½ cups (875 mL) icing sugar, sifted

1 tbsp (15 mL) honey

2 tsp (10 mL) vanilla extract

FILLING AND TOPPING

2 cups (500 mL) store-bought lemon curd

1 cup (250 mL) sweetened shredded coconut, toasted

TWO WAYS TO TOAST COCONUT

1. Bake coconut on a baking sheet in a preheated 350°F (180°C) oven, stirring often, until lightly golden.

2. Place in a frying pan and set over medium heat. Stir almost continuously until lightly golden.

1. Preheat oven to 350°F (180°C). Lightly butter two 8-inch (20 cm) round cake pans. Line bottoms with circles of lightly buttered waxed paper or parchment paper. For cake, in a bowl, using a fork, stir flour with sweetened shredded coconut, baking powder and salt to evenly mix. In a large bowl, using an electric mixer on medium, beat butter with granulated sugar for 3 minutes. Beat in eggs, one at a time, beating well after each addition. Beat in vanilla. On low speed, gradually beat in half of flour mixture, then 1 cup (250 mL) coconut milk (save rest of coconut milk for icing), ending with flour mixture. Divide batter between prepared pans. Smooth tops.

2. Bake in centre of preheated oven until a cake tester inserted into centre of a cake comes out clean, 30 to 40 minutes. Cool in pans on a rack for 10 minutes. Run a knife around inside edge of pans. Turn out cakes onto rack to cool completely.

3. For icing, in a large bowl, using an electric mixer on medium, beat butter until creamy, 2 to 3 minutes. Gradually beat in icing sugar, scraping down sides of bowl as necessary. Mixture will be dry at this point. Beat in honey, vanilla and ¼ cup (50 mL) coconut milk until smooth. (Refrigerate or freeze leftover coconut milk for future use.) Refrigerate icing at least 1 hour before spreading on cake.

4. To ice cake, slice each cake in half horizontally. Place bottom layer on a cake plate. Spread with ⅔ cup (150 mL) lemon curd nearly to the edge. Repeat with remaining cake layers and curd, ending with cake. Spread icing over top and sides of cake. Press toasted coconut into icing on sides of cake. Cake is easier to cut if refrigerated overnight.

GET AHEAD If baking cakes ahead, wrap unfrosted cakes in plastic wrap and store at room temperature overnight. Once frosted, cake will keep, covered and refrigerated, for up to 3 days.

NUTRIENTS PER SLICE 7 G PROTEIN 36 G FAT
102 G CARBOHYDRATES 2 G FIBRE 3 MG IRON
71 MG CALCIUM 271 MG SODIUM 749 CALORIE

Perfect Peach Streusel Pie

PREPARATION TIME 25 MINUTES
BAKING TIME 55 MINUTES
STANDING TIME 10 MINUTES
MAKES 8 SERVINGS

9-inch (23 cm) deep-dish pie shell, store-bought frozen or homemade (page 323)

TOPPING

1 cup (250 mL) all-purpose flour

½ cup (125 mL) chopped pecans or hazelnuts

¼ cup (50 mL) each granulated and lightly packed brown sugar

½ tsp (2 mL) cinnamon

½ cup (125 mL) cold unsalted butter

FILLING

8 ripe peaches

1 tsp (5 mL) grated orange peel (optional)

3 tbsp (45 mL) granulated sugar

3 tbsp (45 mL) cornstarch

¼ tsp (1 mL) each salt and cinnamon

SHORTCUT

To cut down on preparation and baking time, make this into a peach crumble by simply skipping the pastry. Place filling in an empty pie plate and sprinkle with topping. Bake in centre of preheated oven until peaches are tender, about 40 minutes.

1. Position rack on bottom shelf of oven. Preheat oven to 425°F (220°C). Bake empty store-bought pie shell according to package directions, at least 10 minutes. If making homemade pastry, follow blind baking instructions (page 323). Set aside on rack to cool.

2. Meanwhile, in a medium bowl, stir together all topping ingredients except butter. Cut butter into small cubes and add. Using your fingers or a pastry blender, work just until crumbly.

3. For filling, peel peaches, cut in half and discard pits. Slice peaches into thick wedges. You should have about 6 cups (1.5 L). Place in a large bowl and sprinkle with orange peel (if using). In a small bowl, use a fork to stir granulated sugar with cornstarch, salt and cinnamon. Scatter over peaches and toss to evenly coat. Turn peaches and any juices into pie shell. There will be a lot, so mound as best you can. Carefully sprinkle crumble topping over filling. Pick up any that spills onto baking sheet and gently pat back onto pie.

4. Bake on bottom rack of preheated oven for 10 minutes. Reduce oven temperature to 350°F (180°C) and bake until filling is hot, about 45 to 50 more minutes. Check topping after 20 minutes. If browning too quickly, loosely cover with foil. Once pie is baked, cool on a rack for 10 minutes before slicing.

NUTRIENTS PER SERVING 4 G PROTEIN 23 G FAT
50 G CARBOHYDRATES 3 G FIBRE 2 MG IRON
28 MG CALCIUM 199 MG SODIUM 413 CALORIES

Classic Creamy Cheesecake

PREPARATION TIME 25 MINUTES
BAKING TIME 1 HOUR
STANDING TIME 30 MINUTES
REFRIGERATION TIME 4 HOURS
MAKES 12 WEDGES

CRUST

1 ¼ cups (300 mL) graham cracker or chocolate cookie crumbs

2 tbsp (30 mL) granulated sugar

¼ cup (50 mL) unsalted butter, melted

FILLING

3 8-oz (250 g) blocks cream cheese, at room temperature

½ cup (125 mL) regular sour cream

1 ¼ cups (300 mL) granulated sugar

1 tbsp (15 mL) all-purpose flour

2 tsp (10 mL) vanilla extract

4 eggs

TOP THAT!

Chocolate-ganache sauce

Pour ½ cup (125 mL) hot whipping cream over 4 oz (120 g) finely chopped semi-sweet chocolate. Stir until smooth. Drizzle over cheesecake slices.

Fresh fruit

Scatter the unsliced cheesecake with a simple selection of fresh fruits such as figs, raspberries, blackberries, blueberries and ground cherries (also called cape gooseberries).

1. For crust, butter or oil sides of a 10-inch (25 cm) springform pan. For crust, in a large bowl, using a fork, stir graham crumbs with sugar, then stir in butter. Press mixture onto pan bottom. Wrap bottom and sides of pan with foil, making sure it comes to the top edge so water from the water bath won't leak in. Double wrap if necessary. Refrigerate while preparing filling.

2. Preheat oven to 325°F (160°C). Put a kettle of water on to boil. For filling, place cream cheese in a large bowl. Using an electric mixer on medium, beat until smooth, scraping down sides of bowl as necessary. Beat in sour cream, sugar, flour and vanilla. Beat in eggs, one at a time, just until blended. Pour over chilled crust.

3. Place wrapped springform pan in a broiler pan or shallow-sided roasting pan. Place in preheated oven. Pour enough boiling water into broiler pan to come about 1 inch (2.5 cm) up side of foil-wrapped springform pan.

4. Bake in centre of preheated oven until filling is almost set when springform pan is jiggled, about 1 hour. Remove broiler pan to a rack, immediately run a knife around inside pan edge to help prevent cracking. Let stand until water cools, about 30 minutes. Remove pan from water. Discard foil.

5. Cool, then cover with plastic wrap. Refrigerate until chilled, 4 hours. Remove cake from pan.

GET AHEAD Cover cheesecake and refrigerate for up to 3 days, or overwrap with foil and freeze for up to 1 month.

NUTRIENTS PER WEDGE 8 G PROTEIN 30 G FAT
34 G CARBOHYDRATES 0 G FIBRE 1 MG IRON
73 MG CALCIUM 278 MG SODIUM 430 CALORIES

Apple-Cranberry Crumbles

PREPARATION TIME 35 MINUTES
BAKING TIME 45 MINUTES
MAKES 6 TO 8 SERVINGS

1 cup (250 mL) quick or large-flake oats (not instant)

⅓ cup (75 mL) plus 2 tbsp (30 mL) all-purpose flour

1 ⅓ cups (325 mL) lightly packed brown sugar

⅓ cup (75 mL) skin-on whole almonds

⅓ cup (75 mL) unsalted butter, cubed, at room temperature

½ of 300 g pkg fresh or frozen cranberries, thawed, about
    1 ½ cups (375 mL)

8 apples, preferably McIntosh or Granny Smith

1 tsp (5 mL) cinnamon

½ tsp (2 mL) ground nutmeg

¼ cup (50 mL) orange liqueur (optional)

1 tsp (5 mL) vanilla extract

INDULGE

Create a scented whipped
cream by adding pinches
of ground nutmeg,
cinnamon or cardamom
to whipped cream.
Dollop on crisps.

1. Preheat oven to 350°F (180°C). For topping, stir oats with ⅓ cup (75 mL) each flour and sugar in a medium bowl. Coarsely chop almonds, then stir in. Using a fork or your hands, stir or work in butter until crumbly.

2. For filling, coarsely chop cranberries and place in a large bowl. Peel and core apples, slice into very thin wedges, then add to cranberries. Stir in remaining 1 cup (250 mL) sugar, remaining 2 tbsp (30 mL) flour, cinnamon and nutmeg. Toss until evenly mixed. Stir in orange liqueur (if using) and vanilla.

3. Divide apple mixture among 6 to 8 ovenproof coffee cups, ramekins or soufflé dishes that will each hold about 1 ½ cups (375 mL) mounded fruit. Mixture will sink, so make sure to mound it high, then firmly press down. Generously sprinkle with topping. Place on a large, rimmed baking sheet. Bake in centre of preheated oven until apples are tender, 45 to 50 minutes. Great warm or at room temperature.

NUTRIENTS PER SERVING 4 G PROTEIN 12 G FAT
74 G CARBOHYDRATES 6 G FIBRE 2 MG IRON
63 MG CALCIUM 17 MG SODIUM 408 CALORIES

Pumpkin-Coconut Cheesecake

PREPARATION TIME 20 MINUTES
BAKING TIME 1 HOUR, 5 MINUTES
STANDING TIME 40 MINUTES
REFRIGERATION TIME 4 HOURS
MAKES 10 TO 12 WEDGES

2 cups (500 mL) graham cracker crumbs

1 ½ cups (375 mL) sweetened desiccated or flaked coconut, toasted

¾ cup (175 mL) granulated sugar

½ cup (125 mL) unsalted butter, melted

4 eggs

1 cup (250 mL) canned pumpkin purée

½ cup (125 mL) packed brown sugar

1 tsp (5 mL) cinnamon

½ tsp (2 mL) each ground nutmeg and ginger, and salt

2 8-oz (250 g) blocks cream cheese, at room temperature

½ cup (125 mL) whipping cream

1 tsp (5 mL) vanilla extract

TEST KITCHEN TIP

Use pumpkin purée with no spices added. Use regular cream cheese, rather than light or spreadable.

1. Preheat oven to 325°F (160°C). For crust, lightly butter sides and bottom of a 10-inch (25 cm) springform pan. In a bowl, stir graham crumbs with 1 cup (250 mL) coconut, ¼ cup (50 mL) granulated sugar and butter until evenly moist. Press over bottom and partway up sides of prepared pan. Bake in centre of preheated oven until edges are golden, about 10 minutes. Cool on a rack. Keep oven on.

2. Meanwhile, for filling, whisk eggs in a large bowl. Whisk in pumpkin, brown sugar, spices and salt. Cut cheese into cubes and place in a large bowl. Using an electric mixer on medium, beat in remaining ½ cup (125 mL) granulated sugar. Then beat in cream, vanilla and pumpkin mixture, scraping down sides of bowl as necessary, until well mixed. Pour over warm crust.

3. Bake in centre of preheated oven until filling is almost set when pan is jiggled, 55 to 60 minutes. Place pan on a rack to cool. Immediately run a knife around inside pan edge to loosen crust and prevent cracking. Cool to room temperature, about 40 minutes. Then refrigerate until cold, at least 4 hours. Remove from pan. Sprinkle with remaining ½ cup (125 mL) coconut. Slice into wedges.

GET AHEAD Prepare and bake cheesecake. Place pan on a rack and cool to room temperature. Leaving in the pan, loosely cover with plastic wrap and refrigerate for up to 3 days. Or leave in pan and wrap in plastic wrap, then overwrap with foil and freeze for up to 1 month. Defrost cheesecake in the refrigerator for at least 6 hours or overnight. Best to let stand at room temperature for 1 hour before serving. Sprinkle remaining ½ cup (125 mL) toasted coconut overtop. Slice into wedges.

NUTRIENTS PER WEDGE 7 G PROTEIN 32 G FAT
43 G CARBOHYDRATES 2 G FIBRE 2 MG IRON
72 MG CALCIUM 382 MG SODIUM 482 CALORIES

Classic Lemon Loaf

PREPARATION TIME 15 MINUTES
BAKING TIME 55 MINUTES
STANDING TIME 10 MINUTES
MAKES 16 SLICES

1 ¾ cups (425 mL) all-purpose flour

1 tsp (5 mL) baking powder

½ tsp (2 mL) salt

1 large lemon

½ cup (125 mL) unsalted butter, at room temperature

1 ¼ cups (300 mL) granulated sugar

2 eggs

1 tsp (5 mL) vanilla extract

⅔ cup (150 mL) milk

TASTY TWEAKS

• Stir 1 cup (250 mL) chopped shelled pistachios, almonds or pecans into prepared batter.

• Finely grate 1 tbsp (15 mL) fresh ginger and stir into dry batter ingredients along with lemon peel.

• Stir ½ tsp (2 mL) dried tarragon leaves into glaze mixture.

• Add a pinch of crumbled saffron threads to glaze mixture, then warm over medium-low heat. Stir frequently until sugar dissolves and glaze is a golden colour.

1. Preheat oven to 350°F (180°C). Oil a 9- × 5-inch (2 L) loaf pan. In a bowl, use a fork to stir flour with baking powder and salt. Grate peel from half the lemon and stir in. In a bowl, using an electric mixer on medium, beat butter. Gradually beat in 1 cup (250 mL) sugar. Beat for another 2 minutes. Beat in eggs, vanilla and milk. Using a wooden spoon, stir in flour mixture just until batter is moist. Don't overmix. Pour into loaf pan and smooth top.

2. Bake in centre of preheated oven until golden and a cake tester inserted into centre of loaf comes out clean, 55 to 65 minutes. Don't worry if the top of the loaf cracks; because it sets before batter has fully risen, it will split as it bakes.

3. Meanwhile, for glaze, squeeze 3 tbsp (45 mL) juice from lemon into a small bowl. Stir in remaining ¼ cup (50 mL) sugar. Don't worry if sugar doesn't dissolve completely.

4. When loaf is baked, remove pan to a rack. If you'd like the glaze to absorb throughout the loaf, use a skewer to poke several holes through the top and into loaf. Drizzle or brush half of glaze overtop. Cool loaf in pan for 10 minutes, then run a knife around inside of pan. Turn out loaf, then turn top-side up. Drizzle remaining glaze overtop.

GET AHEAD Cool loaf completely before storing. Wrap in plastic wrap and store at room temperature for up to 2 days, or overwrap with foil and freeze for up to 2 months.

NUTRIENTS PER SLICE 3 G PROTEIN 7 G FAT
27 G CARBOHYDRATES 1 G FIBRE 1 MG IRON
28 MG CALCIUM 103 MG SODIUM 177 CALORIES

Grilled Strawberry Shortcake

PREPARATION TIME 5 MINUTES
GRILLING TIME 9 MINUTES
MAKES 6 SERVINGS

CANADIAN STRAWBERRIES

Canadian strawberries are much smaller than imported ones. Use your judgment: If berries are very small, skip cutting or chopping in recipes that call for large ones.

3 cups (750 mL) hulled and chopped ripe strawberries

3 tbsp (45 mL) granulated sugar

2 tbsp (30 mL) orange-flavoured liqueur or orange juice

6 store-bought individual angel food cakes or 283 g store-bought angel food cake or 1 homemade angel food cake

1. Oil grill and heat barbecue to medium. Place strawberries in a very large foil pie plate. Stir in sugar and liqueur. Cover plate tightly with foil. If using a large angel food cake, cut into 6 slices.

2. Place pie plate on grill. Barbecue, lid closed, for 6 minutes, then push to side of grill. Meanwhile, arrange individual cakes or cake wedges on grill. Barbecue, lid open, just until grill marks form, 1 to 2 minutes per side. Remove each cake or wedge as it is done to a plate. Lift up a corner of foil from pie plate. Strawberries should still be chunky but releasing enough juices to make a thin sauce. If necessary, recover and continue grilling until strawberries are saucy, 1 to 3 minutes. Remove from grill and discard foil. Spoon over cakes.

NUTRIENTS PER SERVING 3 G PROTEIN 1 G FAT
31 G CARBOHYDRATES 2 G FIBRE 0 MG IRON
58 MG CALCIUM 266 MG SODIUM 141 CALORIES

Campfire Bananas

PREPARATION TIME 10 MINUTES
GRILLING TIME 8 MINUTES
MAKES 4 SERVINGS

INDULGE

Serve with caramel
gelato or ice cream
and a drizzle of
dulce de leche.

4 large bananas
½ cup (125 mL) mini marshmallows
3 tbsp (45 mL) chocolate chips
3 tbsp (45 mL) chopped almonds or pecans (optional)

1. Heat barbecue to medium or set a grill over a campfire. Peel bananas. Make a lengthwise slit along inside curve of each banana (but don't cut all the way through), then gently open to form a long hollow. Place each banana on a large piece of foil or in a foil or metal pie plate. Divide marshmallows, chocolate chips and almonds (if using) into 4 portions, then stuff each banana with a portion. It's okay if some spills out. Seal foil around bananas or tightly cover pie plate with foil.

2. Place on grill and cook until bananas are warm and chocolate is just starting to melt, about 8 minutes. When opening foil, be careful of any steam. Grab a spoon and eat straight from foil or place packets on plates. Sprinkle with more nuts if you wish.

NUTRIENTS PER SERVING 2 G PROTEIN 3 G FAT
42 G CARBOHYDRATES 3 G FIBRE 1 MG IRON
11 MG CALCIUM 4 MG SODIUM 184 CALORIES

Sugared Phyllo Cups with Fresh Cream and Fruit

PREPARATION TIME 20 MINUTES
BAKING TIME 7 MINUTES
MAKES 12 PHYLLO CUPS

4 sheets frozen phyllo pastry, thawed
¼ cup (50 mL) unsalted butter, melted
2 tbsp (30 mL) granulated sugar
Fresh berries or chopped fruit
2 cups (500 mL) whipped cream

LIME-LACED CREAM

Flavour whipping cream by adding 1 tsp (5 mL) freshly grated lime rind per 1 cup (250 mL) cream before whipping. Then, using an electric mixer on medium-high, whip cream until definite peaks form when beaters are lifted.

1. Preheat oven to 350°F (180°C). Lightly coat or spray a 12-cup muffin tin with oil. Place a phyllo sheet on a large cutting board or the counter. Lightly brush with some of the butter, then sprinkle with 1 ½ tsp (7 mL) sugar. Cover with another phyllo sheet. Line up all edges. Repeat brushing, sprinkling and layering until all phyllo sheets are used, ending with sugar sprinkled overtop. Cut phyllo stack into 12 equal squares.

2. Carefully place 1 square stack in muffin cup, pressing around bottom with your fingers to form a cup. Leave sides of phyllo upright. Do not fold over. Repeat with remaining phyllo square stacks. Prick bottoms of cups with a fork. Bake in centre of preheated oven until crispy and golden, 7 to 9 minutes. Remove to a cooling rack.

3. Fill each cup with a spoonful of fresh fruit and a dollop of whipped cream.

GET AHEAD Store covered phyllo cups at room temperature for up to 2 days. Fill just before serving.

NUTRIENTS PER PHYLLO CUP WITHOUT CREAM OR FRUIT
1 G PROTEIN 4 G FAT 5 G CARBOHYDRATES
2 MG CALCIUM 31 MG SODIUM 63 CALORIES

Watermelon Granita

PREPARATION TIME 10 MINUTES
COOKING TIME 2 MINUTES
FREEZING TIME 3 HOURS,
40 MINUTES
MAKES 5 CUPS (1.25 L)

½ cup (125 mL) granulated sugar
¼ tsp (1 mL) salt
8 cups (2 L) coarsely chopped, peeled seedless watermelon
2 tsp (10 mL) finely grated lime or lemon peel (optional)

1. Combine sugar, 3 tbsp (45 mL) water and salt in a small saucepan and set over medium heat. Stir frequently until mixture starts to bubble and sugar is dissolved, 2 to 3 minutes. Remove from heat.

2. Place half the watermelon cubes in a blender or food processor. Whirl until no chunks remain. Pour into a 9- × 13-inch (3 L) baking dish. Pour sugar mixture into food processor and add remaining watermelon. Whirl until no chunks remain. Pour into baking dish. Add lime or lemon peel (if using). Stir to evenly mix. Cover pan with plastic wrap.

3. Freeze until ice crystals form at edges in dish, about 40 minutes. Using a fork, scrape and stir to evenly distribute ice crystals. Repeat every 40 minutes until frozen, about 3 to 4 more hours.

4. Using a fork or spoon, scrape granita down length of dish, forming icy flakes. Spoon into bowls and serve.

GET AHEAD Prepare Steps 1 to 3, then cover granita and store in freezer for up to 5 days.

USE UP EXTRA WATERMELON

Make a vodka-spiked slushy by cutting watermelon into large chunks, then freezing until firm, about 4 hours. Just before serving, whirl in a blender with vodka, freshly squeezed lime juice and sugar to taste.

NUTRIENTS PER ½ CUP (125 mL) 1 G PROTEIN
1 G FAT 19 G CARBOHYDRATES 1 G FIBRE 0 MG IRON
10 MG CALCIUM 60 MG SODIUM 79 CALORIES

Strawberry-Rhubarb Tiramisu

PREPARATION TIME 30 MINUTES
COOKING TIME 17 MINUTES
REFRIGERATION TIME 6 HOURS,
30 MINUTES
MAKES 12 TO 16 SERVINGS

FRUIT FILLING

4 cups (1 L) sliced fresh rhubarb or 2 300-g pkgs frozen rhubarb

1 cup (250 mL) granulated sugar

2 454-g containers strawberries, about 8 cups (2 L)

CREAM FILLING

475 g container mascarpone cheese

1 orange

½ cup (125 mL) plus 1 tbsp (15 mL) granulated sugar

1 tbsp (15 mL) vanilla extract

2 cups (500 mL) whipping cream

¾ cup (175 mL) orange juice

¼ cup (50 mL) orange-flavoured liqueur, such as Grand Marnier

2 5-oz (150 g) pkgs giant ladyfinger biscuits

COOKING TIP
No liqueur? No problem,
just replace with more
orange juice.

1. For fruit filling, slice rhubarb into 1-inch (2.5 cm) pieces. If using frozen, rinse under cold water to thaw slightly. Pat dry with paper towels. Place in a large saucepan and stir in sugar. (There's no need to add water.) Bring to a boil, stirring often, over medium heat. Boil gently, stirring occasionally, until a thick sauce is formed, 15 to 20 minutes. Slice large strawberries in half and stir into thickened sauce. Stir 2 minutes to slightly cook berries. Don't overcook or they'll lose colour. Refrigerate until cool, about 30 minutes.

2. For cream filling, place mascarpone in a large bowl. Finely grate in peel from orange. Stir in ½ cup (125 mL) sugar and vanilla. In a bowl, using an electric mixer on medium, beat cream with 1 tbsp (15 mL) sugar until soft peaks form when beaters are lifted. Gently stir one-quarter of cream mixture into mascarpone mixture, then gently fold in remainder just until combined.

3. Stir orange juice with liqueur in a pie plate or shallow dish. Working with half the biscuits, dip both sides into juice mixture, then use to line bottom of a 9- × 13-inch (3 L) baking or dessert dish. Spoon half of mascarpone mixture overtop and spread to cover. Spoon half of fruit filling overtop. Repeat layering, beginning with remaining biscuits dipped first in juice mixture. (Pour any leftover juice mixture over biscuits.) Cover biscuits with remaining mascarpone, then remaining fruit filling. Place dish on a baking sheet to catch overflow resulting when dessert settles. Loosely cover with plastic wrap and refrigerate at least 6 hours, and preferably overnight.

GET AHEAD Cover tiramisu and refrigerate for up to 2 days. Berry colour may bleed a little.

NUTRIENTS PER SERVING 7 G PROTEIN 24 G FAT
41 G CARBOHYDRATES 2 G FIBRE 1 MG IRON
68 MG CALCIUM 41 MG SODIUM 400 CALORIES

Sticky Toffee Puddings with Caramel Sauce

PREPARATION TIME 20 MINUTES
COOKING TIME 6 MINUTES
BAKING TIME 40 MINUTES
STANDING TIME 30 MINUTES
MAKES 12 PUDDINGS

½ of 375 g pkg pitted dates, about 1 ¼ cups (300 mL), coarsely chopped

2 tsp (10 mL) baking soda

1 cup (250 mL) all-purpose flour

1 ½ tsp (7 mL) baking powder

¼ tsp (1 mL) ground ginger

½ cup (125 mL) plus 3 tbsp (45 mL) unsalted butter, at room temperature

⅔ cup (150 mL) granulated sugar

2 eggs

1 cup (250 mL) lightly packed brown sugar

½ cup (125 mL) whipping cream

¼ cup (50 mL) Baileys Crème Caramel or Original Irish Cream liqueur

INDULGE
Top with a dollop of whipped cream.

1. Preheat oven to 350°F (180°C). Place dates and ¾ cup (175 mL) water in a medium saucepan. Cover and bring to a boil, stirring occasionally, over medium-high heat. Remove lid and boil gently for 3 minutes, stirring often. Remove from heat and stir in baking soda, then let stand 20 minutes.

2. Meanwhile, lightly butter a 12-cup muffin tin. For a water bath, set aside a roasting pan large enough to hold the muffin tin. Bring a kettle of water to a boil, unplug and set aside.

3. In a medium bowl, using a fork, stir flour with baking powder and ginger. In another medium bowl, using an electric mixer on medium, blend 3 tbsp (45 mL) butter and granulated sugar. Add eggs, one at a time, beating well after each addition and scraping down sides of bowl as necessary. Gradually beat in flour mixture. Stir in date mixture. Spoon batter into prepared muffin tins and fill to just below the rim. Place muffin tin in roasting pan. Place pan on centre oven rack. Pour enough boiling water into roasting pan to come about halfway up sides of muffin pan. Bake in preheated oven for 20 minutes. Reduce oven temperature to 325°F (160°C) and continue to bake until a cake tester inserted into centre of a pudding comes out almost clean, about 20 more minutes. Remove muffin tin from water. Cool on a wire rack for 10 minutes, then run a knife along inside edges and gently turn out.

4. While puddings are baking, prepare sauce. Melt the remaining ½ cup (125 mL) butter in a small saucepan over medium heat. Stir in brown sugar until dissolved. Add cream and liqueur. Increase heat to medium-high and boil gently, uncovered and stirring occasionally, until slightly thickened, about 3 minutes. Serve hot puddings with warm sauce.

GET AHEAD Bake puddings, then wrap and refrigerate for several days, or freeze for up to 2 weeks. To reheat, defrost, then place a few puddings on a microwave-safe dinner plate. Tent with wax paper and microwave on medium just until puddings are warm in the centre, about 1 minute. Repeat with remaining puddings. Sauce will keep well, covered and refrigerated, for up to 2 days. Reheat in microwave on high for 1 minute before serving.

NUTRIENTS PER PUDDING 3 G PROTEIN 16 G FAT
50 G CARBOHYDRATES 2 G FIBRE 1 MG IRON
54 MG CALCIUM 276 MG SODIUM 347 CALORIES

Velvety Chocolate Pudding

PREPARATION TIME 10 MINUTES
COOKING TIME 4 MINUTES
REFRIGERATION TIME 2 HOURS
(OPTIONAL)
MAKES 3 CUPS (750 mL)

3 oz (90 g) semi-sweet chocolate
2 cups (500 mL) milk, preferably homogenized, or half-and-half cream
½ cup (125 mL) granulated sugar
¼ cup (50 mL) cocoa powder
3 tbsp (45 mL) cornstarch
Pinch of salt
2 tsp (10 mL) vanilla extract
Whipped cream (optional)

FLAVOUR BOOST

For a grown-up twist, add Frangelico, Baileys or Grand Marnier. Stir 1 tbsp (15 mL) liqueur into pudding along with the vanilla.

1. Finely chop chocolate. Pour 1 ½ cups (375 mL) milk into a saucepan and set over medium heat. Bring almost to a boil. Meanwhile, in a bowl, whisk sugar with cocoa, cornstarch and salt. Whisk remaining ½ cup (125 mL) milk into sugar mixture until no lumps remain.

2. When milk just starts to boil, gradually whisk in sugar mixture. Using a wooden spoon, stir constantly until pudding thickens and just comes to a boil, 3 to 4 minutes. Reduce heat if pudding is sticking to the pan bottom. Once thickened, remove from heat. Stir in chocolate, then vanilla. Continue stirring until chocolate is completely melted and mixture is smooth, about 1 more minute.

3. Serve warm. Or pour into a large bowl and press a piece of plastic wrap onto surface of pudding and refrigerate, about 2 hours. Pudding thickens as it cools. Just before serving, add a dollop of whipped cream if you wish.

GET AHEAD Pudding will keep well, covered and refrigerated, for up to 3 days (if it sticks around that long).

NUTRIENTS PER ½ CUP (125 mL) 4 G PROTEIN 7 G FAT
36 G CARBOHYDRATES 2 G FIBRE 1 MG IRON
106 MG CALCIUM 41 MG SODIUM 211 CALORIES

Chocolate Cupcakes

PREPARATION TIME 20 MINUTES
BAKING TIME 16 MINUTES
STANDING TIME 15 MINUTES
MAKES 12 CUPCAKES

COCOA 101

Cocoa has the lowest fat content and fewest calories of any chocolate product.

When a recipe for chocolate sauce calls for 1 oz (30 g) unsweetened baking chocolate (about 1 square) you can use 3 tbsp (45 mL) cocoa and 1 tbsp (15 mL) butter instead.

Cocoa will keep for up to 2 years in a covered container at room temperature.

Cocoa contains less caffeine than coffee, tea or cola.

When making brownies using baking chocolate, add a light sprinkling of cocoa to the batter to intensify the chocolate flavour.

1 ¼ cups (300 mL) all-purpose flour
⅓ cup (75 mL) cocoa powder
1 tsp (5 mL) baking powder
½ tsp (2 mL) salt
¼ tsp (1 mL) baking soda
½ cup (125 mL) unsalted butter, at room temperature
1 cup (250 mL) granulated sugar
2 eggs, at room temperature
2 tsp (10 mL) vanilla extract
¾ cup (175 mL) milk

1. Preheat oven to 350°F (180°C). Line a 12-cup muffin tin with paper cups or spray with oil. Place flour in a bowl. Sift in cocoa. Using a fork, stir in baking powder, salt and baking soda. In a large bowl, using an electric mixer on medium, beat butter until creamy, about 1 minute. Beat in sugar, then eggs, one at a time. Don't worry if mixture separates; it'll come together when flour is added. Beat in vanilla. Gradually beat in one-third of flour mixture just until blended, then half of milk. Repeat additions, ending with flour mixture, beating just until blended after each addition. Divide batter among cups, filling about three-quarters full.

2. Bake in centre of preheated oven until a cake tester inserted into centre of a cupcake comes out clean, 16 to 20 minutes. Remove pan to a rack. Cool 15 minutes, then remove cakes to a rack to cool completely before icing. These fluffy and chocolatey miniature cakes make the perfect base for Vanilla Buttercream (opposite page), especially the chocolate variation.

GET AHEAD Store unfrosted cupcakes in an airtight container at room temperature for up to 1 day. Or wrap separately in plastic wrap, overwrap with foil and freeze for up to 1 month. Don't frost until day of serving.

NUTRIENTS PER UNFROSTED CUPCAKE 3 G PROTEIN
9 G FAT 29 G CARBOHYDRATES 1 G FIBRE 1 MG IRON
40 MG CALCIUM 219 MG SODIUM 206 CALORIES

Vanilla Buttercream

PREPARATION TIME 15 MINUTES
COOKING TIME 1 MINUTE
MAKES 4 CUPS (1 L)

CUPCAKE DECORATING 101

How to fill a piping bag
If using a coupler — a plastic base and ring that fits on a piping bag, allowing you to change tips without changing bags — fit the base into the bottom of the bag. Drop tip into ring. Screw ring onto base. If not using coupler, drop tip into bag. Fold top of bag down to make a cuff. Using a spatula, fill bag with buttercream, pushing it down. Fill about three-quarters full. Roll up cuff. Using your hands, squeeze and push buttercream down into tip.

For pretty colours
Beat drops of food colouring, a few at a time, into buttercream.

4 egg whites
1 ⅓ cups (325 mL) granulated sugar
1 ½ cups (375 mL) unsalted butter, at room temperature
3 tbsp (45 mL) vanilla extract

1. Fill bottom of a large saucepan with 1 inch (2.5 cm) water. Bring to a boil, then reduce heat so water is barely simmering. Place egg whites and sugar in a large heatproof bowl that will fit in saucepan but not touch water. Position the bowl over the simmering water. Using an electric mixer on high, beat just until egg mixture is warm and increased in volume, and will hold soft peaks when beaters are lifted, 1 to 2 minutes. The consistency will be thick but not stiff. Remove from heat. Continue beating until mixture and bowl are completely cool, 4 to 6 minutes.

2. Add ½ cup (125 mL) butter and beat until evenly mixed. Repeat with remaining butter in two additions, scraping down sides of bowl as necessary. Once smooth, continue beating on high until pale and fluffy, about 2 minutes. Don't worry if mixture separates. Just continue beating until very smooth. Beat in vanilla.

GET AHEAD Place buttercream in an airtight container and press plastic wrap overtop. Seal and refrigerate for up to 1 week, or freeze for up to 1 month. To prevent splitting, bring to room temperature. Then, using an electric mixer on medium, beat until smooth, 1 to 2 minutes.

TASTY TWEAKS

SPICE: Beat 1 tsp (5 mL) each ground ginger, cardamom and cinnamon into buttercream along with vanilla.

CHOCOLATE: Melt 3 oz (90 g) bittersweet chocolate. Allow it to cool completely. When cool, but not seized, beat into buttercream along with vanilla. Sift 2 tbsp (30 mL) cocoa over buttercream. Continue to beat until evenly mixed.

LEMON: Beat 2 tbsp (30 mL) each freshly squeezed lemon juice and freshly grated lemon peel into buttercream along with vanilla.

NUTRIENTS PER 2 ½ TBSP (37 mL) 1 G PROTEIN
11 G FAT 11 G CARBOHYDRATES 0 G FIBRE 0 MG IRON
4 MG CALCIUM 10 MG SODIUM 139 CALORIES

Lemon-Coconut Shortbread Squares

PREPARATION TIME 15 MINUTES
BAKING TIME 50 MINUTES
MAKES 24 SQUARES

BASE
1 cup (250 mL) all-purpose flour
1 cup (250 mL) sweetened shredded coconut
½ cup (125 mL) sifted icing sugar
½ cup (125 mL) unsalted butter, at room temperature

FILLING
4 lemons
6 eggs
2 ¾ cups (675 mL) granulated sugar
½ cup (125 mL) all-purpose flour
Icing sugar for sifting (optional)

VARIATION

For classic lemon bars, leave out the coconut. When cooled completely, cut into finger-sized portions.

1. Preheat oven to 350°F (180°C). Lightly butter bottom and sides of a 9- × 13-inch (3 L) baking dish. For base, in a large bowl, stir flour with coconut and icing sugar to mix. Cut in butter using your fingers or a pastry blender until mixture resembles coarse crumbs. Turn into prepared baking dish and press evenly over bottom. Base will be thin. Bake in centre of preheated oven just until crust starts to turn golden. Check after 15 minutes of baking, but it may take 20 to 22 minutes in total. Remove from oven and set on a heatproof surface. Reduce oven temperature to 325°F (160°C).

2. For filling, squeeze 1 cup (250 mL) juice from lemons into a large bowl. Add eggs and whisk until blended. Stir sugar with flour, then whisk into egg mixture. Pour over hot baked crust. Make sure oven temperature is reduced to 325°F (160°C), then bake in centre of preheated oven until filling is set when dish is jiggled, 30 to 35 minutes. Set on a rack and cool completely. Cut into 2-inch (5 cm) squares just before serving. Sift with icing sugar if you wish.

GET AHEAD Cover squares in the baking dish and refrigerate for up to 3 days, or overwrap with foil and freeze for up to 1 month. Defrost in refrigerator and cut just before serving.

NUTRIENTS PER SQUARE 3 G PROTEIN 7 G FAT
34 G CARBOHYDRATES 1 G FIBRE 1 MG IRON
10 MG CALCIUM 26 MG SODIUM 199 CALORIES

Best-Ever Brownies

PREPARATION TIME 25 MINUTES
BAKING TIME 43 MINUTES
MAKES 16 BROWNIES

1 cup (250 mL) whole hazelnuts, skin-on, or blanched whole almonds (optional)

1 cup (250 mL) all-purpose flour

¼ cup (50 mL) cocoa powder

¼ tsp (1 mL) salt

6 oz (170 g) semi-sweet chocolate, about 6 squares

½ cup (125 mL) unsalted butter

3 eggs

1 cup (250 mL) granulated sugar

2 tsp (10 mL) vanilla extract

TASTY TWEAKS

• Love chocolate but don't have a sweet tooth? Create a richer, less-sweet flavour by substituting bittersweet for semi-sweet chocolate.

• Spice things up with generous pinches of cinnamon, ground nutmeg or cayenne pepper. Stir into flour before adding to egg mixture.

• Go all out by stirring ½ cup (125 mL) chopped Skor bars, toffee bits or dried cranberries into batter along with nuts.

1. Preheat oven to 325°F (160°C). Spread nuts on a baking sheet. Toast until lightly golden and fragrant, 8 to 12 minutes. Stir halfway through cooking time. Leave oven on. Wrap hazelnuts (if using) in a kitchen towel and let steam 1 minute, then rub in towel to remove skins. When nuts are completely cool, coarsely chop.

2. Meanwhile, coat or spray an 8-inch- (2 L) square baking dish with oil. In a small bowl, using a fork, stir flour with cocoa and salt. Using a serrated knife, coarsely chop chocolate. Place in a medium bowl along with butter.

3. Microwave chocolate and butter on medium until almost melted, about 3 minutes. Use a rubber spatula to stir chocolate halfway through cooking. Stir until smooth. Or place chocolate and butter in a medium saucepan and set over low heat. Stir constantly until melted. Set aside to cool.

4. In a large bowl, whisk eggs, then sugar and vanilla to evenly mix. Using a spatula, scrape in cooled chocolate mixture, then stir to evenly mix. Gradually stir in flour mixture, just until almost mixed. (Overmixing will toughen brownies.) Stir in nuts (if using) until evenly distributed. Spread batter in baking dish. Smooth top.

5. Bake in centre of preheated oven until edges are firm and middle is set, 35 to 45 minutes. Don't overbake. (A toothpick inserted into centre of brownies may have chocolatey crumbs clinging to it.) Remove dish to a rack and cool. Cut into squares.

GET AHEAD Cover brownies and store at room temperature for up to 3 days, or freeze for up to 1 month.

NUTRIENTS PER BROWNIE 3 G PROTEIN 10 G FAT
26 G CARBOHYDRATES 1 G FIBRE 1 MG IRON
13 MG CALCIUM 49 MG SODIUM 202 CALORIES

Triple-Chocolate Ice Cream Sandwiches

PREPARATION TIME 22 MINUTES
BAKING TIME 10 MINUTES
PER BATCH
MAKES 11 ICE-CREAM
SANDWICHES

2 oz (60 g) semi-sweet chocolate, chopped

1 ½ cups (375 mL) all-purpose flour

½ cup (125 mL) cocoa powder

½ tsp (2 mL) each baking soda and salt

¾ cup (175 mL) unsalted butter, at room temperature

¾ cup (175 mL) granulated sugar

½ cup (125 mL) packed brown sugar

2 eggs

2 tsp (10 mL) vanilla extract

1 cup (250 mL) semi-sweet chocolate chips

4 cups (1 L) cherry ice cream

CHATELAINE KITCHEN TIP

Use any ice cream you like — you won't go wrong no matter what you choose.

1. Preheat oven to 350°F (180°C). Place chocolate in a bowl. Microwave on medium until almost melted, 1 to 2 minutes. Stir until smooth. Set aside. Line 2 baking sheets with parchment paper or spray with oil.

2. In a bowl, using a fork, stir flour with cocoa, baking soda and salt. In a large bowl, using an electric mixer on medium-high, beat butter with granulated and brown sugars for 3 minutes. Beat in eggs, one at a time, then vanilla and melted chocolate. On low speed, gradually beat in flour mixture. Stir in chocolate chips. Form dough into balls roughly the size of golf balls and place on baking sheets 3 inches (8 cm) apart. Using your hand, flatten into a cookie shape, ½ inch (1 cm) thick.

3. Bake a sheet at a time in centre of preheated oven, until cookie edges begin to set, about 10 minutes. Cool on baking sheet 5 minutes, then remove to a rack to cool completely. Meanwhile, repeat baking with remaining baking sheet and dough.

4. For sandwiches, place 1 cookie top-side down. Scoop about ⅓ cup (75 mL) ice cream on top. Gently press with a spoon to cover surface of cookie. Cover with another cookie, top-side up. Gently squeeze together.

GET AHEAD Store cooled cookies in an airtight container at room temperature for 3 days, or freeze for up to 1 month. Assembled sandwiches can be frozen in a sealed container for up to 1 month.

NUTRIENTS PER ICE-CREAM SANDWICH 6 G PROTEIN
24 G FAT 65 G CARBOHYDRATES 3 G FIBRE 2 MG IRON
88 MG CALCIUM 209 MG SODIUM 484 CALORIES

Pistachio and Orange Cookies

PREPARATION TIME 20 MINUTES
BAKING TIME 10 MINUTES
PER BATCH
MAKES 32 COOKIES

½ cup (125 mL) salted shelled pistachios

1 orange

2 cups (500 mL) all-purpose flour

½ tsp (2 mL) baking soda

¼ tsp (1 mL) salt (optional)

⅔ cup (150 mL) unsalted butter, at room temperature

1 ¼ cups (300 mL) granulated sugar

2 eggs

2 tsp (10 mL) vanilla extract

NUT TIP

To break nuts in half, place them on a cutting board. Using the bottom of a heavy pan, press until they separate in half (some will be more crushed than others).

1. Preheat oven to 350°F (180°C). Line a large baking sheet with parchment paper or spray with oil. Halve nuts. Finely grate peel from orange.

2. In a medium bowl, using a fork, stir flour with baking soda and salt (if using). (You can skip the salt if the pistachios taste very salty.) In a large bowl, using an electric mixer on medium-high, beat butter with sugar for 3 minutes. Beat in eggs, one at a time, scraping down sides of bowl as necessary. Beat in vanilla. On low speed, gradually beat in flour mixture. Stir in nuts and orange peel.

3. Drop by heaping tbsps (22 mL) onto the baking sheet, at least 2 inches (5 cm) apart. Bake in centre of preheated oven, just until cookies begin to brown around edges, 10 to 12 minutes. Then remove cookies to a rack to cool. Repeat with remaining dough, making sure baking sheet is cooled between batches.

GET AHEAD Store cookies in an airtight container in a cool place or in the refrigerator for up to 2 weeks.

NUTRIENTS PER COOKIE 2 G PROTEIN 5 G FAT
15 G CARBOHYDRATES 0 G FIBRE 1 MG IRON
7 MG CALCIUM 40 MG SODIUM 110 CALORIES

Gingerbread Cookies

PREPARATION TIME 20 MINUTES
REFRIGERATION TIME
30 MINUTES
STANDING TIME 5 MINUTES
BAKING TIME 7 MINUTES
PER BATCH
MAKES 50 COOKIES

VARIATION
Ginger chocolate sparkle cookie

Sift ½ cup (125 mL) cocoa powder into flour mixture. Prepare dough. Roll 1 heaping tsp (7 mL) into a ½-inch (1 cm) ball. Place on a baking sheet. Repeat with remaining dough. Refrigerate until cold, about 15 minutes. Place ¼ cup (50 mL) granulated sugar in a small bowl. In another small bowl, stir ¼ cup (50 mL) icing sugar with 1 tbsp (15 mL) cocoa powder. Roll cold balls in granulated sugar, then in cocoa mixture. Return to oiled baking sheet, placing 1 inch (2.5 cm) apart. Bake until tops of cookies are firm, 7 to 9 minutes. Repeat with remaining dough.

Makes 70 cookies

2 ½ cups (625 mL) all-purpose flour

2 tsp (10 mL) ground ginger

1 ½ tsp (7 mL) cinnamon

½ tsp (2 mL) each ground allspice, salt and baking soda

½ cup (125 mL) unsalted butter, melted

¾ cup (175 mL) lightly packed brown sugar

1 egg

⅓ cup (75 mL) fancy molasses

1. In a large bowl, using a fork, stir flour with ginger, cinnamon, allspice, salt and baking soda. In a medium bowl, using a wooden spoon, beat butter with sugar for 2 minutes. Beat in egg, then molasses. Make a well in centre of flour mixture, then pour in molasses mixture. Stir until most of molasses is absorbed. Gently knead until dough is an even colour. Divide into 4 portions.

2. Shape each into a ball, then flatten into a disc. Wrap separately in plastic wrap and refrigerate until firm, at least 30 minutes.

3. When ready to bake, remove dough from refrigerator. Let stand at room temperature until soft enough to roll, 5 to 10 minutes. Preheat oven to 350°F (180°C). Lightly spray or oil a baking sheet. Place a disc of dough between 2 sheets of waxed paper. Roll dough no thicker than ¼ inch (5 mm). Cut out shapes with cookie cutter. Place on baking sheet about 1 inch (2.5 cm) apart.

4. Bake in centre of preheated oven just until edges begin to darken, 7 to 10 minutes. Remove cookies to a rack to cool. Repeat with remaining dough.

GET AHEAD Wrap each disc of dough (Step 2) separately in plastic wrap and refrigerate for up to 1 week, or overwrap with foil and freeze for up to 1 month. Store baked cookies in an airtight container in a cool place for up to 1 week, or freeze for up to 1 month.

NUTRIENTS PER 2-INCH (5 CM) COOKIE 1 G PROTEIN
2 G FAT 10 G CARBOHYDRATES 0 G FIBRE 1 MG IRON
11 MG CALCIUM 41 MG SODIUM 62 CALORIES

The Ultimate Chocolate-Chip Cookies

PREPARATION TIME 20 MINUTES
BAKING TIME 8 MINUTES
PER BATCH
MAKES 5 DOZEN COOKIES

2 ¼ cups (550 mL) all-purpose flour

1 tsp (5 mL) baking soda

½ tsp (2 mL) salt

1 cup (250 mL) unsalted butter, at room temperature

1 ¼ cups (300 mL) lightly packed brown sugar

1 egg

1 ½ tsp (7 mL) vanilla extract

2 cups (500 mL) dark chocolate chips or coarsely chopped dark chocolate chunks

GO NUTS
Add chopped pecans or skin-on almonds to batter along with the chocolate chips.

1. Preheat oven to 350°F (180°C). Lightly spray a baking sheet with oil. In a medium bowl, using a fork, stir flour with baking soda and salt. In a large bowl, using a wooden spoon or an electric mixer on medium, beat butter with sugar until creamy, about 1 minute. Beat in egg and vanilla. Gradually stir flour mixture into butter mixture just until combined. Mix in chocolate chips.

2. Scoop about 1 tbsp (15 mL) dough and place on prepared baking sheet. Repeat with remaining dough, placing at least 2 inches (5 cm) apart. Don't press down; they will spread as they bake.

3. Bake in centre of preheated oven until cookies are golden around the edges, 8 to 10 minutes. Remove baking sheet to a heatproof surface and leave for 2 minutes. Remove cookies to a rack to cool completely. Cool baking sheet or use another sheet and repeat with remaining dough.

GET AHEAD Form dough into a thick disc and wrap well in plastic wrap. Refrigerate for up to 2 weeks or freeze for up to 1 month. Baked cookies will keep well in a covered container at room temperature for up to 2 days — but we doubt they'll last that long.

NUTRIENTS PER COOKIE 1 G PROTEIN 5 G FAT
12 G CARBOHYDRATES 1 G FIBRE 1 MG IRON
8 MG CALCIUM 44 MG SODIUM 92 CALORIES

entertaining ideas

Hosting a get-together is fun, but let's be honest: it can be stressful too. Not anymore! These simple tips will ease your party-planning stress so that you'll have lots of time to spend with family and friends.

Tips

MENU PLANNING

Consider planning your meal around in-season produce so that you won't find yourself running to several grocery stores in search of hard-to-find ingredients.

TROUBLESHOOTING

It's the guests' responsibility to let you know about their dietary restrictions, but it will make your life simpler if you check in advance of menu planning. Keep limitations in mind when preparing the meal and provide options, but don't feel you have to cater the entire meal to one person's needs.

KEEP IT SIMPLE

Soups and salads are easy to reheat or toss together at the last minute, so select ones you can make in advance.

CHEESE, PLEASE

Kick off the evening with a crowd-pleaser that takes just a few minutes to prepare — a cheese plate. Choose a selection of three to five cheeses, a combination of firm, semi-firm, soft, semi-soft and veined. For example:

- Firm: asiago, mimolette, manchego, parmigiano-reggiano,
- Semi-firm: cheddar, edam, Jarlsberg, gruyère, oka
- Soft: brie, camembert, Explorateur, La Sauvagine
- Semi-soft: gouda, Niagara Gold, esrom, taleggio, havarti
- Veined: Bleu Bénédictin, St. Augur, stilton, Le Ciel de Charlevoix

Plan for 3 to 4 oz (90 to 120 g) cheese per person. For example, if you select three cheeses, purchase about 1 oz (30 g) per person of each type of cheese. Fill out the platter with toasted nuts and dried apricots. If you like, drizzle a gourmet honey over blue cheese to soften its pungent kick. Serve with a selection of crackers and toasted baguette slices.

BE REALISTIC

Serve a maximum of five courses for an intimate sit-down get-together. Choose dishes that can mostly be assembled ahead of time for two or three of the courses.

HUNGRY HORDES

When serving more than eight guests, consider preparing a buffet-style menu — it's easier on the chef and creates a more social atmosphere. (You'll find suggested buffet menus in the Menus section, page 375 — for instance, the Buffet brunch with friends, as well as the Backyard barbecue and Thanksgiving or Christmas menus, which are potentially buffet-style.)

MAIN COURSE

Timing is key when it comes to dinner preparation, so don't stress yourself out by guessing when your main dish is ready. Keep your trusty instant-read meat thermometer on hand to confirm that the roasting meat is done. While it stands, you can pull together the last-minute details for the side dishes. If you're making a vegetarian main such as risotto, pasta or curry, make sure to cover it once it's ready with a lid or foil so that it doesn't dry out while waiting to be served.

KEEP IT WARM

Never underestimate the importance of a warm plate — it adds a touch of class to your meal, while ensuring that it isn't cold when it hits the table. Just tuck your dinner plates into the oven once the main course is done and the heat is turned off. If you're making a stove-top dish, preheat the oven to 200°F (90°C). A few minutes before your meal is ready to serve, place plates in the oven to warm.

RAISING THE BAR

For a small get-together, going with a self-serve bar can be a life-saver. Mix up a special cocktail that matches the menu and provide a selection of wine and beer. Follow this guide and adjust according to your guest count:

12 to 18 guests:

- 3 to 4 bottles white wine
- 3 to 4 bottles red wine
- 24 bottles domestic beer
- 24 bottles imported beer

Drinks

HOMEMADE CAPPUCCINO

Brew some strong coffee, then half-fill a 2 cup (500 mL) measuring cup with milk. (Skim milk gives the best foam.) Microwave until almost boiling, about 1 minute and 20 seconds. Place a whisk in the milk. Holding the handle between your palms, vigorously rub your hands together so the whisk spins back and forth, creating foam. Partially fill a mug with the coffee, then pour in the hot milk, holding the foam back with a spoon. Ladle on the foam, then dust with cinnamon and cocoa powder.

MAKES 1 SERVING (RECIPE IS EASILY DOUBLED)

HOT CHOCOLATE

Simmer a few slices of fresh ginger in milk until gently infused, about 3 to 5 minutes. Mix cocoa powder and granulated sugar together (about 1 tablespoon/15 mL of each) in a mug, then strain in the hot milk and stir to combine. To up the comfort quotient, add a splash of rum. No marshmallow required.

MAKES 1 SERVING (RECIPE IS EASILY DOUBLED)

STRAWBERRY LEMONADE

Finely grate 1 tsp (5 mL) peel from a lemon. Squeeze ⅔ cup (150 mL) juice from 2 to 3 lemons. Place 2 cups (500 mL) chopped fresh strawberries, lemon peel, ¾ cup (175 mL) granulated sugar and 1 cup (250 mL) ice-cold water in a blender. Blend until puréed. Strain through a sieve into a large pitcher. Stir in lemon juice and 2 cups (500 mL) ice-cold water. If mixture is too thick, stir in more water or lemon juice. Pour into glasses and add ice cubes. Lemonade tastes best the day it's made. To make this a boozy lemonade, prepare as directed, then stir in ⅓ cup (75 mL) vodka or gin and 2 tbsp (30 mL) orange-flavoured liqueur. Taste and add more if you like.

MAKES 4 ½ CUPS (1.125 L)

MANGO CAIPIRINHA

Using the back of a wooden spoon or pestle, mash 2 thick lime wedges in a short, wide glass. (Be careful not to crush lime skin too much or you'll end up with a bitter taste.) Remove wedges. Stir 1 tsp (5 mL) sugar into lime juice. Superfine sugar works well because it dissolves easily. If you can't find it at the grocery store, simply pulse granulated sugar in a food processor until finely ground. Or just use granulated sugar. Pour in ¼ cup (50 mL) mango juice and 3 tbsp (45 mL) cachaça (vodka works in a pinch too). Add crushed ice.

MAKES 1 SERVING (RECIPE IS EASILY DOUBLED)

CRANBERRY-RUM COCKTAIL

Pour ½ cup (125 mL) white rum into a pitcher. Add 1 thin slice peeled fresh ginger. Using the handle of a wooden spoon, gently crush ginger to release juices. Stir in 2 cups (500 mL) cold cranberry or raspberry cocktail. Pour into sugar-rimmed martini glasses and float frozen cranberries in each glass.

MAKES 2 ½ CUPS (625 mL)

PURPLE GRAPE SPRITZER

In a large pitcher, stir 1 cup (250 mL) purple grape juice with ½ cup (125 mL) gin or vodka, 1 tbsp (15 mL) orange-flavoured liqueur and two 355 mL cans chilled soda water. Pour into tall glasses filled with ice cubes. Top with spirals of orange peel or garnish glasses with tiny champagne grapes.

MAKES 4 CUPS (1 L)

CLEMENTINE SPARKLE

Squeeze juice from 7 clementines into a large measuring cup. Juice should measure about 1 cup (250 mL). Stir in 2 tbsp (30 mL) orange-flavoured liqueur. Divide mixture among 6 or 8 short-stemmed glasses or champagne flutes. Divide a 750 mL bottle chilled sparkling wine among the glasses, topping up the clementine mixture. Garnish with clementine slices or fresh raspberries.

MAKES 4 CUPS (1 L)

CLASSIC MARGARITA

Pour a little salt onto a saucer. Pinch a lime wedge around the rims of 4 cocktail glasses, then dip the rims in salt to evenly coat. In a martini shaker or small pitcher, stir ½ cup (125 mL) tequila with ¼ cup (50 mL) Grand Marnier. Squeeze in 2 tbsp (30 mL) juice from lime. Add ice cubes and shake well if using a martini shaker or, if using a pitcher, stir together. Taste, then stir in more lime juice, 1 tbsp (15 mL) at a time, if you like. Strain into 4 small cocktail glasses and serve on the rocks. Garnish with a twist of lime.

MAKES 4 SERVINGS

SAKE POM-TINI

Mix ½ cup (125 mL) pomegranate juice, 5 tbsp (75 mL) gin and 1 ½ tsp (7 mL) sake in a highball glass filled with ice. Add a splash of sparkling water and a squeeze of lemon.

MAKES 1 SERVING (RECIPE IS EASILY DOUBLED)

BLOOD-ORANGE SCREWDRIVER

In a large pitcher, stir ½ cup (125 mL) vodka with 2 tbsp (30 mL) orange liqueur, 1 tbsp (15 mL) brandy and 2 cups (500 mL) freshly squeezed blood orange juice or other orange juice. Refrigerate until cold, at least 1 hour. Pour into tall fluted glasses. Garnish with strips of orange peel.

MAKES 2 ⅔ CUPS (650 mL)

PEACH BUBBLY

Peel 1 large ripe peach (preferably freestone) if you wish. Slice in half and remove pit. Slice each half into thin wedges. Divide slices among 8 champagne flutes. Pour 1 cup (250 mL) peach nectar into flutes, then divide a 750 mL bottle sparkling wine or champagne among the glasses. Thread raspberries or blueberries onto 8 small wooden skewers. Place one in each glass as a garnish. Serve immediately.

MAKES 8 SERVINGS

CLASSIC MOJITO

Place 24 large mint leaves and ¼ cup (50 mL) granulated sugar in a pitcher. Using a wooden spoon, mash leaves with sugar against side of pitcher to release flavour. Add 1 cup (250 mL) freshly squeezed lime juice (you will need about 10 limes). Stir in 1 cup (250 mL) white rum until sugar dissolves. Stir in 1 cup (250 mL) soda water. Fill glasses with ice. Top with mojito mixture. Garnish each glass with a sprig of mint.

MAKES 4 TO 6 SERVINGS

SPIKED MINT ICED TEA

Remove leaves from 1 bunch fresh mint. Place in a large pitcher. Using the back of a wooden spoon, mash leaves against side of pitcher to release flavour. Thinly slice 1 large lemon or lime and add to pitcher. Fill pitcher with ice cubes, then pour in four 340 mL cans or one 2 L bottle iced tea. Add ½ cup (125 mL) gin or vodka if you wish. Stir well, then pour into tall glasses.

MAKES 8 CUPS (2 L)

REFRESHING ICED TEA

Place 4 tea bags in 2 cups (500 mL) boiling water. Leave for 15 minutes. Remove bags. Stir in ¼ cup (50 mL) granulated sugar until dissolved. Pour into a pitcher. Fill with ice cubes, then add 2 ½ cups (625 mL) cold water.

MAKES 6 SERVINGS

SPICY CAESAR

Pour a little celery salt onto a saucer. Pinch a lemon wedge around the rim of a tall glass, then dip the rim in the salt to evenly coat. Fill the glass with ice. Top with a shot or two of vodka. Add a dash or two of Worcestershire and Tabasco sauces. Squeeze in the juice from lemon wedge. Fill glass with Clamato juice. Top with a lemon wedge and pickled beans or garlic scapes if you wish.

MAKES 1 SERVING (RECIPE IS EASILY DOUBLED)

Menus

THANKSGIVING OR CHRISTMAS DINNER FOR 12

Salad course
Roasted Plum and Spinach Salad (page 64) or Perfect Roast Chicken (page 123)

Main course and sides
Perfect Prime Rib (page 166)
Brussels Sprouts in Parmesan Cream (page 310)
Multi-Coloured Carrots with Ginger Brown Butter (page 319)
Jewelled Rice (page 301)
Greek Herb-Roasted Potatoes (page 307)

Dessert
Sticky Toffee Puddings with Caramel (page 352) or
Lemon-Coconut Shortbread Squares (page 358)
Pumpkin-Coconut Cheesecake (page 339) or Classic Creamy Cheesecake (page 336)

Drink
Cranberry-Rum Cocktail (page 373)

NEW YEAR'S EVE DINNER FOR 6 TO 8

Appetizers
Thai Turkey Meatballs (page 60)
Smoked Trout and Mango Bites (page 59)
Gorgonzola and Clementine Toasts (page 41)

Soup course
Fabulous French Onion Soup (page 94)

Main course and sides
Trio of Lamb (page 194)
Asparagus with Pine-Nut Butter (page 287)
Coconut Milk–Infused Rice (page 303)

Dessert
Hazelnut Meringue Cake (page 328)

Drink
Sake Pom-Tini (page 373)

DINNER FOR 2 (VALENTINE'S DAY–WORTHY)

Appetizer
Quick Caprese-Style Toasts (page 39)

Main course and side
Shared Steak with Shiitake Mushroom Sauce (page 154)
Baby Zucchini with Blue Cheese (page 288)

Dessert
Best-Ever Brownies (page 361)

Drink
Blood-Orange Screwdriver (page 374)
Homemade Cappuccino (page 372) or Hot Chocolate (page 372) (with dessert)

CHRISTMAS BREAKFAST FOR 8 TO 12

Main courses
Cheddar, Pepper and Potato Bake with Perfect Soft-Boiled Eggs (page 32)
Roasted Sugary Rum Bacon (page 31)

Drink
Clementine Sparkle (page 373)

CLASSIC AND EASY DINNER FOR 4 TO 6

Main course and salad
Homemade Mushroom Meat Lasagna (page 230)
Classic Caesar Salad (page 67)

Dessert
Sugared Phyllo Cups with Fresh Cream and Fruit (page 346)

FRIDAY FAMILY NIGHT FOR 4

Salad course
Warm Balsamic-Soaked Mushroom and Spinach Salad (page 89)

Main course and side
Quick Roast with Garlicky Cherry Tomatoes (page 163)
Shortcut Scalloped Potatoes (page 306)

Dessert
Velvety Chocolate Pudding (page 355)

BUFFET BRUNCH WITH FRIENDS FOR 6

Main courses
Smoked-Salmon Nachos (page 14)
Baked Croque Monsieur (page 7)
Easy Arugula and Hazelnut Salad (page 86)
Fresh Fruit Salad with Lime-Ginger Drizzle (page 17)

Drink
Purple Grape Spritzer (page 373) or Peach Bubbly (page 374)

BIRTHDAY DINNER FOR 4 TO 5

Main course and sides
Butterflied Chili-Lime Chicken with Roasted Garlic (page 116)
Rapini Sauté (page 315)
Chunky Sweet Potato Fries with Herbed Yogourt Dip (page 304)

Dessert
Coconut-Lemon Cake (page 332)

BACKYARD BARBECUE FOR 6 TO 8

Salads
Warm Curried-Potato Salad (page 73)
Minted Summer Tomatoes (page 70)
Green Salad with Three Homemade Dressings: Ginger-Sesame Drizzle, Provençal Vinaigrette and Buttermilk Dressing (page 79)

Main course and sides
Fiery Asian Burgers (page 143) and/or Portobello Burgers (page 270)
Husk-On Barbecued Corn with Herbed Butter (page 294)
Grilled Sweet Peppers with Basil Drizzle (page 293)

Dessert
Triple-Chocolate Ice-Cream Sandwiches (page 362) or Campfire Bananas (page 344)

Drink
Strawberry Lemonade (page 372)

SUMMER DINNER FOR 6

Starter
Smoky Brie with Wild Blueberry Sauce (page 44) or Spiked Pepper Gazpacho (page 100)

Main course and sides
BBQ Chicken with Piri Piri Sauce (page 120) or Roasted Halibut with Minted Pea Coulis (page 210)
Chili-Garlic Beans (page 313)
Orecchiette with Herbed Garlic Tomatoes (page 251)

Dessert
Free-Form Berry Pie (page 327) or Grilled Strawberry Shortcake (page 343)

VEGETARIAN ENTERTAINING FOR 2 TO 4

Appetizer
Savoury Sesame-Tofu Cakes (page 266)

Main course and side salad
Baked Tomato Risotto (page 280) or Grilled Eggplant Parmesan (page 269)
Roasted Vegetable and Kale Salad with Maple Dressing (page 256)

Dessert
Watermelon Granita (page 349)

About the Nutrient Analysis

Computer-assisted nutrient analysis of the recipes was performed by Info Access (1988) Inc., Don Mills, Ontario, using the nutritional accounting component of the CBORD Menu Management System. The nutrient database was the Canadian Nutrient File, supplemented when necessary with documented data from reliable sources.

The analysis is based on:

- Imperial weights and measures (except for foods typically packaged and used in metric quantity),
- Larger number of servings (i.e., smaller portion) when there is a range,
- Smaller ingredient quantity when there is a range, and
- First ingredient listed when there is a choice of ingredients, unless listed otherwise.

Unless otherwise stated, recipes were analyzed using canola vegetable oil, 2% milk, 1% to 2% yogourt and large eggs. Calculation of meat and poultry recipes assumed that only the lean portion, without skin, was eaten. When the recipes called for lightly oiled pans, it was assumed that 1 tsp oil was used. Salt was included only when a specific amount was given. Optional ingredients and garnishes in unspecified amounts were not included in the calculations.

Nutrient Information on Recipes

- Nutrient values have been rounded to the nearest whole number. Non-zero values less than 0.5 are shown as "trace."
- Good and excellent sources of vitamins (A, C, thiamine, riboflavin, niacin, B6, folacin, B12) and minerals (calcium and iron) have been identified according to the criteria established for nutrition labelling (*2003 Guide to Food Labelling and Advertising,* Canadian Food Inspection Agency).
- A serving that supplies 15% of the Daily Value (DV) for a vitamin or mineral (30% for vitamin C) is a good source of that nutrient. An excellent source must supply 25% of the DV (50% for vitamin C).
- A serving providing at least 2 g of dietary fibre is considered a moderate source. Servings providing 4 g and 6 g are high and very high sources respectively (*2003 Guide to Food Labelling and Advertising*).

index

Chatelaine

Featuring More of
What You Want

Chatelaine delivers real ideas, real inspiration and real solutions.

More style. More health. More food ... in every issue!

Get your free trial issue NOW
Chatelaine.com/classics1